# CRUSHING THE DEVIL

# PEDRO OKORO

# CRUSHING THE DEVIL

## Your Guide to Spiritual Warfare and **Victory in Christ**

"And being ready to punish all disobedience when your obedience is fulfilled."

2 CORINTHIANS 10:6

To:
the memory of my late older brother
Kingsley Sienakereho Okoro
(September 10, 1962 to June 23, 2002)
Gone
But never forgotten

# ACKNOWLEDGMENTS

My appreciation goes to my wife, Ola, and my daughters, Jess and Mychaela, for bearing with me in the last four years as I worked hard to give birth to this dream. Over this period, there were many long days and very many late nights as I translated my vision into the finished product that it is now. Not only did you persevere with me, you encouraged me, prayed with me, prayed *for* me, laughed at me, and laughed *with* me! You are simply the best.

To my parents, Mr. and Mrs. Joseph Okoro, I wish to say a special thank you. Papa and Mama, I am grateful to you for shooting me like an arrow from the bow of a skillful warrior toward my destiny. I couldn't have asked for more.

My thanks and gratitude also go to Dr. Paul Jinadu, the General Overseer of the New Covenant Church worldwide and my father in the ministry. You believed in me and gave me a platform to minister. Thank you so much.

How can I forget the congregation at the New Covenant Church, Wallington, where I have taught some of the truths contained in this book? Thank you for validating my ministry. Thank you for allowing me to work with you in this journey of life.

Similarly, I'd like to appreciate Dr. Hugh Osgood, senior minister of the Cornerstone Christian Center, Bromley, United Kingdom; founder and president, Churches in Communities International; and co-chair, UK Charismatic and Pentecostal Leaders' Conference; for taking time out of his busy schedule to write the foreword. I am deeply honored.

My gratitude likewise goes to my publishers, Deep River Books, for agreeing to work with me on this project. Thank you for your foresight. I am very much obliged.

And last but by no means least, I would like to thank my editor, Rachel Starr Thomson: author, performer, and writing coach. The professionalism, insight, and spirit of excellence which you displayed as you went through the manuscript are truly inspirational and deeply appreciated. Thank you for the constructive criticism; I am grateful for your helpful comments. Rachel, you are indeed a star!

# TABLE OF CONTENTS

# A Poem-Satan, You're Under Arrest

## Satan, You're Under Arrest!

This is a citizen's arrest
For I bear on my body the Lord's crest
Heaven is my final destination
And a citizen I am of God's holy nation

*Devil, you are fired*
*You will never ever be required*
*For all the calamities you inspire*
*I pour on you the Lord's unquenchable fire*
*I don't want you around me, devil*
*'Cause you are Machiavellian and so full of evil*

I am arresting you, devil
You're so jam-packed with evil
I arrest you on reasonable suspicion
Of various counts of gross insubordination

*Devil, you are fired*
*No more are you hired*
*For all the misfortunes you inspire*
*I pour on you the Lord's unquenchable fire*
*I don't like you one bit, devil*
*'Cause you are conniving and brimming with evil*

I arrest you in the name of Jesus
God's Son who came to save us
And deliver us from your oppression
Following Adam's initial transgression

*Devil, you are fired*
*You were never ever required*
*For all the devastation you inspire*
*I pour on you the Lord's unquenchable fire*

# CRUSHING THE DEVIL

*I don't want you near me, devil*
*'Cause you are deceitful and busting with evil*

To remain silent when questioned is your right
But of this important fact you must not lose sight
It would harm your defense if later you rely
On something you could have said today in reply
For the avoidance of doubt whatever you say
Will stand against you at your trial on judgment day

*Devil, you are fired*
*No more will you ever be hired*
*For all the catastrophes you inspire*
*I pour on you the Lord's unquenchable fire*
*I don't like you at all, devil*
*'Cause you are sly and so satiated with evil*

Your failure to carry out my instructions as a child of God
Appears from others to be a familiar pattern you have trod
Your willful disobedience amounts to a declaration of war
Enough is enough, I cannot continue with you as before

*Devil, you are fired*
*You were never ever required*
*For all the disasters you inspire*
*I pour on you the Lord's unquenchable fire*
*I can't stand you, devil*
*'Cause you are devious and overflowing with evil*

I now break your yoke, destroy your burdens and bind you
In the name of the exalted Lord Jesus who was born a Jew
Who on the cross of Calvary became sin and was of evil men slain
But rose from the dead and sat at the right hand of God to reign

*Devil, you are fired*
*No more are you hired*
*For all the tragedies you inspire*
*I pour on you the Lord's unquenchable fire*

# POEM

*I don't like you, devil*
*'Cause you are a very bad devil*

I scatter your assignments, your mission
I frustrate and thwart your goals, your vision
I deny you reinforcement of any provision
I bind you and refuse you any sort of permission
I forbid you my sphere of influence to permeate
I decree today, "Thou shall not within my space operate!"

*Devil, you are fired*
*You could never ever have been hired*
*For all the adversities you inspire*
*I pour on you the Lord's unquenchable fire*
*I don't want you around me anymore, devil*
*'Cause you are devious and so full of evil*

Satan, in the name of Jesus I put an end to your repression
I declare that henceforth I am free from every demonic oppression
By the power in the name of Jesus I undo every satanic subjugation
With the authority in the Word of God I put a stop to every devilish
     domination

*Devil, you are fired*
*You were not even ever hired*
*For all the debacles you inspire*
*I pour on you the Lord's unquenchable fire*
*In the name of Jesus I bind you, devil*
*You who epitomize all that is evil*

From now on I say no to your suppression
From this time forth I exercise my power of expression
I destroy, demolish, and dismantle the power of concealed sin
I proclaim, profess, and confess that I am in Christ, yes "I am in"
For whom the Son makes free is liberated, triumphant, and victorious
Thank you, Jesus, for helping me in all things to become auspicious

# CRUSHING THE DEVIL

*Devil, you are fired*
*You could never ever have been required*
*For all the fiascos you inspire*
*I pour on you the Lord's unquenchable fire*
*Now get thee behind me, devil*
*You scheming sneaky crafty cunning conniving embodiment of evil*

# FOREWORD

I love it when the cover of a book leaves you in no doubt as to its contents. This book is truly "your guide to spiritual warfare and victory in Christ." Whichever way you want to emphasise the subtitle, it effectively describes the pages that follow.

Firstly, Pedro Okoro has succeeded in writing *your* guide. Every reader will have the sense of being taken on a personal journey. At each step, the writer's disarming graciousness adds unexpected weight to his exhortations to rise and fight.

Secondly, this book is truly a *guide*. Pedro Okoro maps out the ground with care and precision. Whenever he moves onto controversial territory (and he is not afraid of treading in areas where I might be cautious to go), he never forces his opinions but shares frankly how he sees things and leaves us room to draw our own conclusions.

Thirdly, the *spiritual warfare* focus is never lost from view. This is not a book on spiritual diplomacy; it is about a fight, albeit a fight that utilizes the courtroom insights of a lawyer as well as the battlefield strategies of a warrior. Those of us who know the writer may admire his gentlemanly diplomacy in day-to-day pleasantries, but there is clearly another side that comes with his spiritual maturity—he is a warrior whose tactics extend beyond trench warfare.

Fourthly, and supremely, this book is about *victory in Christ,* and here I could let my enthusiasm run away with me. We all need books that remind us of the triumph that is ours in Christ, and here is a book that helps us root that triumph in reality and not in mere triumphalism. As the author leads us on a personal journey, we encounter a whole welter of information and practical counsel. When issues that he guides you to seem to be particularly relevant in your circumstances, do take the time to use the "Food for Reflection," "Prayer Features," and "Action Points" at the end of each chapter to ensure that what you have read is well applied. It is this practical approach that excites me.

Everyone will find something in this book that will cause them to stand firmer—feet shod, helmet set, belt tightened, breastplate secured, shield held high, sword at the ready—well-equipped to overcome all the onslaughts of the Enemy.

Pedro, thank you for taking the time to write this book; there will be very many whose lives are changed through your clearly presented insights. Reader, I am confident that you will be among that number.

DR. HUGH OSGOOD, FOUNDER AND PRESIDENT
CHURCHES IN COMMUNITIES INTERNATIONAL
CO-CHAIR, UK CHARISMATIC AND PENTECOSTAL LEADERS' CONFERENCE
LONDON, 2011

Prologue

# THE GOOD IS THE ENEMY OF THE BEST

———✦———

*You have stayed at this mountain long enough. It is time to break camp and move on.*
*Go...Look, I am giving all this land to you!*

DEUTERONOMY 1:6–8, NLT

It was a beautiful summer's evening in the year of our Lord 2000. I heard God so clearly it was surreal. I was at the solemn assembly, a monthly prayer meeting of the leaders and intercessors of the New Covenant Church, which is held on the last Wednesday of every month in Streatham, South London. "Son, it's time to move," I heard the Lord say to me. "Not yet, Lord," I protested. "I have a great job. I work for a fantastic law firm, and I have been invited to become a partner. I am happy where I am. The future couldn't be better and brighter!"

"Son," the Lord continued, "the good is the Enemy of the best. Until you depart from the good, you cannot enter my best for your life."

Prior to attending this meeting, I had been prayerfully thinking about my future. I was at a point where I wanted to start a new law practice with an associate. However, I had my trepidations, my fears, my worries, my apprehensions, and my anxieties...who wouldn't? I thought to myself: "Why should I leave certainty for uncertainty? Why should I give up the security of my job for the risk of the unknown? What if it doesn't work?" After all, I had a wife and a young daughter to look after! I was at a crossroads, and I had to decide one way or another. That night after my encounter with the Lord, I knew what to do. I had to step out in faith—and I did. I decided to launch out into the deep.

You see, ordinarily, *good* is, well, good! A *good thing* is always desirable, pleasing, attractive, and sought after. *Good* is suggestive of high quality, distinction, fineness, superiority.

However, as I found out on that Wednesday evening back in 2000, in the global picture of God's plan for your life, the *good* can be the Enemy of the better. And the *better* is the foe of the best. Until the good is cleared out of the way, you cannot receive that which is better, and you cannot receive the best until you are willing to let go of the better. Put differently, until Miss Barbara Better is taken off the scene, Mr. Benjamin Best will not appear.

Whatever your station or position in life, there is always room for improvement, enhancement, and perfection. I say this with a great sense of humility. Regardless of what you are enjoying at the moment, the Lord says that he has something better for you! No matter what you have achieved, attained, or accomplished in this world, there are more challenges and blessings ahead. God says that you have stayed long enough on this mountain. It is time to press forward to take more territories and receive more trophies. There is more work to be done. There are yet more victories to be won, more successes to be achieved, more triumphs to be obtained, and more accomplishments to be made.

In Deuteronomy 1:6–8, we read that God spoke to Moses in Horeb, the mountain of the Lord. God told him that the nation of Israel had stayed long enough on that spot and that it was time to move on. That probably came as a surprise to them! Horeb was God's mountain. It represented the presence of the Lord. The Israelites had experienced divine encounters on this mountain. Why would they want to move from this place that had come to signify God's presence? Like Peter on the Mount of Transfiguration, they probably wanted to build tents in Horeb and make it their permanent home. However, God had better ideas, because as good as Horeb was, it was not their final destination. It was not the Promised Land. It was at best a bus stop. They were but pilgrims at Horeb. God had something better in store for them. The only way they could get into the Promised Land and obtain God's best was for them to move forward. There was no other way.

In like manner, where you are at today is the adversary and rival of where God wants to take you. The good that you enjoy today and to which you have become so accustomed is the Enemy of those better things which God has planned for you. The better things that you currently take pleasure in are standing in the way of God's best for you. They are the opponents of your progress!

God has the most incredible, unimaginable, inconceivable, and indescribable intention and design for your life. His plans for you—yes, you!—are amazing, magnificent, wonderful, glorious, awesome, breathtaking, and awe-inspiring. In Jeremiah 29:11, we read that his thoughts and plans are for your well-being, not for evil, in order to give you a future and a hope. He wants to give you an expected end.

However, for you to get to where you belong, for you to *reach* where God is taking you, for you to arrive at God's destination for your life, you must first know who you are. To move into what God has in mind for you, it is necessary to discover your purpose, to know where you are going, and to understand the reason for your existence. Without an understanding of purpose, misuse is inevitable; abuse unavoidable. Purpose gives rise to discipline, restraint, and self-control, which are crucial, fundamental tools for success in the journey of life.

Have you ever wondered why you did not rapture and go to heaven the day you became a Christian? It is because God has work for you to do here on earth! Having gone to heaven, Jesus expects you to be his body on earth. You are *his* hands, *his* feet, *his* voice. The Bible says in Ephesians 2:8–10, "By faith are ye saved…We are his workmanship created in Christ Jesus unto good works."

The New Living Translation says in verse 10, "For we are God's masterpiece. He created us anew in Christ Jesus, so we *can do the good things he planned for us long ago*" (emphasis mine).

Before salvation, our good works do not count for anything before God. At best they are like filthy, grimy, grubby rags. However, having saved you, God now expects you to get busy working with him and for him. He expects good quality work which will bring glory and honor to his name. The use of the word *masterpiece* in Ephesians suggests that God has invested something very special in you. He therefore expects a return on his investment.

In the Gospel of Luke, chapter 19, Jesus tells a parable in verses 12 and 13. It more or less goes like this: A certain nobleman went into a far country to receive for himself a kingdom and to return. Before leaving, he called ten of his servants, delivered to them ten mina (the New Living Translation says the servants received ten pounds of silver) and said to them, "Do business till I come."

On his return, the man called his servants and asked them to give an account of their stewardship in his absence. In the same way, you are called to be about the Lord's business, to occupy yourself with matters of the Lord's kingdom, and to be engaged in the Lord's pursuits until the Lord returns in his second advent. Clearly, there is a lot of work to be done here on earth. And someday you will give an account of your labors.

But it isn't going to be easy. In fact, the Bible teaches that we have an active, destructive, and intelligent enemy. That reality is the reason I'm writing this book. In the journey of life, the Enemy will do his utmost to derail you, to stop you from realizing your full potential and accomplishing your purpose. To make it easy for you to fail and fall, he adapts his temptations and tricks to suit your natural inclinations and desires. He will modify his lure to match your lifestyle. Look out for the longings of your eyes, the desires of your physical body, and the pride of life, which are referred to in 1 John 2:16. The truth is, you can fit most temptations into one of these three categories.

The devil doesn't really have any new schemes, ideas, or initiatives. He keeps on recycling and reusing the same old temptations, adorning them in different attires. He started his temptations with Adam and Eve when he deceived them in the garden of Eden. Eve clearly responded to the lust of the eyes, the yearnings of the flesh, and the pride of life:

> So when the woman saw that the tree was good for food, *that it was* pleasant to the eyes, *and a tree* desirable to make one wise, *she took of its fruit and ate. She also gave to her husband with her, and he ate.*

GENESIS 3:6, EMPHASIS SUPPLIED

Satan tried the same trick with Jesus when he tempted him in the desert after Jesus had fasted for forty days and forty nights. Having fasted for so long, the Lord must have been famished! Satan, *being aware of this,* adapted the temptation to suit Jesus's immediate circumstances in a bid to make him succumb. You can read the story in Matthew 4:1–10 (I'll quote parts of it from the International Standard Version). Satan tells him that *since* he is the Son of God, he should turn the stones into bread. We see the Enemy attempting to use the desires of the physical body when he tells Jesus to turn the stones into bread.

In the second temptation, Satan tells Jesus that *since* he is the Son of God, he should throw himself down from the pinnacle of the temple in the holy city. Satan then shows off his knowledge of the Scriptures when he tells Jesus, "It is written, 'God will put his angels in charge of you,' and 'with their hands they will hold you up, so that you will never hit your foot against a rock.'" Here we see the devil's attempt to use the pride of life to derail Jesus.

In the third temptation, we are told that the devil took Jesus to the top of an exceedingly high mountain and showed him all the kingdoms of the world with their glory, splendor, and magnificence. After Jesus had taken in the sights, Satan said to him, "All these things I will give you if you will fall down and worship me." There is no doubt in my mind that this third temptation is a clear attempt by the devil to make Jesus fall through the lust of the eyes.

If the Enemy tried the same ruse with Jesus, he will try it with you; no doubt about that! And unless you watch and pray, you could be caught unawares. This book aims to help you stay aware and alert to the Enemy's designs.

After the fall, man came under what I call the *Adamic curse*. By this I mean the curse which came upon the whole of humanity because of Adam's transgression and which manifested primarily in eternal separation from God (i.e. spiritual death), which eventually led to physical death, sickness, and disease, as well as poverty. On the cross of Calvary, Jesus defeated the devil, destroyed his stronghold over man, and freed man from the effects of the Adamic curse. Paul puts it beautifully in his letter to the church in Colossae, as follows:

> *When you were stuck in your old sin-dead life, you were incapable of responding to God. God brought you alive—right along with Christ! Think of it! All sins forgiven, the slate wiped clean, that old arrest warrant canceled and nailed to Christ's cross. He stripped all the spiritual tyrants in the universe of their sham authority at the Cross and marched them naked through the streets.*

COLOSSIANS 2:14–15, MSG

Having triumphed over the Enemy, Jesus boldly declared in Matthew 28:18 that all authority in heaven and on earth has been given unto him. Paul later elucidated this profound statement of the Lord when he said in Philippians 2:9–11 that "therefore, God elevated him to the place of highest honor and gave him the name above all other names, that at the name of Jesus every knee should bow, in heaven and on earth and under the earth, and every tongue confess that Jesus Christ is Lord, to the glory of God the Father" (NLT).

For those who receive Jesus into their hearts and become born again, the Lord delegates his authority to them and empowers them to exercise authority over the devil. Jesus couldn't be clearer when he told his followers after his resurrection in Mark 16:17 that "these are the miraculous signs that will accompany believers: they will use the power and authority of my name to force demons out of people. They will speak new languages" (GW).

In other words, as a believer, you have the authority to tell the devil what to do *in the name of Jesus,* and he will obey! However, there are times when the Enemy will oppose and resist you. He may choose to stand in the way of the answer to your prayers. He may even resolve to ignore and disobey your lawful instructions. For those times, God has made adequate provision to enable you to punish the Enemy's disobedience.

This book has been written to deal with those tricky situations when the Enemy is recalcitrant, obstinate, unruly, and disobedient. It seeks to unpack such crucial and critical theological issues as who you are in Christ Jesus, your authority over the Enemy, spiritual warfare, and strategy in spiritual warfare. Come along on this journey of discovery as we unmask the devil and uncover demonic schemes and methods. It is my prayer and hope that this book will open your eyes to discover why and how the Enemy disobeys and to understand how best to handle his disobedience.

It is my desire that you will fully understand the reality of spiritual warfare. As you read this book, may you discover God's superabundant provision to enable you to emerge victorious at all times. May you also wholly appreciate and take hold of all the supplies and weapons and every grace that God has made available to you for your spiritual battles on this side of eternity.

Chapter One

# RIGHT, CAPACITY, ABILITY

—⟡—

*But to all who believed him and accepted him, he*
*gave the right to become children of God.*

JOHN 1:12, NLT

P eter John Anthony Jones was an enigma. His life was a sensational human-
interest story: dynamic, interesting, and yet paradoxical. Peter lived in a
sleepy village in the county of Shropshire in the United Kingdom. He was
a poor, wretched old man who had the word POVERTY written all over him in
bold, capital letters...or so it seemed during his lifetime.

At the age of seventy, Peter Jones lived alone in a modest two-bedroom, mid-
terraced house. There was no mortgage on his property. He did not have a wife or
children. In fact, Mr. Jones did not seem to have any relatives at all! He could barely
pay his bills, and in the winter, he would hardly heat his home because he could
not afford the gas bill. One year, he was dragged before the local magistrates for
not paying his council tax bill. But for the generosity of an anonymous benefactor
who came to Mr. Jones's rescue when he read about his case in the local newspaper,
he would have served a custodial sentence in jail.

Jones depended on his neighbors for handouts. He would even beg for groceries. His only apparent income was his state pension. He shopped in the local
charity shop on the high street for his clothes. At Christmas, the neighbors would
take turns inviting him for Christmas dinner. Everybody thought he was poverty
stricken and destitute. The neighbors felt that he could barely make ends meet.
That was until he died one winter from exposure to cold.

Following Jones's death, his neighbors were shocked when they saw his will.
They were so astonished that they must have thought they were dreaming! They
had to look at his bank statements to be sure the will was authentic: somehow, this

elderly beggar had left £4.9 million to a charity. "Peter, a multimillionaire?" they asked in utter disbelief. "How could he be so rich, yet so poor? How could he have £4.9 million sitting in his bank account but live a life of lack, deficiency, and penury like a penniless and poverty-stricken pauper? And to die in such awful circumstances; to pass away in such abject poverty; ostensibly because he could not even heat his home!"

In reality, Peter Jones was a mystery. He had been a public-school educated boy, the only child of middle-class parents. He studied classics at an Ivy League university and graduated with a second-class honors upper degree when he was just twenty-two years old. He had a bright future ahead of him. We do not know what he did between the ages of twenty-two, when he left university, and sixty-five, when he moved into his two-bedroom terrace in Shropshire. We *do* know that he came into his vast wealth following the tragic death of his parents in an airplane crash. Part of it was his inheritance; the rest came from insurance payouts following the accident.

Two years after his parents' funeral, Peter Jones made a will giving all of his wealth to charity. He then moved to Shropshire and became a recluse. He obviously knew that he had this money, because his will was detailed and clear as to what to do with it. However, he decided not to spend a penny of it on himself. So he depended on his state pension and the generosity of his neighbors to eke out a living. He made a knowledgeable decision and stuck with it. He knew the score.

Peter Jones's story is similar to those of a growing number of people around the world who have been nicknamed "Millionaires in Rags" by CNN/*Money* contributing writer Les Christie, a designation which I am keen to adopt and make use of in this book. In my view, a millionaire in rags is a person who has at least £1 million (or US$1.4 million) of his own money but who, for whatever reason—including but not limited to ignorance, a personal choice, or mental incapacity—refuses, neglects, or fails to make use of the money for his own benefit and lives instead like a pauper. Let us take a look at some of their fascinating and sometimes bizarre life stories.

## MILLIONAIRES IN RAGS

### Joseph Leek

The first person in our roll call of modern-day millionaires in rags is Joseph Leek. Born in 1912, Joseph Leek willed nearly US$1.8 million to a charity that provides guide dogs for the blind. Despite having millions in his bank account, the ninety-year-old British man lived like a pauper during his lifetime, using a twenty-year-old car, watching television at a neighbor's house to save on electricity, putting off essential home repairs, and buying secondhand clothes from charity shops. Nobody, not even his own family, had any idea that Leek had that kind of money! Not surprisingly, it is unclear how he made his money. When he died, his family and the neighbors got the shock of their lives when they discovered that he was in fact a millionaire!

## REVEREND VERTRUE SHARP

The Reverend Vertrue Sharp (his real name!) was another millionaire in rags. A minister of the gospel, he raised hay and cattle in addition to preaching and teaching. To Reverend Sharp, self-denial and making sacrifices in order to help others was not difficult at all. He worked very hard and saved every penny he made. Over the course of his lifetime he amassed an enormous amount of wealth. As the saying goes, he took care of the pennies, and so the millions took care of themselves.

By the time he died in 1999, Sharp had so much money that he was able to leave an estate worth about US$2 million (yes, US$2 million!) to the East Tennessee Children's Hospital, the University of Tennessee Medical Center, and various other charities in the United States.

## MARY GUTHRIE ESSAME

Even more intriguing is the story of Mary Guthrie Essame, a retired nurse who lived in an old Victorian house in East Sussex. Miss Essame was a spinster who lived modestly in very humble surroundings. She dressed herself in secondhand clothes and used shoes which she bought from charity shops. Her neighbors were shocked to learn that her estate amounted to a whopping US$10 million when she died in January 2002. It is thought that she inherited her massive wealth, although no one is certain.

She willed her immense fortune to a host of local charities. Her friend and neighbor, Ms. Monica Unter, told the local newspaper that Miss Essame clad herself in such worn clothes and old shoes that no one knew how well off she was!

ROBERTA LANGTRY

Roberta Langtry was an anonymous philanthropist, a modestly paid Toronto elementary school teacher, and a multimillionaire, all rolled into one! Upon her death she bequeathed more than CAD$4.3 million (US$3.8 million) of her estate to the Nature Conservancy of Canada (NCC), a charity that buys environmentally sensitive land and turns it into nature reserves. She had been a modest supporter of NCC's work since 1999.

While she was alive, Ms. Langtry made a number of large, anonymous gifts to individuals she knew were in need. Recipients would receive envelopes from an unknown benefactor in the amounts of US$25,000 or US$30,000. Yet, her friends and coworkers were unaware of her wealth.

According to reports, Langtry was born in Manitoba. She began teaching around the age of sixteen. Most of her fifty-five years as a teacher and speech therapist were with the East York Board of Education. She never married and had no children. Langtry lived in her aunt's modest bungalow, sharing it until her aunt died in the early 1990s and then living alone until she herself died. The Alberta Teachers' Association stated in a news report that the executor of Langtry's estate speculated that her wealth flourished as a result of her having purchased shares of IBM in the 1940s and 1950s and holding the stock until her death.[1]

MR. JOE TEMECZKO

Another millionaire in rags worth looking at was Mr. Joe Temeczko, a Polish immigrant and former prisoner of war who did odd jobs and handyman work. He had no family and lived in a humble house which he filled with stuff he scavenged from the streets. We do not know how Temeczko acquired his immense wealth. What we do know is that he roamed his Minneapolis neighborhood looking for throwaways to fix up and sell or give away.

According to Les Christie,[2] attorney William Wangensteen described himself as "blown away" when Temeczko's bank called a few years ago, trying to enlist Wangensteen's support in persuading the little old man with the thick accent to convert his million-dollar bank account into more lucrative investments. Before that, Wangensteen had no idea that the handyman who rotated the attorney's screens and storm windows every spring and fall was so rich. Wangensteen says Temeczko would get free food from local charities and read newspapers in the store so he wouldn't have to buy them.

Temeczko took the news of the September 11, 2001 attacks hard; he had his will rewritten, leaving US$1.4 million to the city of New York. He died a few weeks later in October 2001 at age eighty-six. Temeczko's bequest helped fund a park renovation as well as "The Daffodil Project," in which thousands of volunteers planted more than two million flower bulbs across New York City as a living memorial to the victims of the September 11 attacks.

## JACK WITHAM

This roll call of millionaires in rags would be incomplete without the fascinating story of Jack Witham. He was a reclusive pensioner who lived the life of a pauper in Southampton, United Kingdom. He left £6 million to a children's hospice in his will.

A retired surveyor, Mr. Jack Witham lived alone above a garage in a flat he stuffed with bargains found as he wandered around car boot sales. The self-effacing and modest-living millionaire had made his fortune by investing in property, and his biggest extravagance was a season ticket to see his beloved Southampton Football Club. Nicknamed "Saints," the Southampton Football Club were in the premiership, the top flight of English League Soccer, when Witham died in Southampton at the age of seventy-nine in November 2004.

A friend of Witham's, Susanne Fry, told *The Telegraph:* "Jack was a very private man. If you saw him you wouldn't think he had two ha'pennies to rub together. He just didn't spend the money on himself. I wouldn't describe him as an eccentric but he had a slightly odd way of living."[3]

His bequest helped the Naomi House Children's Hospice near Winchester, Hampshire, to build a new center for seriously ill teenagers. "It's a complete bolt out of the blue. We knew nothing about it until we received a letter from his executors," hospice manager Mr Ray Kipling told *The Telegraph.*

## FATHER ANTHONY WOJTUS

Last but by no means least in this strange list is Father Anthony Wojtus, a diocesan priest in Wheeling-Charleston, West Virginia, who died without a will while living in appalling conditions. According to the *National Catholic Reporter,* twelve brothers and sisters in Poland received about US$150,000 each from the estate of this Kanawha County priest, who lived like a pauper despite having nearly US$2 million stashed away in cash and investments.[4]

For nearly three years, Chief Tax Deputy Allen Bleigh and members of the tax department investigated the estate of Fr. Anthony Wojtus. Following his death in 2007, the millionaire priest was discovered to have been living in squalor. Wojtus left no will or known family members. The county was appointed as estate administrator shortly after the priest's death, leaving officials with the job of tracking down next of kin.

Wojtus was a retired member of the Wheeling-Charleston Diocese. It is not clear how Wojtus made his enormous riches. However, Father Anthony Cincinnati, the episcopal vicar for clergy in the diocese, said priests are not required to take a vow of poverty but are supposed to live simple lives.

These stories illustrate an important point: If you have millions of pounds sterling or United States dollars sitting in your personal bank account, you have the right to use the money as you please. However, if for whatever reason you do not *exercise* the right to use that money, you will live in poverty like our millionaires in rags—even though, to all intents and purposes, you are stupendously wealthy.

## WEALTHY—BUT REFUSING TO ACCEPT IT

There are also cases of people who become entitled to stupendous wealth but refuse to accept it, preferring instead to live in poverty. Dr. Grigory "Grisha" Perelman, a Russian scientist, is one such person. He is said to be a math genius, and he won fame in August 2006 for apparently spurning a one-million-dollar prize and then moving in with his mother in a humble flat in St. Petersburg, where he is unemployed and coexists on her £30-a-month pension.[5]

There is no doubt that this man is brilliant. The eccentric recluse stunned the math world when he solved a century-old puzzle known as the Poincaré Conjecture. Dr. Perelman has some small savings from his time as a lecturer, but is apparently reluctant to supplement them with the US$1 million offered by the Clay Mathematics Institute in Cambridge, Massachusetts, for solving one of the world's seven "Millennium Problems."

Unlike the stories of many millionaires in rags, we do have some insight into the reason for Perelman's apparently inexplicable decision. Grigory Perelman's predicament stems from an acrimonious split with a leading Russian mathematical institute, the Steklov, in 2003. When the institute in St. Petersburg failed to reelect him as a member, Dr. Perelman, forty, was left feeling an "absolutely ungifted and untalented person," said a friend. He had a crisis of confidence and cut himself off.

To my mind, there can be only three reasons why you would have so much and neglect to use it. *Ignorance* would be the main rationale, because you cannot spend what you do not know to be yours. The second reason would be *a conscious decision not to spend it on yourself,* or in the case of people like Dr. Perelman, *a deliberate decision not to accept the money in the first place.* The final reason is a *lack of mental capacity,* which would probably be another form of ignorance. If you were mentally incapable, you wouldn't know what belonged to you, would you?

## SPIRITUAL MILLIONAIRES IN RAGS

"But what is the allegory?" you may rightly ask. "How does this relate to me as a Christian?" Well, the truth of the matter is that in Christ Jesus we have the *right* or *ability* to become children of God—but like millionaires in rags, many of us do not use it.

> *But to all who believed him and accepted him, he*
> *gave the right to become children of God.*
>
> JOHN 1:12, NLT

When we are born into God's family through our faith in Jesus, God gives us the *capacity* or *capability* to live as his children. This is our *right* as believers, people who have accepted Jesus into our lives as our personal Savior and Lord. But this is merely a *right, "the capability to become."* Nothing more. And dare I say, *nothing less!*

The word translated "right" in this passage is the Greek word ĕxousia (pronounced ex-oo-see-ah). Depending on the context, it can be translated as *privilege, capacity, authority, jurisdiction, power, strength,* or *liberty.*[6] It is the ability or strength with which one is endued, which he has the option to exercise. In other words, a right is simply an entitlement, a privilege, a prerogative. It is not necessarily the *acting upon* that right.

Capability is ability that has not yet been put to full use. As we have seen from Peter Jones's story, for a right to be worth anything, it has to be *exercised,* or put to use, by the person who is entitled to it. In Christ Jesus, we all start on a level playing field. What we make of ourselves in the Christian race depends entirely upon us.

What we do with this right determines how far we go with God. How deep we get in our walk with God is determined by whether or not this capacity to live as his children remains dormant or is maximized. In other words, you could be a spiritual millionaire in rags if you do not take ownership of what is yours in Christ Jesus. To my mind, the majority of Christians fall into the category of spiritual millionaires in rags because they fail to be all they can be in Jesus.

## IGNORANCE IS NOT BLISS; IT IS REMISS

Four more stories further illustrate this line of reasoning, but from the point of view of ignorance. These four cases demonstrate the truth that *without an understanding of the things that are rightfully yours,* you will be unable to appropriate them for your personal use and benefit.

The first story is of a seventy-seven-year-old retired academic named Miss Jean Preston, who died in Oxford, in the United Kingdom, in 2006. She owned two small altar paintings of saints in medieval clothing. She had found them in a box of odds and ends in America in the 1960s when she was the curator of historic manuscripts at a museum. She thought them "quite nice" and told her father, an amateur collector, about them. He paid a modest sum for them and passed them down to his daughter when he died in 1974. The two paintings were found hanging behind a door in her spare room after her death.

Subsequent to her death, her family decided to value the paintings. The art historian Mr. Michael Liversidge identified them as fifteenth-century masterpieces completed by Fra Angelico in 1439 which had been missing for two hundred years! Fra Angelico was a Dominican friar in the monastery at Fiesole in Italy. The portraits had been kept among similar paintings by the artist in the Church of San Marco in Florence until it was ransacked during the Napoleonic Wars in the 1800s. Six of the eight panels were recovered, but the location of the remaining two was regarded as one of the art world's great mysteries—that is, until Miss Jean Preston died.

The two works of art were sold for £1.7 million at the Duke's Auction in Dorchester, Dorset, on April 19, 2007.[7] Can you imagine hanging two portraits, worth so much money, behind the door of your spare room? Why did she not insure them or store them in a high-security vault like other people who own such treasured paintings do? The answer is obvious: she did not know the true worth or value of the paintings. In other words, she was *ignorant.*

Although she owned these treasures, Jean Preston lived a modest life. In the words of *The Guardian,* "Miss Preston, an expert on medieval texts, carried on living an unassuming life, travelling everywhere by bus or on foot, buying her clothes from a catalogue and eating frozen meals, not realizing she had a fortune hanging behind the door of her spare bedroom. It was only after her death…that the panels came to light, to the shock of Miss Preston's family and the art world."[7]

In fairness to Miss Preston, we do not know what she would have done had she known the real worth of the two masterpieces. However, the fact remains that she lived a humble and self-effacing life even though she could have lived a millionaire lifestyle complete with all the trimmings: luxurious homes, designer clothes and jewelry, expensive cars, the finest food and drinks, and an array of domestic staff at her beck and call. She had a right which she failed to employ for her own benefit.

The story is also told of an illiterate woman who lived in the United States in the eighteenth century. She had an only son who was extremely wealthy and looked after her. She lived in a beautiful house with two maids, a butler, and a chauffeur, all paid for by her doting, loving, and caring son. Unfortunately, he died before she did. Following his death, the money stopped. She fell into really hard times and began to live in abject poverty. She lost her maids and could barely heat her home.

One day, her vicar was visiting when he noticed a peculiar item hanging on her wall. He asked her why she had framed it and if she knew what it was. The lady explained that on her son's death, she had received a parcel from his attorney with a beautiful piece of paper. It was from her son, and as it was the only thing she possessed that reminded her of him, she had decided to frame it and hang it on her wall.

The vicar explained that it was a check for US$500,000 and that all she had to do was pay it into her bank account and she would have so much money she would not know what to do with it. The check represented the net proceeds of her late son's estate, which she was entitled to as the sole beneficiary. The lady was so overwhelmed that she started to weep tears of joy. Here she was, living on the poverty line, when in reality she had the *entitlement* to US$500,000, an amount which today would be worth in excess of US$10 million! Why did this lady not exercise her entitlement to the money? The answer is simple. *Ignorance.*

Our third story comes from London in the United Kingdom. On November

11, 2010, a Chinese vase sold at auction for US$69 million. The urn had been sitting in the loft in a house owned by a brother and sister in Pinner, a suburb of London, for years. It was only discovered during a routine house clearance. The brother and sister were stunned when it sold for a world-record-breaking US$69 million. The eighteenth-century piece of Qianlong Era porcelain had been expected to fetch between £800,000 and £1.2 million when it went under the hammer. The vase was believed to have been acquired by an English family during the 1930s or earlier; the auctioneer, Bainbridges, said how it reached northwest London would never be known.

According to *The Harrow Times*, the owners, who had inherited the urn, had little or no idea of the fortune it would make them when they found it.[8] The vase is understood to have been carried off by a private buyer from China for what is believed to be the highest sum for any Chinese artwork ever sold at auction. Its eye-watering price shocked both the auctioneer and the owners. Helen Porter of Bainbridges said: "They had no idea what they had. They were hopeful but they didn't dare believe until the hammer went down. When it did, the sister had to go out of the room and have a breath of fresh air."

Can you imagine having a treasure worth a life-changing *US$69 million* and leaving it to rot away in your attic? The simple reason why this vase sat in the loft all those years until it was discovered is *ignorance!* Nobody knew the vase's true value until it went under the hammer. However, the truth is that the brother and sister did not become millionaires the day the Chinese vase was sold on that cold November morning at auction in Ruislip, West London. They became multimillionaires the very day *they inherited the property with all its contents.* The fact that they did not know that they owned such a treasure is irrelevant!

Our final story concerns a certain Mr. James O'Neil, a young Irishman who was said to have been born in November 1825. According to the story, in the spring of 1850, he boarded a ship to New York in the United States from Southampton in the United Kingdom. He was the oldest of nine children. He and his eight brothers and sisters were the children of Jack and Johanna O'Neil, potato farmers who lost everything in the Great Famine.

In 1850, James O'Neil was emigrating from Shannon in Ireland to Springfield, Illinois. He was fleeing the Great Famine in search of a better life for himself, with the aim of eventually returning to help those of his siblings who survived the widespread starvation occasioned by the famine. He bought his ticket with all his life savings. It was his first ever journey abroad. After paying for his ticket, he had just enough money left for his onward journey from New York to Springfield. He packed some food to eat on the ship because he thought that his ticket covered only his travel and lodgings.

After about four days on the ship, O'Neil ran out of food. He thought he would do without food for a few days and see how things went. By the second day, he was so hungry that he would do anything to get a morsel of food into his mouth. When he could no longer cope with the hunger, he made his way to the dining room for dinner. He thought to himself that he would eat and offer to work as a cleaner in the kitchen in return. It was a Sunday evening. He had the most amazing roast dinner he had ever eaten in all his life; then waited for his bill.

When the bill was not forthcoming, he called one of the waitresses aside and explained his predicament to her. The stewardess explained to him that his ticket included free food because he had paid for full board and lodging. In other words, he didn't need to have gone hungry for those two days! The day he bought his ticket and boarded the ship, he became entitled to three meals daily on the ship whether he knew it or not. Can you imagine the needless pain he suffered because of his ignorance?

"How does this apply to me as a born-again Christian?" you might ask. In every way! In case you didn't know, the single most important reason why Christians do not exert or make use of their entitlement in Christ Jesus is *ignorance,* or as the Bible puts it beautifully, "lack of knowledge."

*My people are destroyed for lack of knowledge.*

HOSEA 4:6

Notice that Hosea actually says, *"My people* are destroyed"! It is God's people, God's children—not unbelievers, not the dying world, but his own people whom he has redeemed unto himself by the precious blood of Jesus—who are being destroyed, wiped out, defeated, and crushed! Why would God's chosen people be destroyed?

The simple answer is because they are either too busy to read and study the Scriptures or they are not interested in reading and studying the Scriptures, and as a result, they demonstrate an embarrassing lack of knowledge and understanding.

The word "destroyed" here connotes defeat with all its ramifications: shattered dreams and lives ruined. It also denotes bondage or slavery to sin, as well as an inability to achieve anything in life. The word "destroyed" signifies a life of poverty, a lack of fulfillment, and an inability to either discover or fulfill one's purpose in life.

The tragedy—I would even say the *catastrophe*—of life in this day and age is that God's people simply do not know who they are in Christ Jesus. They go through life trying to be somebody else and living a lie. One of the tricks of the Enemy is to keep them from the knowledge of this vital truth, to keep them from understanding the power and purpose of salvation. It is crucial to know who we are and what we have *in Christ*. This knowledge is freely available to us in the pages of Scripture. For the Christian, ignorance is not bliss; it is negligence and carelessness.

> *"As hunger is cured by food, so ignorance is cured by study."*
>
> CHINESE PROVERB

The question that comes to mind is, of course, "How do we acquire this knowledge and this understanding?" Or in the words of the Chinese proverb, how does a person cure ignorance? The short answer is that knowledge comes by revelation through the study of the Scriptures. It is for those who are prepared to do that little bit extra which distinguishes them from ordinary folk and makes them *extra*ordinary; those who want to draw close to God; those who long to know God, his ways, his principles; those who desire God more than their necessary food; those who thirst for righteousness; those who are really serious about finding God and want him more than anything else, as found in Jeremiah 29:13–14, MSG.

To put it differently, this essential knowledge is only available to those who call out to God…those who dig deep.

> *Deep calls unto deep at the noise of Your waterfalls; all*
> *Your waves and billows have gone over me.*
>
> PSALM 42:7

Knowledge is available to those who ASK: i.e., those who *ask, seek,* and *knock.* The reason is uncomplicated. As we are told in Matthew 7:7, when you ask with anticipation you receive; when you seek wholeheartedly you find; when you knock persistently the door is opened. There must be faith, desire, and perseverance. The combination is unstoppable.

However, it is not enough *merely* to ask, seek, and knock. You must also *retain*. You must receive with thanks and appropriate what you are given. You must hold on to what you find and exercise what you possess. When the door is opened, you must enter in expectantly. "But how?" I hear you ask. By verbalizing the truth. By acknowledging that it is yours. By speaking it into your situation and circumstances. By letting the Word of God become flesh to you and allowing it to be a part of your daily routine and everyday life.

The apostle Paul puts it superbly in his epistle to Philemon in the Bible book of the same name:

> *That the sharing of your faith may become effective by*
> *the acknowledgment of every good thing which is in you in Christ Jesus.*

PHILEMON 1:6

The Word of God can be real to you. All the resources of heaven are at your disposal. God has given you all things to enjoy in Jesus Christ. However, you have a part to play. *Only you* can determine how far you go with God. God is willing and able to go with you all the way. Are you ready to walk with him? The ball is in your court.

## FOOD FOR REFLECTION

- Are you in Christ Jesus?
- Are you exercising your right to be a child of God?
- What other entitlements do you have in Christ Jesus?
- Are you a spiritual millionaire in rags?
- How do you retain what God has given you?
- What is the solution or cure for ignorance?
- Has it ever occurred to you that the difference between an ordinary person and an extraordinary person is the *extra* bit?
- How do you show faith, desire, and perseverance?

## PRAYER FEATURES

- Lord, create in me a hunger for you and a thirst for righteousness. Let it be a driving force that cannot be stopped, a fire that cannot be quenched.
- Lord, open my eyes to see myself the way you see me.

- Lord, teach me your principles.
- Lord, please help me not to be a spiritual millionaire in rags!

## ACTION POINTS

- If you are not a Christian, and you want to become one, invite Jesus into your heart and ask him to become your personal Savior and Lord. You will need to pray the sinner's prayer.[9]
- If you are a Christian, rededicate your life afresh to God and to his worship.
- Make a conscious decision to spend more time with God in daily fellowship and devotion. If you spent ten minutes previously, make it twenty minutes. If you spent fifteen minutes before, make it thirty minutes. If thirty minutes previously, make it one hour.

Chapter Two

# WHO ARE YOU?

———ᴏ/ᴏ/ᴏ———

*For the creation waits with eager longing for the revealing of the sons of God.*

Romans 8:19, rsv

Originally, man was not merely or simply a human being. He was created to be like God and to have fellowship and a personal relationship with God. The Bible states in Genesis 1:27 that man was made in the very likeness and image of God. He had the attributes of a deity. In other words, he was created to be a reflection of God's nature, character, and personality; he was a partaker of the divine nature. Of course, God and man were not exactly alike even then. Unlike God, man was a creation made from dust, with a beginning. Unlike God, he did not have the knowledge of good and evil.

However, like God, man was ideal and perfect. Like God, he was a spirit with divine attributes. He could have face-to-face communication with God. Like God, he could call unto the deep. It also seems to me that originally, before the fall, man would have been in a position to speak things into existence. This view is based on my understanding of a combination of Scriptures, notably Proverbs 18:21 "The tongue has the power of life and death" (NIV) and Job 22:28 "You will also declare a thing, and it will be established for you, so light will shine on your ways". See also Job 22:28 in The New American Standard Bible "You will also decree a thing, and it will be established for you; and light will shine on your ways" and The New Century Version, which says, "Anything you decide will be done, and light will shine on your ways."

*When I look at the night sky and see the work of your fingers—the moon and the stars you have set in place—what are mortals that you should think of us, mere humans that you should care for us? For you made us only a little lower than God, and you crowned us with glory and honor. You put us in charge of everything you made, giving us authority over all things.*

PSALM 8:3–6, NLT

In effect man was as God in that he was created by the One True God, the Almighty, to be the "god" of the earth and ruler over creation.

*So God created man in His own image; in the image of God He created him; male and female He created them.*

GENESIS 1:27

*I said, "You are gods, and all of you are children of the Most High."*

PSALM 82:6

Any question of who we are as human beings must take this origin into account. (And please note I'm talking *original intention,* not giving an excuse for present-day arrogance.)

## EVOLUTION VERSUS CREATION

Of course, the above is not the story we commonly hear in regards to our origins. Modern man is asking an entirely different set of questions: Is man a product of evolution? Did he occur as a result of the accidental coming together of various chemicals in a massive explosion?

What is evolution? *The Oxford Concise Science Dictionary* defines evolution as "the gradual process by which the present diversity of plant and animal life arose from the earliest and most primitive organisms, which is believed to have been continuing for the past 3000 million years."

Charles Darwin's book *The Origin of Species by Means of Natural Selection* is generally regarded as the foundation of evolutionary biology, the branch of biology which is primarily concerned about the origin of species from a common descent, as well as their change, multiplication, and diversity over time. *The Origin of Species* introduced the theory that populations evolve over the course of generations through a process of natural selection which ensures the survival of the fittest.

This story has become the dominant explanation of human life in our day, but it stands in sharp contrast to the teachings of the Bible. Was Darwin right or wrong? Is man the product of evolution, or did a loving God create him? Contrary to popular belief, evolution is not an established fact—and even in scientific circles, there is growing doubt as to its credibility.

Let us see what Adam Sedgwick, one of Darwin's contemporaries, thought of his theory of evolution. In his book *Evolution or Creation,* H. Enoch tells us the following story:

> Adam Sedgwick, author of the famous *Student's Text Book of Zoology,* after reading the book, *The Origin of Species,* expressed his opinion to Darwin in the following words: "I have read your book with more pain than pleasure. Parts of it I admired greatly, parts I laughed till my sides were almost sore: other parts I read with absolute sorrow because I think them utterly false and grievously mischievous."

H. Enoch then goes on to say, "As feared by this great man of science, the evolutionary idea of civilization has grown into a practical method of thought and code of conduct, affecting the reasoning and actions of every part of the human race. Human conduct is modelled on the philosophy that finds current acceptance."[1]

Dr. Wernher von Braun is an eminent and celebrated scientist widely regarded as the father of the American rocket and space program. His crowning achievement was to lead the development of the Saturn V booster rocket that helped land the first men on the moon in July 1969. In 1975 he received the National Medal of Science, which is an honor bestowed by the president of the United States to individuals in science and engineering who have made important contributions to the advancement of knowledge in the fields of behavioral and social sciences, biology, chemistry, engineering, mathematics, and physics.

In a letter originally published in 1988, this renowned and distinguished scientist stated as follows:

> For me, the idea of a creation is not conceivable without invoking the necessity of design. One cannot be exposed to the law and order of the Universe without concluding that there must be design and purpose behind it all. In the world around us, we can behold the obvious manifestations of an ordered, structured plan or design. We can see the will of the species to live and propagate. And we are humbled by the powerful forces at work

on a galactic scale, and the purposeful orderliness of nature that endows a tiny and ungainly seed with the ability to develop into a beautiful flower.

The better we understand the intricacies of the Universe and all it harbors, the more reason we have found to marvel at the inherent design upon which it is based. While the admission of a design for the Universe ultimately raises the question of a Designer (a subject outside the realm of science), the scientific method does not allow us to exclude data which lead to the conclusion that the Universe, life, and man are based on design. To be forced to believe only one conclusion—that everything in the Universe happened by chance—would violate the very objectivity of science itself. Certainly there are those who argue that the Universe evolved via a random process, but what random process could produce the brain of a man or the human eye?

Some people suggest that science has been unable to prove the existence of a Designer. They admit that many of the miracles in the world around us are hard to understand, and they do not deny that the Universe, as modern science sees it, is indeed a far more wondrous thing than the creation that medieval man could perceive. But they still maintain that since science has provided us with so many answers, the day will soon arrive when we will be able to understand even the creation of the fundamental laws of nature without invoking divine intent. They challenge science to prove the existence of God. *But must we really light a candle to see the Sun?* Many men who are intelligent and of good faith say they cannot visualize a Designer. Well, can a physicist visualize an electron? The electron is materially inconceivable, and yet it is so perfectly known through its effects that we use it to illuminate our cities, guide our airliners through the night skies and take the most accurate measurements.

What strange rationale makes some physicists accept the inconceivable electron as real, while refusing to accept the reality of a Designer on the ground that they cannot conceive of Him? I am afraid that, although they really do not understand the electron either, they are ready to accept it because they managed to produce a rather clumsy mechanical model of it borrowed from rather limited experience in other fields, yet they would not know how to begin building a model of God.

I have discussed the aspect of a Grand Designer at some length because it might be that the primary resistance to acknowledging the "case for design" as a viable scientific alternative to the current "case for chance" lies in the inconceivability, in some scientists' minds, of a Designer. The inconceivability of some ultimate issue (which always will lie outside scientific resolution) should not be allowed to rule out any theory that explains the interrelationship of observed data and is useful for prediction.

We at NASA often are asked what the real reason was for the amazing string of successes we have had with our Apollo flights to the Moon. I think the only honest answer we could give was that we tried to never overlook anything. It is in that same sense of scientific honesty that I endorse the presentation of alternative theories for the origin of the Universe, life, and man in the science classroom. It would be an error to overlook the possibility that the Universe was planned rather than happening by chance.[2]

I couldn't agree more! There is too much structure to man's life from birth to death for him to have evolved from apes—or from anything else, for that matter! Human beings are too complex and wonderful to be the result of an accident or the consequence of evolution.

*For You formed my inward parts;*
*You covered me in my mother's womb.*
*I will praise You, for I am fearfully and wonderfully made;*
*Marvelous are Your works,*
*And that my soul knows very well.*

PSALM 139:13–14

Let us take the blood vessels as an example. They consist of arteries, veins, and capillaries. During blood circulation, the arteries carry blood from the heart, the veins carry the blood back to the heart, and the capillaries connect the arteries to veins. The Franklin Institute tells us that if all the blood vessels of an average child were taken out of his body and laid out in one line, they would be over 60,000 miles long! That is about 97,000 kilometers! An average adult's blood vessels would be close to 100,000 miles long if laid out in one line, or 156,200 kilometers.[3]

Just to put this into context, let us take a quick look at the distances between some major cities of the world. The distance between New York City and London is 3,471 miles (5,585 kilometers); the distance from New York City to Los Angeles is 2,462 miles (3,961 kilometers); the distance between New York City and Jakarta, Indonesia, is 10,053 miles (16,179 kilometers); the distance from Los Angeles to Manila, Philippines, is 7,295 miles (11,740 kilometers); the distance from Los Angeles to Chicago is 1,749 miles (2,815 kilometers); and the distance between London and New Zealand is 11,654 miles (18,755 kilometers).

The sheer size, extent, and magnitude of the blood vessels tell us two things: the awesomeness of God's work in man and the fact that as human beings, every one of us is a walking wonder, an amazing work of art.

What of the human brain? The brain and spinal cord make up the central nervous system of the body. The brain is said to comprise over ten billion nerve cells and in excess of fifty billion other cells! It is the site of consciousness, thought, and creativity. The brain is simply extraordinary! According to The Franklin Institute, "Your brain houses your cherished memories and future hopes. It orchestrates the symphony of consciousness that gives you purpose and passion, motion and emotion."[4] Could this have come about by accident? I don't think so.

In his book *Darwin's Black Box: The Biochemical Challenge to Evolution*, Michael J. Behe, Professor of Biological Sciences at Lehigh University, argues that the organic world is so complex, particularly at the level of molecular biology and biochemistry, that Darwinian evolution cannot possibly have led to it. According to Behe, the most convincing evidence for design is not to be found in the stars or the fossils, but in biochemical systems. In his view, Darwinism, whatever it may explain at the organismic level, fails to account for the evolution of the complex biochemical machinery that is found in every living cell. He states that for the Darwinian theory of evolution to be true, it has to account for the molecular structure of life, and that it is the purpose of his book to show that it does not.

Why does the existence of these (and many other) systems rule out evolution? Simply because they are "irreducibly complex," as Behe puts it, meaning that if they are missing just one of their many parts, they cannot function. Behe tells us that irreducibly complex systems cannot evolve in a Darwinian fashion. He then goes on to say,

> To a person who does not feel obliged to restrict his search to unintelligent causes, the straightforward conclusion is that many biochemical systems were designed. They were designed not by the laws of nature, not by

chance and necessity; rather, they were *planned.* The designer knew what the systems would look like when they were completed, then took steps to bring the systems about. Life on earth at its most fundamental level, in its most critical components, is the product of intelligent activity. The conclusion of intelligent design flows naturally from the data itself—not from sacred books or sectarian beliefs.[5]

Now let us take a look at the human heart. The heart is the engine of the human body which pumps blood all around the body. Scientists say that in the average person, the pumping of the heart (called the cardiac cycle) occurs about seventy-two times per minute. The cardiac output of the average human heart over a lifetime is said to be about one million liters! With the average heart rate of seventy-two beats per minute, the heart beats around 2.5 billion times during the lifetime of an average person! Isn't that just incredible? Could this really be the result of evolution?

Dr. Michael Denton, a molecular biologist and medical doctor, in his book *Evolution: A Theory in Crisis,* sets out to explain the gathering scientific evidence against evolution in its traditional form. He argues that the scientific theory of evolution by natural selection is a theory in crisis, enabling us to understand why an increasing number of research scientists are questioning strict Darwinism.

He states that "The popular conception of a triumphant Darwin increasingly confident after 1859 in his views of evolution is a travesty. On the contrary, by the time the last edition of the *Origin* was published in 1872, he had become plagued with self-doubt and frustrated by his inability to meet the many objections which had been leveled at his theory."[6]

According to Denton, the theory's claims to account for the relationship between classes and orders, let alone the origin of life, appear to be based on shaky foundations at best. As he put it, "Neither speciation nor even the most trivial type of evolution had ever actually been observed directly in nature. [Darwin] provided no direct evidence that natural selection had ever caused any biological change in nature and the concept was in itself flawed because it was impossible to reconcile with the theory of heredity in vogue at that time. The idea of evolution on a grand scale was entirely speculative and Darwin was quite unable to demonstrate the "infinitude of connecting links," the existence of which he repeatedly admitted was crucial to his theory."[6]

What of fingerprints? Just like DNA, the fingerprint is unique to each individual. According to Maria Timmins in her article "All About Fingerprints":

A fingerprint is a "friction ridge skin" arrangement. This covers the palm surface of the hands, fingers and the corresponding areas on the soles of the feet, and it consists of tiny ridges and furrows. On the tips of your fingers the ridges are arranged into different patterns and this is your fingerprint. As the arrangement of these ridges and furrows is unique to the individual and does not alter throughout life, it can be used for identification purposes.

How do we get the marks on our fingers? The friction ridge skin develops between 6 and 24 weeks of foetal development. Skin cells grow on the surface of the skin and fuse to form the ridges. As these ridges form, some fuse, some branch and others break to form individual ridge features and ridge patterns. The arrangement of the ridges is fully formed by the 24th week.

Why are fingerprints unique? Factors that affect the rate of ridge development include environmental e.g. temperature and genetic. These random factors combine to ensure that the ridges and ridge features form at different rates. As the same pregnancy can never be recreated, the same ridge development can't. Therefore, even identical twins have different fingerprints.[7]

In other words, no two people in the world have the same set of fingerprints. And this is despite the fact that the population of the world is currently estimated by the United States Census Bureau to be 7,000,000,000!

Having regard to the blood vessels, the human brain, DNA, the human heart, and the fingerprint, can anyone say with any degree of confidence that God did not create man? To my mind, the answer is a resounding and unequivocal no.

What a piece of work is a man, how noble in reason, how infinite in faculties, in form and moving, how express and admirable in action, how like an angel in apprehension, how like a god. (William Shakespeare, *Hamlet*[8])

Without a shadow of doubt, God created man. Man was designed, planned, and well thought-out. He was a deliberate part of God's plan, not a last-minute addition. From Genesis 1:26, we can picture God the Father calling a meeting of the Trinity in heaven, and at the end of the meeting they agreed as follows: "Let us make human beings in our image, to be like us" (NLT). After that, God formed man from the dust of the earth. Finally, he gave him the breath of life, and man was transformed from a lifeless object to a living being.

## GOD MADE ADEQUATE PROVISION FOR MAN'S MISSION

Before God made man, he provided everything that man would need, which is why man was made on the last day of creation. Man was not an afterthought! Besides all of the physical things he needed to live, God made adequate provision for man's mission. Man had all the resources he required to fulfill his purpose. All the raw materials needed to discover, accomplish, and carry out his destiny were at his disposal in the beautiful garden of Eden.

Despite the fact that he was the last to be created by God, man was in fact the most important of all God's creation. He obtained significance in two ways. First, he was born great by virtue of the fact that he was made in the image of God, to be like God. Second, he had greatness thrust upon him insofar as God blessed him and gave him authority and control over the rest of creation.

Man had authority and dominion. He was born to rule, to reign. He was formed to preside over all creation. He had a divine mandate to direct, to control, and to take charge. He had a duty to fill the earth and to govern it. In a nutshell, he was king of the earth.

*Then God blessed them, and God said to them, "Be fruitful and multiply; fill the earth and subdue it; have dominion over the fish of the sea, over the birds of the air, and over every living thing that moves on the earth."*

GENESIS 1:28

However, man committed high treason in the garden of Eden when he disobeyed God. God had given him a specific instruction not to eat of the fruit of the Tree of the Knowledge of Good and Evil, else he would die. Like many of us today, the first man was caught up with the yearning of his eyes, the craving of his body, and the pride of his life. After all, the fruit was good to look at, it was desirable for food, and it could make one wise! He made the wrong choice. By the single act of disobedience recorded in Genesis 3, humanity rejected God. At that moment, *in that very instant,* man died spiritually because he lost fellowship and communion and contact with God.

When man sinned, he fell from grace and favor. He lost his position. He lost his robes of righteousness and became naked. He lost his God-given authority, which he handed over to Satan as he fell. He became a slave to Satan and sin, and at that precise moment, in that split second, Satan automatically, immediately, and *instantaneously* became the god of this world.

> *Then the devil, taking [Jesus] up on a high mountain, showed Him all the kingdoms of the world in a moment of time. And the devil said to Him, "All this authority I will give you, and their glory; for this has been delivered to me, and I give it to whomever I wish."*

LUKE 4:5–6, EMPHASIS SUPPLIED

> *Satan, who is the god of this world, has blinded the minds of those who don't believe. They are unable to see the glorious light of the Good News.*

2 CORINTHIANS 4:4, NLT

When Adam fell, he took the whole universe down with him. Having done the crime, he had to serve the time. God had no choice but to drive man from Eden to prevent him from eating the fruit of the Tree of Life; otherwise man would have become immortal in his fallen state, which would have been a real nightmare for God! Adam was driven from the garden of Eden to serve his time in the prison that is this world. The whole of creation came under the Adamic curse alongside him. That curse is manifested primarily in death, poverty, and disease.

As it's painted in Genesis and seen in our experience, death is both spiritual and physical: spiritual death being separation from God and physical death, when we stop breathing and give up the ghost. As for poverty, the earth's resources were cursed so that man would have to work extra hard to eke out a living. All living things are now subject to different types of diseases, infirmities, and sicknesses. Women particularly have a hard time at childbirth:

> *[God] told the Woman: "I'll multiply your pains in childbirth; you'll give birth to your babies in pain. You'll want to please your husband, but he'll lord it over you." He told the Man: "Because you listened to your wife and ate from the tree that I commanded you not to eat from, 'Don't eat from this tree,' the very ground is cursed because of you; getting food from the ground will be as painful as having babies is for your wife; you'll be working in pain all your*

*life long. The ground will sprout thorns and weeds, you'll get your food the hard way, planting and tilling and harvesting, sweating in the fields from dawn to dusk, until you return to that ground yourself, dead and buried; you started out as dirt, you'll end up dirt."*

GENESIS 3:16–19, MSG

Not surprisingly, God had a rescue package. After all, he is all-knowing, and nothing catches him unawares. He told the serpent that one day the seed of the woman would bruise his head, while the serpent would at best bruise his heel.

In addition, there was a need for a connection between God and man. A kind of God-Man: someone who was God and man at the same time. Someone who would understand the righteousness and justice of God as well as the frailties of man; an arbitrator who could bridge the gap between both, lay his hands on them, and reconcile them. This need is seen throughout the Old Testament:

*Then Job answered: "Truly I know that it is so: But how can a man be just before God? If one wished to contend with him, one could not answer him once in a thousand times…For he is not a man, as I am, that I might answer him, that we should come to trial together. There is no umpire between us, who might lay his hand upon us both."*

JOB 9:1–3, 32–33, RSV

Put differently, God wanted a kinsman-redeemer. What is that? *The Chambers 21st Century Dictionary* describes a *kinsman* as "a relative by blood or marriage." The same dictionary defines *redeemer* as "One who redeems: The Redeemer [is] A name for Jesus Christ." It then defines *redeemed* as follows: "[In] Christianity, said of Christ: to free (humanity) from sin by his death on the cross."

A kinsman-redeemer is therefore a person who redeems his relative or kinsman; he is the next of kin who settles a debt which his family member is unable to pay. The kinsman-redeemer is able to put himself in the place of the relation he is assisting because, being his kinsman, he understands his problems. Jesus is called our kinsman-redeemer because he came to the earth in the form of a man and thus became physically related to the human race. He then paid the price for man's debt by his death on the cross of Calvary—crushing the devil's head even as the devil "bruised his heel."

God didn't have to look too far to find the link, the kinsman-redeemer, the sacrificial lamb. Jesus was the Lamb of God. In John 1:29, John the Baptist declared concerning Jesus, "Behold! The Lamb of God who takes away the sin of the world!" Although God is a God of love, he is also a God of justice. In his justice, somebody had to die, because Ezekiel 18:20 sets out a spiritual law in very clear terms: namely, that the penalty for sin is death. Hebrews 9:22 reinforces the fact that "without the shedding of blood, there is no forgiveness" (NLT).

As there was nobody else who could shed his blood to redeem mankind, Jesus offered to die in our place. He became the sacrificial lamb without blemish, spot, or wrinkle, who died in our place once and for all. He became the one upon whom was laid the sin and iniquity of us all.

> *Under the old system, the blood of goats and bulls and the ashes of a young cow could cleanse people's bodies from ceremonial impurity. Just think how much more the blood of Christ will purify our consciences from sinful deeds so that we can worship the living God. For by the power of the eternal Spirit, Christ offered himself to God as a perfect sacrifice for our sins. That is why he is the one who mediates a new covenant between God and people, so that all who are called can receive the eternal inheritance God has promised them. For Christ died to set them free from the penalty of the sins they had committed under that first covenant.*
>
> HEBREWS 9:13–15, NLT

You can see that even in the mess that Adam created, there was to be a Messiah. Jesus Christ, the second person of the Trinity, fit the bill perfectly. He volunteered to be the atonement for man's sin. He was God, but he did not mind coming into this world to become a man. He would understand both God and man. He would be a sinless man. He would be a perfect sacrifice. And so he was. He died on the cross of Calvary and rose from the dead after three days. For man, he became the way, the truth, and the road back to God.

> *Think of yourselves the way Christ Jesus thought of himself. He had equal status with God but didn't think so much of himself that he had to cling to the advantages of that status no matter what. Not at all. When the time came, he set aside the privileges of deity and took on the status of a slave, became human! Having become human, he stayed human. It was an incredibly humbling*

*process. He didn't claim special privileges. Instead, he lived a selfless, obedient life and then died a selfless, obedient death—and the worst kind of death at that—a crucifixion.*

PHILIPPIANS 2:5–8, MSG

*Jesus said, "I am the Road, also the Truth, also the Life. No one gets to the Father apart from me."*

JOHN 14:6, MSG

The apostle Paul looks at Jesus in Romans 5 as "the second Adam"—the second beginning for mankind. The first Adam disobeyed and lost out to the devil. The second Adam obeyed and retrieved man's lost authority. In his death and resurrection, Jesus destroyed the power of sin and broke the curse. He came to restore man to God's original place, plan, and purpose.

In Adam, all sinned and came under the dominion and condemnation of Satan. On the other hand, in Jesus there is salvation and redemption. He restores as many as accept his vicarious sacrifice to their original location and standing. In him there is full restoration. In the words of the Latin phrase so often used by lawyers, *restitutio in integrum*—reinstatement and return to man's original position before the fall.

So, who are you? The answer to that question can only be found in the second Adam, Jesus Christ. Without him we are nothing, we are lost, and we are on a one-way ticket to hell.

## YOU ARE MORE THAN A CONQUEROR

*Who shall separate us from the love of Christ? Shall tribulation, or distress, or persecution, or famine, or nakedness, or peril, or sword? As it is written: "For Your sake we are killed all day long; we are accounted as sheep for the slaughter." Yet in all these things we are more than conquerors through Him who loved us.*

ROMANS 8:35–37

A conqueror is a victor, one who has conquered and triumphed over his adversary. As children of God, we are not just conquerors; we are described as "more than conquerors." Put differently, the margin of our victory is so great that we do not merely have a conquest, we have *overwhelming* victory! Why? Simply because no matter how great the powers of this world, the Greater One indwells us. The Holy Spirit who dwells within us is greater than the devil in the world. We are victorious in Christ Jesus. Outside of him, we are but meat for the Enemy. However, *in* him we overcome, because he destroyed all the work of the devil at Calvary, and as we are told in Acts 17:28, in him we live and move and have our being. Second Corinthians 2:14 adds it voice to this truth, reminding us that the Lord causes us to triumph always in all things.

This very notion of triumph shows that there is a battle. You are involved in spiritual warfare. But no matter how difficult the battle may get, God expects you to have the mentality of a conqueror. See yourself as a victor *in Christ Jesus,* and go about life with a holy swagger!

## You Are Redeemed

*He has delivered us from the power of darkness and conveyed us into the kingdom of the Son of His love, in whom we have redemption through His blood, the forgiveness of sins.*

Colossians 1:13–14

The use of the word "redeem" here means to save from the bondage of sin. It means to ransom, to set free; it stands for the rescue of a person from the power and consequences of sin. It also connotes the recovery of ownership of something by paying a specified sum.

The story is told of a young girl who made a beautiful work of art that she loved and treasured. Unfortunately, she lost the artwork when her family moved to a new home. She was so terribly upset that she became inconsolable. One day, she went to a garage sale near the local park and saw her beloved artwork on display with a price tag of £10. She went to the shop owner and told him that the artwork was hers. She informed him that she had made it, that it bore her signature, and that she wanted it back.

The old man gently stroked his gray hair and smiled playfully at her as he told her that she might have made the artwork, but it no longer belonged to her; although he sympathized with her plight, the painting was now his. If she wanted it, she would have to pay for it. Not wanting to let money come between her and her beloved artwork, she ran back home to ask her parents for the money. She then returned to the seller with the money and paid for the painting. Afterwards, she told herself that she now owned the artwork twice: first when she had made it and secondly when she paid the price for it.

God did exactly the same thing for man. God made man in his image, to be like him. And so man belonged to God originally. However, man sold out to the devil. Jesus therefore had to pay the ultimate price to buy man back to God. The price was his very life, as he shed his precious blood at Calvary. In redemption, there is a complete restoration of all that was lost in Adam. And so in Jesus, we are set free from the Adamic curse, and we recover all: eternal life, divine health, and heavenly provision.

## You Are Righteous

*God made him who had no sin to be sin for us, so that in him we might become the righteousness of God.*

2 Corinthians 5:21, niv

Those who accept Jesus's sacrificial death are made new. *Positionally* they are righteous before God; that is to say, they have right standing with God. This is because when God looks at them, he sees what Jesus accomplished on their behalf through his death on the cross of Calvary. They have been made perfect. Yet, *experientially,* Christians are still in a growth process. They have *been* made perfect, yet they *are* being made holy. Said another way: by his death and resurrection, Jesus makes us perfect, yet we are being progressively made holy, cleansed, and set apart daily.

Having been saved by God, it is now your responsibility to pursue righteousness not just *positionally* but *in reality.* Both you and God have a part to play here. In the words of the apostle Paul, "Therefore, my beloved…work out your own salvation with fear and trembling; for it is God who works in you both to will and to do for His good pleasure" (Philippians 2:12–13). Now that you have become a child of God, you can (and indeed should) encourage and facilitate this process, while being entirely dependent upon God and allowing the Holy Spirit to work in you. Let me make it clear that this isn't something we do in our power, but out of our new birth in the Holy Spirit. For this to happen, you need to:

- Constantly renew your mind with the Word. Spend quality time on the Word of God. Study it, meditate upon it, live it, and make it an integral part of your daily routine.

- Cultivate, develop, and nurture all the fruits of the Spirit: love, joy, peace, patience, kindness, goodness, faithfulness, gentleness, and self-control. This happens as you yield control of your life to the Holy Spirit. In addition, you need to desire these fruits. You need to pray them into your life. Displaying the fruit of the Spirit is crucial because we know who people really are by their outgrowth—by their fruit.

- Know God. Not just his acts, but also his ways. This comes by revelation through the study of the Word of God. As you draw close to him and seek him in daily devotion and fellowship, he will draw close to you and reveal himself to you. You need to be sincere in your desire for God. You need to seek him wholeheartedly.

- Please God. To please God is to be set apart for God. To be separated for him alone. To be removed from every common use. To sanctify and consecrate yourself for God. Knowing God and his principles should make it less challenging for you to live your life for him.

- Accept the discipline and guidance which Jesus gives. You do this by giving Jesus Christ total control of all your desires and goals. In addition to being your Savior, he becomes your Lord as well. You allow him to take over the reins of your life. You enthrone him in your heart. You become his disciple.

## YOU ARE A JOINT HEIR WITH JESUS

*And if children, then heirs—heirs of God and joint heirs with Christ, if indeed we suffer with Him, that we may also be glorified together.*

ROMANS 8:17

An *heir* is a person who inherits, or is entitled by law or the terms of a will to inherit, the estate of another person. Hebrews 1:2 tells us that Jesus has been appointed heir of all things and made so much better than the angels, because he obtained a more excellent name than the angels through inheritance. As a child of God, you automatically become an heir of God and a joint heir with Jesus Christ. As God's heir, you have access to all spiritual blessings through Jesus Christ. Not only that, but as a joint heir with Jesus Christ, you become a joint beneficiary of all the things that Jesus is entitled to.

Paul states in Romans 8:22 that the whole of creation is groaning and waiting in eager anticipation for *your* manifestation as a son of God. If there was ever a time for Christians to exercise their right to be children of God, it is now! The world is crying out for people who can do exploits because they know their God. This is the time to arise and shine and bring glory and honor to God. Mankind is desperately waiting for people who will display the manifold wisdom of God. Even the Lord Jesus Christ is waiting…for his enemies to be made his footstool (John 1:12; Daniel 11:32; Isaiah 60:1; Ephesians 3:10–11; Hebrews 10:13).

## YOU ARE A CHILD OF GOD

*For as many as are led by the Spirit of God, these are sons of God. For you did not receive the spirit of bondage again to fear, but you received the Spirit of adoption by whom we cry out, "Abba, Father." The Spirit Himself bears witness with our spirit that we are children of God.*

### ROMANS 8:14–16

That's right! You are a child of the Most High God. You can actually call God Almighty, the Creator of the heavens and the earth, *Father*. Isn't that amazing, that mere mortals like you and me can call the Ancient of Days, the Maker of the universe, the Creator of all things, the One who upholds all things in place by his word, our Father? Some religions teach that God neither begets nor is he begotten—i.e. that God is neither a child nor does he have children. Much as I respect their viewpoint, they are very sadly mistaken. The Bible, the *only* true Word of God, teaches emphatically and categorically that Jesus was God's only begotten Son and that as many as receive Jesus into their hearts as Lord and Savior are given the right to become children of God through the atoning sacrifice of Jesus Christ.

Not only are you a child of the King of Kings, you are also a walking wonder. No matter what you look like, you are a masterpiece, beautifully put together by a caring and loving God. You are unique and special. You are so exceptional and important that if you were the only person in the world, Jesus would still have died for you.

*Oh yes, you shaped me first inside, then out; you formed me in my mother's womb. I thank you, High God—you're breathtaking! Body and soul, I am marvelously made! I worship in adoration—what a creation! You know me inside and out, you know every bone in my body; you know exactly how I was made, bit by bit, how I was sculpted from nothing into something. Like an open book, you watched me grow from conception to birth; all the stages of my life were spread out before you, the days of my life all prepared before I'd even lived one day.*

PSALM 139:13–16, MSG

Regardless of what your parents may have told you about the circumstances surrounding your conception and birth, you are not an accident of history. Even if your parents did not plan to have a child when you were born, the fact remains that God created you for a specific purpose, his purpose. It is also the case that you can only find out the purpose of a thing from its manufacturer. It is therefore not for you as the one who was created, to *determine* your purpose, the reason for your existence. It is for you to *discover* your purpose by asking the Creator why he created you! And the really interesting bit is that if you ask him, he will reveal your purpose to you.

## YOU ARE A PARTAKER OF THE DIVINE NATURE

*Grace and peace be multiplied to you in the knowledge of God and of Jesus our Lord, as His divine power has given to us all things that pertain to life and godliness, through the knowledge of Him who called us by glory and virtue, by which have been given to us exceedingly great and precious promises, that through these you may be partakers of the divine nature, having escaped the corruption that is in the world through lust.*

2 PETER 1:2–4

As a born-again child of God who has been regenerated and redeemed, you become a partaker of God's divine nature. This is hardly surprising, because as part of the process of being born again, God's own seed, the divine sperm, has come to dwell in you, making it impossible for you to want to commit sin willfully and habitually. We are born again, not of corruptible seed, but of an incorruptible seed (1 Peter 1:23).

At the new birth, God imparts part of his nature to us. There is no ambiguity in the apostle Peter's use of the words "divine nature." The words mean exactly what they say: that the divine nature, the very nature of God, has come into us; and so we don't need to try to explain them away, or worse still, dilute them as some teachers have attempted to do. Without a doubt, every true believer in Christ Jesus is a recipient of the very nature and life of God. In Christ Jesus, you are a participant of God's nature.

## HOW DO YOU EXERCISE YOUR RIGHT TO BE A CHILD OF GOD?

### KNOW WHAT THE BIBLE SAYS ABOUT BEING A CHILD OF GOD.

Search the Scriptures. Highlight the passages that tell you about your inheritance as a child of God. Study them, commit them to memory, meditate upon them, and make them a part of your everyday life. Make them a part of your daily routine. This is very important because your future is tied up in your daily routine!

### SEE YOURSELF AS A CHILD OF GOD AND LIVE AS ONE.

See yourself the way God sees you. God sees you through the accomplished work at Calvary. When he looks at you, he sees what Jesus did on the cross. You are victorious. You are an overcomer. You are a child of the Most High God. You are a partaker of the divine nature. You are a joint heir with Jesus. The Holy Spirit who dwells within you is greater than the devil in the world.

### ACKNOWLEDGE EVERY GOOD GIFT YOU HAVE AS A CHILD OF GOD, AND PUT THESE GIFTS TO USE FOR YOUR OWN BENEFIT.

Identify everything that is yours in Jesus Christ. Ask God for a revelation of all the gifts you have in Jesus Christ. Seek to activate those gifts and talents which may lie latent within you. Ask for grace to put all your gifts to use for God's glory. Desire, covet, and ask God for the gifts of the Spirit that are relevant to your life and ministry. Appropriate the benefits of the ministry of the blood of Jesus, which is upon the mercy seat in the tabernacle in heaven crying better things on your behalf than the blood of Abel (Hebrews 12:24).

### DETERMINE NOT TO BE A SPIRITUAL MILLIONAIRE IN RAGS.

Make use of all God's abundant provision for your life here on earth. Determine to avail yourself of whatever resource is available for your journey on this side of eternity. From James 4:2 we understand that sometimes the only reason we do not receive from God is that we fail to ask. We do everything else: we moan, we grumble, we whinge, we complain, we start a pity party, we even cry…we do the whole lot except pray. Believe me when I say that there is an abundance of resources and spare parts in heaven which we need to draw upon in our journey through life.

Make use of God's provision. Do not get to heaven to discover that you had so much but lived beneath the poverty line because of ignorance.

## FOOD FOR REFLECTION

- Who are you?
- Do you consider yourself to be a child of God and a joint heir with Christ Jesus?
- What does it mean to be a joint heir?
- What is your purpose in life?
- Is there a difference between your standing positionally and your standing in reality?
- How do you see the word "impossible"?

## PRAYER FEATURES

- Lord, I acknowledge your accomplished work at Calvary. Please give me a revelation of all that I am in Christ Jesus.
- Lord, help me to work out my salvation even as you help me both to will and do your good pleasure for my life.
- Lord, reveal yourself to me.
- Lord, help me to discover my purpose in life, the reason why you redeemed me.
- Lord, open my eyes to see myself the way you see me.
- Lord, give me a revelation of the truth that if I have faith as small as a mustard seed, nothing will be impossible for me.

## ACTION POINTS

- Make a conscious effort to discover your purpose in life. Start by identifying your talents and gifts. Those should usually give you an inclination of your calling.
- Identify and make a list of all the Bible promises that relate to who you are in Jesus. Personalize them and speak them to yourself on a regular basis.
- Make a list of the things you have always wanted to undertake but which you thought were impossible. Now, prayerfully, have a go at them, one at a time.

# Chapter Three

# SPIRITUAL WARFARE

—⟨ɷɷ⟩—

*The weapons we fight with are not the weapons of the world.*
*On the contrary, they have divine power to demolish strongholds.*
*We demolish arguments and every pretension that sets itself up against the knowledge*
*of God, and we take captive every thought to make it obedient to Christ.*

2 CORINTHIANS 10:4–5, NIV

Spiritual warfare is very real. There is a furious, fierce, and ferocious battle raging in the realm of the spirit between the forces of God and the forces of evil. Warfare happens every day, all the time. Whether you believe it or not, you are in a battlefield. You are in warfare. The moment you become a Christian, the devil's grip over your life is broken, you cease to be his child, and you become a threat to him. He begins to see you as his enemy and seeks to either win you back or destroy you. You are therefore immediately thrust onto the front line of this brutal battle whether you appreciate it or not, whether you like it or not, and whether you *know* it or not.

The first thing you need to know is who your enemy is and who it is not. Paul makes it very clear in Ephesians 6 that we are not fighting against people made of flesh and blood, but against the evil rulers and authorities of the unseen world, against those mighty powers of darkness who rule this world, and against wicked spirits in the heavenly realms. In other words, you are fighting an enemy who is a spirit. You are waging war against an enemy who is invisible to the naked eye. To stand a chance, you must rely totally, utterly, and completely on God, because he is spirit. He can see the end of a thing from its beginning and is in fact the Lord of Hosts (or "Lord of heaven's armies," in today's English). Our weapons are mighty through God, and we are nothing without him. The battle is really his; you are merely a battle-axe, a sword, or an arrow in his hands.

On the cross of Calvary, Jesus obtained victory over sin, sickness, and death. He triumphed over the Enemy through his death and resurrection. Jesus Christ's triumph at Calvary means that in this warfare, our victory has been predetermined. Jesus, the greater one, far superior to the Enemy, is with you, therefore you are assured of triumph and victory. This is the only battle where the outcome is pre-ordained and predestined, even before the fighting begins. How remarkable is that!

*For this purpose the Son of God was manifested, that He might destroy the works of the devil.*

1 JOHN 3:8

*And you, being dead in your trespasses and the uncircumcision of your flesh, He has made alive together with Him, having forgiven you all trespasses, having wiped out the handwriting of requirements that was against us, which was contrary to us. And He has taken it out of the way, having nailed it to the cross. Having disarmed principalities and powers, He made a public spectacle of them, triumphing over them in it.*

COLOSSIANS 2:13–15

*No, despite all these things, overwhelming victory is ours through Christ, who loved us.*

ROMANS 8:37, NLT

This battle continues until you depart from this world. As you go on in this battle, spectators are urging you on. The saints triumphant, i.e., the Christians who have died and gone ahead of us to heaven, have become "a cloud of witnesses" who are cheering you on.

## WHAT SHOULD BE YOUR OBJECTIVE IN SPIRITUAL WARFARE?

### TO ENFORCE JESUS'S VICTORY

Jesus came to redeem mankind from sin, but to achieve this objective he had to first destroy all the work of the Enemy. Through his death on the cross of Calvary and his subsequent resurrection from the dead on the third day, Jesus completely disarmed the devil and his cohorts. After winning the victory on the cross, Jesus then empowered his followers ("as many as receive him") to enforce his triumph by giving them authority and power over the devil and all his power. In Luke 10:19, Jesus said, "I have given you authority to trample on snakes and scorpions and to overcome all the power of the enemy; nothing will harm you" (NIV). In the words of Jeremiah 51:20, you become his "battle-ax and weapons of war: for with you I will break the nation in pieces; with you I will destroy kingdoms."

Having returned to heaven, Jesus is now waiting until his enemies are made his footstool. That will be the final and ultimate consummation of his victory. The Bible says in Hebrews 10:12–14, "But this Man, after He had offered one sacrifice for sins forever, sat down at the right hand of God, from that time waiting till His enemies are made His footstool. For by one offering He has perfected forever those who are being sanctified."

You make Jesus's enemies into his footstool by enforcing the victory through the name of Jesus, a name which has been exalted by God above every other name. It is now for the church, which is the body of Christ—that is, the *ordinary Christian*—to enforce the victory that Jesus won on the cross of Calvary over two thousand years ago. You do this by exercising your authority over the Enemy and living your life in victory.

## To make known to the adversary the manifold wisdom of God

One of the main goals and purposes of spiritual warfare is for born-again children of God to show and demonstrate to the adversary and his cohorts the manifold, multifarious, and diverse wisdom of God.

> *To the intent that now the manifold wisdom of God might be made known by the church to the principalities and powers in the heavenly places according to the eternal purpose which [God] accomplished in Christ Jesus our Lord.*
>
> EPHESIANS 3:10–11

The word translated "manifold" is from the Greek *poulupoikilos* (pol-oo-poy-kil-os) and can mean much-variegated, exhibiting different colors, especially as irregular patches or streaks.[1] The word can also be translated *multifarious* and *diverse*. There is also a sense in which the wisdom of God is unfathomable because it cannot be fully explored or understood. There is always a new layer, a new level, a new quality of God's wisdom to be discovered and displayed. There will always be a new aspect, a new dimension of God's wisdom, to be experienced.

You display God's awesome wisdom to the Enemy as you outsmart him in this battle. You do this as you depend totally upon the Holy Spirit in this conflict. You do not depend on your experience or expertise; instead, you completely rely on the leading, direction, and guidance of the Holy Spirit, acknowledging him in all your ways.

## To destroy the Enemy's strongholds

A *stronghold* is an iron grip, a fortress in the minds and lives of people. In the mind, it can be an idea that has taken root and become a strong opinion, sometimes through brainwashing, wrong teaching, or a traumatic experience. On the other hand, in the daily lives of people a stronghold can be a bad habit or particular way of doing things which militates against any kind of spiritual progress. Through such strongholds, the Enemy has blinded the minds of the people of this world so that they cannot perceive the glorious light of the gospel.

The Enemy erects and maintains strongholds in people's lives and minds to prevent them from understanding the truth of the gospel and accepting the atonement offered by Jesus Christ. In effect, what the Enemy does is to take hold of these people and lock them up in his territory so that they become blind to the basic truth of God's Word. Have you ever come across somebody who is highly intelligent yet cannot understand the simple truths about the atonement? You have seen the walls of a stronghold.

These strongholds must crumble if people are to be set free from the grip of the Evil One. As Paul said in 2 Timothy 3:5, some of them have a form of godliness but deny the power of salvation. However, at the name of Jesus every knee must bow—without any exceptions. God expects you and me to destroy these strongholds and to set the people free because his desire is that everyone would know Jesus as personal Savior and Lord.

## To cast down arguments and every high thing that exalts itself against the knowledge of God

To enable him to maintain his stranglehold on people, the Enemy sets up defense mechanisms in their minds. These are argumentative barricades, hedges, fences, partitions, and dividing walls that he helps them erect around their minds and hearts. Some of them are mind-control techniques, which denounce God and promote the power of the subconscious mind. Others are moral codes, which teach morality and goodness with no reference to God whatsoever—they effectively add the letter "o" to *God* to create the word *good.*

With the weapons of our warfare (which are listed in the next section of this chapter), we are able to tear down and destroy every proud line of reasoning that keeps people from knowing God. You are able to demolish the barriers that the Enemy has erected in people's minds against the truth of God's Word. These weapons create an opening through which the glorious truth of the good news of Jesus can shine. With the Word going in as a seed and gaining ground, the Holy Spirit is able to bring conviction for sin.

## To bring every thought into captivity to the obedience of Christ

The mind is a battlefield. The battles of life are lost and won in the mind. Whatever you accept in your mind invariably becomes a reality. The Enemy knows this, and so he aggressively tries to attack the mind. When he tempts us, he starts by dropping a thought or suggestion or idea into the mind.

Just as you cannot stop a bird from flying over your head, in the same way you cannot stop the devil from dropping ideas into your mind. However, in the same way that you *can* stop a bird from building a nest on your head, you can stop the Enemy's suggestions from wandering without restriction and taking root in your mind. If left untamed, the thought or suggestion or idea takes root, grows, and becomes part of your outlook. You adopt it as something that is acceptable. That is why we are admonished in Proverbs 4:23 to guard our minds with due care and diligence.

With the weapons that God has made available to you, he expects you to capture and hold captive every thought and idea that comes into your mind, and to examine these against the backdrop of the Word of God. Those thoughts that are in line with God's will and purpose for your life are to be released and allowed to move freely within your mind. However, those thoughts and ideas that are contrary to the Word of God are to be held perpetually captive and cast out of your mind in the name of Jesus!

## WHAT WEAPONS DO YOU HAVE?

Every war has its own weapons. In ancient times, Roman soldiers carried two javelins, a sword, a dagger, and a shield when they went to war. The sword was carried in a sheath strapped high on the right side of the soldier's body. This enabled it to be drawn easily without interfering with the shield, which was carried with the left hand.

There is a reason for the variety. When a skilled hunter goes with his bow and arrow into the meadows in search of game, he carries at least one bow and a quiver full of arrows of different shapes, lengths, and sizes. When he sees a potential target, he reaches for his quiver and selects the arrow that is best suited for the particular prey before shooting.

The 2003 invasion of Iraq was spearheaded by the United States and backed by British forces as well as smaller contingents from Australia, Spain, Poland, and Denmark. In the course of the Iraq War, the United States forces have used the following weapons:

- M4 Carbines
- M16 Assault Rifles
- M9 Pistols
- M249 Squad Automatic Weapons
- M240 Machine Guns
- M2 Machine Guns (.50 Caliber)
- MK 19 Automatic Grenade Guns
- M203 Grenade Launchers

In the same way, God has provided you with a variety of spiritual weapons to enable you to fight and win this battle. Although God has preordained the outcome of the conflict in your favor, you must nonetheless make use of God's supplies. To do otherwise is to leave you open to attack by the Enemy.

*A final word: Be strong in the Lord and in his mighty power. Put on all of God's armor so that you will be able to stand firm against all strategies of the devil. For we are not fighting against flesh-and-blood enemies, but against evil rulers and authorities of the unseen world, against mighty powers in this dark world, and against evil spirits in the heavenly places. Therefore, put on every piece of God's armor so you will be able to resist the enemy in the time of evil. Then after the battle you will still be standing firm. Stand your ground, putting on the belt of truth and the body armor of God's righteousness. For shoes, put on the peace that comes from the Good News so that you will be fully prepared. In addition to all of these, hold up the shield of faith to stop the fiery arrows of the devil. Put on salvation as your helmet, and take the sword of the Spirit, which is the word of God. Pray in the Spirit at all times and on every occasion. Stay alert and be persistent in your prayers for all believers everywhere.*

EPHESIANS 6:10–18, NLT

The imagery of Ephesians 6 is that of a Roman soldier:

## THE BREASTPLATE OF RIGHTEOUSNESS

A breastplate is a piece of armor which is worn over the upper body to protect the vital organs around the chest from injury. In ancient times, the breastplate was the front portion of the plate armor worn by soldiers. As a piece of spiritual armor, the breastplate of righteousness protects the vital organs in our chest area from the Enemy's attack. In other words, if we are not in right standing with God, then our vital organs (such as the heart) are bare, unprotected, and susceptible to the Enemy's damage.

## THE HELMET OF SALVATION

In olden times, soldiers wore helmets as part of their armor to protect their heads from attack in battle. Today, motorcyclists and bicyclists wear helmets to greatly reduce injuries and fatalities in traffic accidents.

On March 18, 2009, the actress Natasha Richardson, who starred opposite Lindsay Lohan in *The Parent Trap* and Jennifer Lopez in *Maid in Manhattan,* died while on a skiing holiday in Canada. Her death was caused when she banged her head in a fall. The actress was skiing with an instructor at the Mont Tremblant Resort outside Montreal when the accident occurred. She was not wearing a crash helmet. Had she worn a helmet, she might not have died. In the same manner, salvation is the protective gear that protects the head from attack in spiritual warfare.

## THE SHIELD OF FAITH

The shield is primarily a defensive weapon against javelins and arrows in warfare. In spiritual warfare, the shield is used to stop the fiery arrows aimed at us by the Enemy. These flaming arrows come in different guises and include fear, doubt, evil desire, lust, and hate.

Not only does the shield of faith protect your vital organs from the Enemy's onslaught, it also safeguards the other armor pieces. Your faith is that vital weapon that can be maneuvered toward each and every attack, no matter its size or the direction it is coming from.

Faith is your trust in God as Savior and Deliverer. It is the evidence and proof you have in your heart of spiritual truths and God's provision, even when you have not yet seen their physical manifestation. God's spoken word to you inspires your faith, and as you study the Word of God and listen to God speak to you through the pages of the Bible, your faith in God grows.

## THE SWORD OF THE SPIRIT, WHICH IS THE WORD OF GOD

A sword is an offensive weapon. The Word of God is our spiritual sword. But what is the Word of God? There are two Greek words which are both interchangeably translated as the "word" of God in the Bible—*logos* and *rhema*. *Logos* is often used to identify the written Word of God as revealed in Scriptures.

On other hand, *rhema* is a specific word of God which we receive from God. Sometimes, when studying the Scriptures, a particular verse leaps at you or burns within your spirit. In those circumstances, that specific Scripture becomes a rhema from God for you regarding your particular situation. That word then inspires your faith, and you are subsequently able to use it as a double-edged sword to deal with the circumstances you face.

The Word of God seems to be the only offensive weapon which you have in your spiritual armory. It is quite powerful, and in the words of Hebrews 4:12, "It is sharper than the sharpest two-edged sword" (NLT). You make use of this weapon when you speak God's Word to the Enemy concerning the situation you face. We see the example of Jesus, in Matthew 4, who constantly referred to the Scriptures when he was tempted, often prefacing his counterattacks by saying "it is written."

## YOUR FEET PROTECTED WITH THE PEACE OF THE GOOD NEWS

As a soldier of Christ, you need to wear protective gear for your feet as you march valiantly to battle. It is not enough to wear just any old sandals! Your footwear must be appropriate in terms of size and comfort; if not, you will not be able to walk and run when necessary. The good news of the gospel is your footwear.

If you do not share the good news of Jesus with the unsaved, you risk going into battle with your feet not properly protected. As Paul exclaims in Romans 10:15, how beautiful are the feet of those who preach the good news of salvation!

## How I Love the Name of Jesus!

You also have the name of Jesus. This is one of the greatest weapons at the disposal of the Christian in spiritual warfare. At the name of Jesus, the Enemy and his cohorts quake with fear and terror.

> *Therefore God elevated him to the place of highest honor and gave him the name above all other names, that at the name of Jesus every knee should bow, in heaven and on earth and under the earth, and every tongue confess that Jesus Christ is Lord, to the glory of God the Father.*
>
> PHILIPPIANS 2:9–11, NLT

The name of Jesus provides answers. At the mention of the Name, doors that have been shut in the realm of the spirit fling open. The Name brings deliverance to the oppressed. At the mention of the name of Jesus, the hurting receive healing and succor. At the mention of the name of Jesus, every tongue must confess that he is Lord.

The name of the Lord also offers protection. It is a tower of protection for the righteous from the flaming arrows of the Enemy. The Bible tells us in Proverbs 18:10 that "the name of the Lord is a strong tower; the righteous run to it and are safe." So whenever you perceive any form of danger, peril, or threat, call upon the name of the Lord!

## No Turning Back

In this battle, there is no room for turning back. You have to be on the offensive. You have to keep attacking the Enemy. And on account of this, your back is left bare. You cannot afford to turn back once you have put your hand to the plow and agreed to follow Jesus! To do otherwise is to leave yourself open to the Enemy's attack.

There must be complete and utter dependence on God for the following reasons:

- God has won the victory already, and our work is to enforce what he has done.

- God is our source. Our authority is derived from our relationship with God.
- We are fighting an Enemy who is unseen. Although we do not see him, he is clearly at work.
- Without God we are nothing. For in him we move and live and have our being.
- Second Corinthians 10:4 tells us that the weapons of our warfare are not carnal but mighty in God for pulling down strongholds.

As our authority over the Enemy emanates from our relationship with Jesus, we can only exercise this authority in his name. You can only address the Enemy in the name of Jesus, saying, for instance, "Satan, I command you to come out in Jesus's name" or "You spirit of infirmity, I rebuke you in the name of the Lord Jesus Christ." You may also say, "You spirit of fear, I resist you in the name of Jesus" or "Lack, I bind you in Jesus's name."

*And these signs will follow those who believe: in My name they will cast out demons.*

MARK 16:17

## THE CENTRALITY OF FAITH

In spiritual warfare, faith is the currency that releases your prayer. It is the instrument (or weapon, if you like) that activates and sets loose the answers to your prayers. In Mark 5:34, Jesus told a woman who had been suffering from chronic bleeding for twelve years, who had spent all her money on doctors to no avail and had become a social outcast, "Daughter, *your faith has made you well.* Go in peace! Be cured from your illness" (GW, emphasis supplied).

This lady, through her faith, was able to activate and set in motion the divine solution to her long-term problem. You can do the same today, even with the tiniest amount of faith. Jesus couldn't be clearer when he said in Matthew 17:20, "For assuredly, I say to you, if you have faith as a mustard seed, you will say to this mountain, 'Move from here to there,' and it will move; and nothing will be impossible for you."

You must, however, learn to PUSH—that is, to Pray Until Something Happens. You must remain and continue in the place and attitude of warfare until your faith can take hold of the answer to your petition. In Mark 11:24, Jesus said, "That's why I tell you to have faith that you have already received whatever you pray for, and it will be yours" (GW).

## THE POWER OF AGREEMENT

There is nothing as potent as agreement and unity of heart in spiritual warfare. In fact, in relation to the building of the Tower of Babel in the Old Testament book of Genesis, God said that nothing would be impossible or too difficult for the people because they were united and spoke the same language. (In this case, as we're told in Genesis 11, the people had united *against* God, and God broke their power by breaking their unity.)

When we as Christians agree, we bring God into the situation and he takes over. This is because the Scriptures say in Matthew 18:19 that if two people shall agree on earth concerning anything they ask, "My Father in heaven will do it for" them (NLT). In other words, when two people come together to pray in agreement, that is, if they are singing from the same hymn sheet in a harmonious tune on any issue they pray about, God does the work for them. Do you need God to fight a particular battle for you? Then agree with your spouse, your friend, or your prayer partner in the place of prayer, and see the Lord of heaven's armies set out to work on your behalf!

## GOD INHABITS YOUR PRAISES

The Bible tells us in Psalm 22:3 that God inhabits praises, making praise an awesome weapon in spiritual warfare. Through praise, you are able to take hold of your enemy by the scruff of the neck. Although one can pray amiss, I believe that it is impossible to praise God amiss! To praise God is to extol him, to eulogize him, to worship him, and to sing his praises for who he is. It is also to thank him for what he has done for you.

Paul takes praise to a new dimension when he admonishes us in 1 Thessalonians 5:18 to give thanks to God in everything because "this is the will of God in Christ Jesus." This is a call to a lifestyle of *thanksliving! Thanksliving* is a way of life where you give thanks and praise to God in every situation, no matter what happens to you. Even when things don't go as planned, you still give thanks to God, knowing that, as Paul tells us in Romans 8:28, God is able to make everything work out for your good, including those things which were meant for evil by the devil. In Genesis 50:20, Joseph testified of God's goodness when he told his brothers who had sold him into slavery, "Even though you planned evil against me, God planned good to come out of it. This was to keep many people alive, as he is doing now" (GW).

When you learn to praise God in any and every situation—no matter what the devil throws at you—I believe that the devil will avoid you like a plague.

## THE DYNAMITE OF ANOINTING

The anointing of the Holy Spirit comes with power. You receive the anointing through the baptism of the Holy Spirit. You can also receive the anointing through the laying on of hands and through being anointed with oil, as Aaron the Old Testament priest was. The word translated *power* in Acts 1:8 ("But you shall receive power when the Holy Spirit has come upon you") is the Greek word *dunamis,* from which we get *dynamite,* the high explosive invented by Swedish chemist and engineer Alfred Nobel. So every child of God who is filled with the Holy Spirit is a portable dynamite, capable of wreaking havoc and mayhem in the camp of the Evil One! With the anointing also comes the power to be an effective witness for the Lord. As you share your testimony of what God has done for you and you lead many people to the Lord, you are effectively depopulating the kingdom of darkness. This is part of spiritual warfare.

In addition, by reason of the anointing, you can destroy from your neck any and every yoke that is not of God. You are also able to cast down every burden that is not of God from off your shoulders and the shoulders of those to whom you minister.

## THE BLOOD OF JESUS SPEAKS BETTER THINGS

The blood of Jesus is one the greatest weapons we have in this warfare. The blood is powerful. First of all, it cleanses us from all unrighteousness. Then it speaks. However, unlike the blood of Abel, which cried out to God for vengeance when his brother Cain killed him, the blood of Jesus speaks forgiveness on your behalf. All you have to do is plead the blood of Jesus over your life and over the particular situation you are dealing with. The Enemy cannot stand the blood of Jesus. When the angel of death sees the blood, he will most definitely pass over you. (See 1 John 1:7; Hebrews 12:24, and Exodus 12:13).

## THE IMPORTANCE OF YOUR TESTIMONY

In this battle, the words that come out of your mouth are significant. What you say is very important, because you have within your mouth the power to create and destroy. What you say about your relationship with God is even more crucial. That is your testimony: how God saved you from darkness and perdition, what God has done for you in the past, how he is faithful, always on time, never late, and never too early. Let the Enemy hear your testimony. Tell him how God has come to your rescue in the past and proclaim that he will deliver you again and again. This is one of your weapons.

## THE HELP OF FASTING

There is also a place for fasting in spiritual warfare. In fact, it is one of the major weapons God has provided to his church. In Matthew 17:21, when his disciples could not cast out an evil spirit, Jesus told them that "this kind does not go out except by prayer and fasting." Fasting and prayer go side by side. Without prayer, fasting is nothing more than starvation or an exercise in dieting. With prayer, fasting enables you to discipline your body. It helps you to mortify the evil desires of your flesh. It helps your spirit to come alive. In Matthew 6:16, we read, "Moreover, when you fast…" The use of word "when" suggests that fasting is a given. We are *expected* to fast. It is not a question of *if,* but of *when* and how often.

In her book *The Power of Prayer and Fasting,* television host Marilyn Hickey makes a compelling case for biblical fasting and prayer. She deals with the issue so well that I hope you will indulge me as I quote copiously from her book.

In what she calls "key reasons to fast and pray," she says, "I…encourage every believer to fast and pray for two very important reasons."

1.  THE SCRIPTURES TEACH US TO FAST AND PRAY
    The Bible has a great deal to say about both fasting and praying, including commands to fast and pray. The Bible also gives us examples of people who fasted and prayed, using different types of fasts for different reasons, all of which are very positive results. Jesus fasted and prayed. Jesus' disciples fasted and prayed after the Resurrection. Many of the Old Testament heroes and heroines of faith fasted and prayed. The followers of John the Baptist fasted and prayed. Many people in the early church fasted and prayed. What the Scriptures have taught

69

us directly and by the examples of the saints is surely something we are to do.

2. FASTING AND PRAYER PUT YOU INTO THE BEST POSSIBLE POSITION FOR A BREAKTHROUGH

That breakthrough might be in the realm of the spirit. It may be in the realm of your emotions or personal habits. It may be in the realm of a very practical area of life, such as a relationship or finances. What I have seen repeatedly through the years—not only in the Scriptures but in countless personal stories that others have told me—is that periods of fasting and prayer produce great spiritual results, many of which fall into the realm of a break-through. What wasn't a reality…suddenly was. What hadn't worked…suddenly did. The unwanted situation or object that was there…suddenly wasn't there. The relationship that was unloving…suddenly was loving. The job that hadn't material-ized…suddenly did.

The very simple and direct conclusions I draw are these: First, if the Bible teaches us to do something, I want to do it. I want to obey the Lord in every way that He commands me to obey Him. And second, if fasting and praying are means to a breakthrough that God has for me, I want to undertake those disciplines so I might experience that breakthrough!

Every person I know needs a breakthrough in some area of his or her life. I am no exception. I need breakthroughs all the time…If you have any need in your life, you need a breakthrough from God to meet that need! Fasting and prayer break the yoke of bondage and bring about a release of God's presence, power, and provision.[2]

## HIS PRESENCE CAN MAKE ALL THE DIFFERENCE

The presence of the Lord is another weapon in spiritual warfare. The Bible says in Psalm 16:11 that in God's presence is fullness of joy. In John 6:16–21, we read a story that powerfully illustrates the power of God's presence. The dis-ciples of Jesus attempted to cross a great lake. However, a ferocious storm blew against them and threatened to capsize their boat. The wind was relentless and unrelenting. They toiled and worked all night, managing to go only a few miles.

At about three or four in the morning, Jesus appeared to them, walking on the sea. Initially, they were afraid. He told them, "It is I; do not be afraid." Then they *willingly received* him into the boat.

Amazingly, the moment Jesus got in the boat, they were *instantly* transported supernaturally to their destination. This was instantaneous. It was immediate. It happened right away. This experience of the disciples teaches us that when you willingly invite God into your "space" and abide in his presence, you can expect the miraculous to happen. It also shows that for you as a child of God engaged in spiritual warfare, safety is not in the absence of danger but in the presence of the Lord.

## Holy Spirit, I Need You

You need the help of the Holy Spirit in this battle. His ministry is so crucial on this side of eternity that Jesus told his disciples in John 16:7 that it was better for him to go back to heaven because if he didn't, the Holy Spirit (described by The Amplified Bible as the Comforter, Counselor, Helper, Advocate, Intercessor, Strengthener, and Standby) would not come. The Holy Spirit knows all things and so is able to guide you and keep you ahead of the devil in all things at all times.

Sometime in 2003, my younger daughter was very ill. She was only a few months old at the time. She couldn't retain anything. Whatever she took in basically came back out through her mouth. She was very dehydrated and had lost a fair bit of weight. I remember thinking to myself that I had to do something quickly; if not, she might well slip away from us. One night as my wife and I prayed for her, I fell into a trance and saw a strange man sitting on one of the small sofas in my front room. This was a revelation by the Holy Spirit. I told my wife what I had seen, and we both prayed. We addressed the stranger and in the name of Jesus commanded him to leave our house. Shortly afterwards, my daughter improved and became well again.

We achieved victory because we depended on the Holy Spirit and acted on the revelation which he gave to us.

## WHAT DOES GOD EXPECT FROM YOU AS A SOLDIER?

### To endure hardness as a good soldier

When in the battlefield, soldiers forsake all the usual luxuries to live in tents which they erect for themselves. Usually they have to improvise for most things which civilians take for granted in a developed economy, like lights and running water. They have to be able to endure harsh conditions. In like manner, Paul enjoined Timothy in 2 Timothy 2:3 to endure hardness as a good soldier of Christ. You must learn to give thanks in all things; when you have and when you don't, because God never changes. Our walk with God must continue regardless of the physical conditions in which we find ourselves.

## To be separated from the affairs of civilian life

When soldiers go to war, they separate themselves from civilian pursuits. All they care about is the instructions of their commanding officers, whom they seek to please at all costs. As a Christian, though you live in this world, you are nonetheless not of this world. You are a traveler on your way to the Promised Land. You are in transit here on earth. Your focus and attention must be on finishing the race. Your desire must be to please Jesus Christ, who is the commander in chief.

## To have the mentality of a winner

You need to develop a winning mentality. You are born of God and have the divine seed dwelling within you. If God is for you, then it is impossible for you to fail. Just think about this: if God gave Jesus Christ (the very best of the best) to die for you when you were his enemy wallowing in sin, now that you have become his child, his heir, and a joint heir with Jesus Christ, do you think he would withhold any good thing from you? I don't think so! Sometimes we give up too easily. You must realize at all times that the battle is not over until God says so.

## To watch and pray

Usually when we pray, we close our eyes as a sign of submission to God and also to help us concentrate and avoid distractions. On the other hand, the biblical concept of being watchful in prayer involves staying wide awake, with all your senses and faculties fully awake and alert. On the face of it, the call in Matthew 26:41 to "watch and pray" would appear to be a contradiction in terms. However, the admonition is that you need to be *prayerfully observant* of the world we live in. You must be conscious of the things going on around you because every now and then, God uses them to tell you about the times and seasons in which you live. It is therefore not sufficient merely to pray; you must also be vigilant. Both should go hand in hand.

# SPIRITUAL WARFARE

## TO DO THE RIGHT THING AT THE RIGHT TIME

David was one of the greatest kings to ever reign over Israel. Although he had many faults, yet he was a man after God's own heart. And today, he is one of the human forefathers of our Lord Jesus Christ. Yet, one of the greatest mistakes of his life was committing adultery with Bathsheba, a married woman, and subsequently killing her husband in an attempt to cover up his tracks. (Read the story in 2 Samuel 11.)

It all happened when David decided to stay at home at the time when kings went to battle. One day during this self-imposed holiday, he went to the penthouse suite of his palace, and lo and behold, there was Bathsheba having a shower. He liked what he saw, and he sent for her. She soon became pregnant, and the rest is history.

If David had gone to war, he would not have been in the penthouse, he would not have seen Bathsheba, he would not have sinned with her, and he would not have killed her husband. He was at the *right place* at the *wrong time!*

## FOOD FOR REFLECTION

- What is your understanding of spiritual warfare?
- What experience do you have of spiritual warfare?
- Which of the weapons of spiritual warfare do you consider most important? Why?
- What would you say is the main objective of spiritual warfare?
- Have you ever been tempted to give up your faith as a Christian? What implication would giving in have in view of the fact there is no weapon for your back?
- How do you fast? How often should one fast?

## PRAYER FEATURES

- I destroy every weapon of the Enemy formed or fashioned against me in the name of the Lord Jesus.
- Lord, teach me to endure hardness like a good soldier of yours.
- Lord, open my eyes to understand that in you I am victorious.
- Lord, grant me a revelation of the true purpose of spiritual warfare.

## ACTION POINTS

- Identify the spiritual weapons you have in Jesus.

- Identify the essential requirements for joining the Royal Marines or the United States Marine Corps, and then attempt to relate them to your life as a Christian soldier.
- Think of the areas of your life where you need to be more disciplined and make a determined effort to apply self-discipline in those areas.
- If you do not already fast regularly, decide to fast and pray at least one day a month, say from 6.00 A.M to 6.00 P.M.

Chapter Four

# STRATEGY IN SPIRITUAL WARFARE

*Do you think it's possible in broad daylight to enter the house of an awake, able-bodied man, and walk off with his possessions unless you tie him up first? Tie him up, though, and you can clean him out.*

MARK 3:27, MSG

Tactics and strategy are as important in spiritual warfare as they are when nations go to war in this world. Jesus clearly reinforces this spiritual principle when he teaches us in the passage from Mark's gospel quoted above that if you want to plunder the Enemy's goods, you must first disarm him. He is definitely referring to the devil, because the New Living Translation puts it this way: "Let me illustrate this further. Who is powerful enough to enter the house of a strong man like Satan and plunder his goods? Only…someone who could tie him up and then plunder his house."

To tie up a strong man like the devil, you do not require physical brawn but spiritual brains. In other words, what you need to defeat the devil is divine strategy!

The Old Testament story of Queen Esther as told in Esther 3–8 illustrates the importance of strategy in spiritual warfare. Haman, who was the king's right-hand man, hated Esther's uncle Mordecai so much that he convinced the king to issue a decree that all Jews—young and old, men, women, and children—must be slaughtered and annihilated on a specified date. Esther decided to fast and took her destiny into her hands when she went into the king's inner chamber uninvited, a course of action which could have resulted in her death. The king received her and asked her what she wanted. Esther replied, "If it pleases the king, let the king and Haman come today to a banquet I have prepared for the king."

At the banquet, the king again asked Esther what her request was. This time, she said her request was for the king and Haman to return the following day to another banquet. That night, the king had trouble sleeping, so he ordered an attendant to bring the history book of his reign so it could be read to him. In this way, he discovered that Mordecai had saved his life previously, and nothing had been done to show the king's appreciation.

By the time Esther made her request the following day, Mordecai was in the king's very good books! Esther's intercession for her people was successful because the king was fully on their side. *If Esther had made her request on the first day she approached the king, before he read the history book, the result might have been very different.* Inviting the king back for another banquet was nothing short of a divinely inspired and miraculous strategy.

In spiritual warfare, Jesus is seen as the Lord of Hosts, the Man of War. The battle is his, and the Holy Spirit is the military strategist and tactician. The Holy Spirit dictates the plan or line of attack, determines the weapons to be used in the battle, and directs the focus of attack. This is not surprising, because:

- The battle is the Lord's.
- God sees the end of a thing from its beginning.
- Jesus defeated the Enemy on the cross of Calvary, and all we are required to do is to enforce the victory.
- The Enemy we fight is invisible to us but visible to the Holy Spirit.
- God is all-knowing and all-powerful.

It is imperative to seek guidance from God through the Holy Spirit for each and every battle we face in life. To do otherwise is to walk into one of the many traps, snares, and ambushes of the Enemy.

## THE GIBEONITES TRICK JOSHUA

The book of Joshua shares a classic case of entrapment which happened because, for once in his life, Joshua, the mighty man of God, made a decision based on the externals—what he could see, his expertise, and his understanding—instead of asking God for direction. The story goes like this: the people of Gibeon, who were Canaanite dwellers in the Promised Land destined to be wiped out by Israel, heard that Joshua had miraculously defeated the nearby cities of Jericho and Ai. Scared, they cooked up a ruse.

We continue this intriguing story in Joshua 9:4–27, as translated in *The Message:*

*They posed as travelers: their donkeys loaded with patched sacks and mended wineskins, threadbare sandals on their feet, tattered clothes on their bodies, nothing but dry crusts and crumbs for food. They came to Joshua at Gilgal and spoke to the men of Israel, "We've come from a far-off country; make a covenant with us." The men of Israel said to these Hivites, "How do we know you aren't local people? How could we then make a covenant with you?" They said to Joshua, "We'll be your servants." Joshua said, "Who are you now? Where did you come from?"*

*They said, "From a far-off country, very far away. Your servants came because we'd heard such great things about God, your God—all those things he did in Egypt! And the two Amorite kings across the Jordan, King Sihon of Heshbon and King Og of Bashan, who ruled in Ashtaroth! Our leaders and everybody else in our country told us, 'Pack up some food for the road and go meet them. Tell them, We're your servants; make a covenant with us.' This bread was warm from the oven when we packed it and left to come and see you. Now look at it—crusts and crumbs. And our cracked and mended wineskins, good as new when we filled them. And our clothes and sandals, in tatters from the long, hard traveling."*

*The men of Israel looked them over and accepted the evidence. But they didn't ask God about it. So Joshua made peace with them and formalized it with a covenant to guarantee their lives. The leaders of the congregation swore to it. And then, three days after making this covenant, they learned that they were next-door neighbors who had been living there all along! The People of Israel broke camp and set out; three days later they reached their towns— Gibeon, Kephirah, Beeroth, and Kiriath Jearim. But the People of Israel didn't attack them; the leaders of the congregation had given their word before the God of Israel. But the congregation was up in arms over their leaders.*

*The leaders were united in their response to the congregation: "We promised them in the presence of the God of Israel. We can't lay a hand on them now. But we can do this: We will let them live so we don't get blamed for breaking our promise." Then the leaders continued, "We'll let them live, but they will be woodcutters and water carriers for the entire congregation." And that's what happened; the leaders' promise was kept.*

*But Joshua called the Gibeonites together and said, "Why did you lie to us, telling us, 'We live far, far away from you,' when you're our next-door neighbors? For that you are cursed. From now on it's menial labor for you—woodcutters and water carriers for the house of my God." They answered Joshua, "We got the message loud and clear that God, your God, commanded through his servant Moses: to give you the whole country and destroy everyone living in it. We were terrified because of you; that's why we did this. That's it. We're at your mercy. Whatever you decide is right for us, do it." And that's what they did. Joshua delivered them from the power of the People of Israel so they didn't kill them. But he made them woodcutters and water carriers for the congregation and for the Altar of God at the place God chooses. They still are.*

Seek God, depend on him. As we are enjoined in Proverbs 3:5–6, "Trust in the Lord with all your heart; do not depend on your own understanding. Seek his will in all you do, and he will show you which path to take" (NLT).

## BIBLE STRATEGIES REVISITED

### THE WALLS OF JERICHO COME TUMBLING DOWN

This account, found in Joshua 6:1–20, is the wonderful and true story of how Joshua and the nation of Israel overcame Jericho by the most unconventional of military strategies. So what really happened?

*Now the gates of Jericho were tightly shut because the people were afraid of the Israelites. No one was allowed to go out or in. But the Lord said to Joshua, "I have given you Jericho, its king, and all its strong warriors. You and your fighting men should march around the town once a day for six days. Seven priests will walk ahead of the Ark, each carrying a ram's horn. On the seventh day you are to march around the town seven times, with the priests blowing the horns. When you hear the priests give one long blast on the rams' horns, have all the people shout as loud as they can. Then the walls of the town will collapse, and the people can charge straight into the town."*

*So Joshua called together the priests and said, "Take up the Ark of the Lord's Covenant, and assign seven priests to walk in front of it, each carrying a ram's horn." Then he gave orders to the people: "March around the town, and the armed men will lead the way in front of the Ark of the Lord." After Joshua spoke to the people, the seven priests with the rams' horns started marching in the presence of the Lord, blowing the horns as they marched. And the Ark of the Lord's Covenant followed behind them. Some of the armed men marched in front of the priests with the horns and some behind the Ark, with the priests continually blowing the horns. "Do not shout; do not even talk," Joshua commanded. "Not a single word from any of you until I tell you to shout. Then shout!" So the Ark of the Lord was carried around the town once that day, and then everyone returned to spend the night in the camp.*

*Joshua got up early the next morning, and the priests again carried the Ark of the Lord. The seven priests with the rams' horns marched in front of the Ark of the Lord, blowing their horns. Again the armed men marched both in front of the priests with the horns and behind the Ark of the Lord. All this time the priests were blowing their horns. On the second day they again marched around the town once and returned to the camp. They followed this pattern for six days.*

*On the seventh day the Israelites got up at dawn and marched around the town as they had done before. But this time they went around the town seven times. The seventh time around, as the priests sounded the long blast on their horns, Joshua commanded the people, "Shout! For the Lord has given you the town! Jericho and everything in it must be completely destroyed as an offering to the Lord. Only Rahab the prostitute and the others in her house will be spared, for she protected our spies. Do not take any of the things set apart for destruction, or you yourselves will be completely destroyed, and you will bring trouble on the camp of Israel. Everything made from silver, gold, bronze, or iron is sacred to the Lord and must be brought into his treasury." When the people heard the sound of the rams' horns, they shouted as loud as they could. Suddenly, the walls of Jericho collapsed, and the Israelites charged straight into the town and captured it.*

NLT

All Joshua did was to be willing and obedient. He dared to take God at his word and followed God's instructions to the letter. He was not put to shame. The walls of the city fell down, and Joshua and his people had a memorable victory. In the same way, learn to trust God and take him at his word.

# CRUSHING THE DEVIL

## GIDEON GOES TO WAR WITH THREE HUNDRED MEN AND DEFEATS THE MIDIANITES

Gideon, by the direct instruction of Almighty God, overcame the Midianites, who had become a snare to the nation of Israel, with only three hundred men. How did this happen? This is the story which is found in Judges 7:1–25.

*So Jerub-baal (that is, Gideon) and his army got up early and went as far as the spring of Harod. The armies of Midian were camped north of them in the valley near the hill of Moreh. The Lord said to Gideon, "You have too many warriors with you. If I let all of you fight the Midianites, the Israelites will boast to me that they saved themselves by their own strength. Therefore, tell the people, 'Whoever is timid or afraid may leave this mountain and go home.'" So 22,000 of them went home, leaving only 10,000 who were willing to fight. But the Lord told Gideon, "There are still too many! Bring them down to the spring, and I will test them to determine who will go with you and who will not." When Gideon took his warriors down to the water, the Lord told him, "Divide the men into two groups. In one group put all those who cup water in their hands and lap it up with their tongues like dogs. In the other group put all those who kneel down and drink with their mouths in the stream." Only 300 of the men drank from their hands. All the others got down on their knees and drank with their mouths in the stream.*

*The Lord told Gideon, "With these 300 men I will rescue you and give you victory over the Midianites. Send all the others home." So Gideon collected the provisions and rams' horns of the other warriors and sent them home. But he kept the 300 men with him. The Midianite camp was in the valley just below Gideon. That night the Lord said, "Get up! Go down into the Midianite camp, for I have given you victory over them! But if you are afraid to attack, go down to the camp with your servant Purah. Listen to what the Midianites are saying, and you will be greatly encouraged. Then you will be eager to attack." So Gideon took Purah and went down to the edge of the enemy camp. The armies of Midian, Amalek, and the people of the east had settled in the valley like a swarm of locusts. Their camels were like grains of sand on the seashore—too many to count! Gideon crept up just as a man was telling his companion about a dream. The man said, "I had this dream, and in my dream a loaf of barley bread came tumbling down into the Midianite camp.*

It hit a tent, turned it over, and knocked it flat!"

His companion answered, "Your dream can mean only one thing—God has given Gideon son of Joash, the Israelite, victory over Midian and all its allies!"

When Gideon heard the dream and its interpretation, he bowed in worship before the Lord. Then he returned to the Israelite camp and shouted, "Get up! For the Lord has given you victory over the Midianite hordes!" He divided the 300 men into three groups and gave each man a ram's horn and a clay jar with a torch in it. Then he said to them, "Keep your eyes on me. When I come to the edge of the camp, do just as I do. As soon as I and those with me blow the rams' horns, blow your horns, too, all around the entire camp, and shout, 'For the Lord and for Gideon!'"

It was just after midnight, after the changing of the guard, when Gideon and the 100 men with him reached the edge of the Midianite camp. Suddenly, they blew the rams' horns and broke their clay jars. Then all three groups blew their horns and broke their jars. They held the blazing torches in their left hands and the horns in their right hands, and they all shouted, "A sword for the Lord and for Gideon!"

Each man stood at his position around the camp and watched as all the Midianites rushed around in a panic, shouting as they ran to escape. When the 300 Israelites blew their rams' horns, the Lord caused the warriors in the camp to fight against each other with their swords. Those who were not killed fled to places as far away as Beth-shittah near Zererah and to the border of Abel-meholah near Tabbath.

Then Gideon sent for the warriors of Naphtali, Asher, and Manasseh, who joined in chasing the army of Midian. Gideon also sent messengers throughout the hill country of Ephraim, saying, "Come down to attack the Midianites. Cut them off at the shallow crossings of the Jordan River at Bethbarah." So all the men of Ephraim did as they were told. They captured Oreb and Zeeb, the two Midianite commanders, killing Oreb at the rock of Oreb, and Zeeb at the winepress of Zeeb. And they continued to chase the Midianites. Afterward the Israelites brought the heads of Oreb and Zeeb to Gideon, who was by the Jordan River.

NLT

Gideon depended totally and entirely upon God and obeyed God, using God's strategy even when God's instruction to go with only three hundred soldiers did not make much sense. In the end, God showed himself strong on Gideon's behalf. Like Gideon, you can be entirely reliant on God.

## JESUS PRAYS ALL NIGHT BEFORE CHOOSING HIS DISCIPLES

Just before he chose his twelve disciples, the Lord Jesus spent a considerable amount of time in prayer. We are told the story in Luke 6:12–16:

> *At about that same time he climbed a mountain to pray. He was there all night in prayer before God. The next day he summoned his disciples; from them he selected twelve he designated as apostles [or "sent ones"]: Simon, whom he named Peter, Andrew, his brother, James, John, Philip, Bartholomew, Matthew, Thomas, James son of Alphaeus, Simon, called the Zealot, Judas son of James, who betrayed him.*
>
> MSG

Coming before he made such an important decision, this time of prayer would have helped Jesus to connect with God the Father in a personal way. He would have sought wisdom, insight, and direction from the Father. Seeking guidance from God in prayer before making decisions is a good rule of thumb. Now, if Jesus could pray *all night*, I don't know how you can expect to live victoriously without making prayer a vital part of your daily routine.

## THE APOSTLES FAST AND PRAY TO RELEASE PAUL AND SILAS

In this story, we're looking at the early church. They knew the Lord in his humanity and had witnessed firsthand the miracles performed by Jesus. They were also present on the day of Pentecost when the Holy Spirit was first released to the church. Yet, they fasted and prayed. Acts 13:1–4 tells us the story:

> *The congregation in Antioch was blessed with a number of prophet-preachers and teachers: Barnabas, Simon, nicknamed Niger, Lucius the Cyrenian, Man-aen, an advisor to the ruler Herod, [and] Saul. One day, as they were wor-shiping God—they were also fasting as they waited for guidance—the Holy Spirit spoke: "Take Barnabas and Saul and commission them for the work I*

*have called them to do." So they commissioned them.*

*In that circle of intensity and obedience, of fasting and praying, they laid hands on heads [of these first missionaries] and sent them off [on the first of Paul's famous, world-changing missionary journeys].*

MSG

Here, the early apostles teach us the importance of seeking guidance from God through prayer and fasting. This must be a regular part of one's spiritual routine.

## SPIRITUAL WARFARE IS NOT DIPLOMACY

In spiritual warfare, you take by force what is rightfully yours. You take it by coercion or compulsion. You take it by binding the devil. You do not take the kingdom by begging for it, and certainly not through diplomacy!

*And from the days of John the Baptist until now the kingdom of heaven suffers violence, and the violent take it by force.*

MATTHEW 11:12

*But no one can go into a strong man's house and ransack his household goods right and left and seize them as plunder unless he first binds the strong man; then indeed he may [thoroughly] plunder his house.*

MARK 3:27, AB

*And these signs will follow those who believe: in My name they will cast out demons; they will speak with new tongues; they will take up serpents; and if they drink anything deadly, it will by no means hurt them; they will lay hands on the sick, and they will recover.*

MARK 16:17–18

In spiritual warfare, you stand on the Word of God and use your authority as a child of God to command the Enemy using the name of Jesus.

*Thou shalt also decree a thing, and it shall be established unto thee: and the light shall shine upon thy ways.*

JOB 22:28, KJV

*Assuredly, I say to you, whatever you bind on earth will be bound in heaven, and whatever you loose on earth will be loosed in heaven.*

MATTHEW 18:18

You do not plead with the devil; nor do you negotiate with him. You bind him in the name of Jesus. This is because the only language the Enemy understands is the language of compulsion *using the name of Jesus.*

## THE VIOLENT TAKE IT BY FORCE

Before we move on, let us attempt to unpack what the Bible means when it says "the kingdom of heaven suffers violence, and the violent take it by force." Is God advocating the use of arms in our Christian strategy? Far from it! We must remember that Paul instructs in 2 Corinthians 10:3–4 that although "we are human…we don't wage war as humans do. We use God's mighty weapons, not worldly weapons" (NLT). In other words, the call to "violence" is not an invitation to physical aggression but to violence in the spirit.

What does the word "violent" as used in the passage in Matthew mean? How do we become violent in the spirit? Let us take a look at each of the letters in the word VIOLENT.

### V STANDS FOR VEHEMENT, VISION, AND VIGOR

- Be vehement.

  The kingdom of heaven is not a matter of eating and drinking, as Paul states in Romans 14:17. Being a child of God is therefore not a leisurely walk in the park, but serious business with a lot of responsibility. It is no wonder, then, that Christians are called soldiers! God expects you to be passionate in expressing your faith. You must be ready to give an answer to anybody who asks you for a reason for your beliefs. Your faith must be expressed with strong feeling and a firm conviction.

  Human interaction often calls for gentleness and sensitivity. However, *in dealing with the devil and his many cohorts*, we must be vehement in our approach and come across at all times as forceful, categorical, and emphatic.

- Have a vision.

With vision comes discipline. On the other hand, without a vision there is no purpose and little self-control. Jesus was able to endure the pain and the agony of the cross because he had a revelation of the glory and the joy that was set before him. Joseph gladly suffered the pain of the pit, eagerly said no to Potiphar's beautiful wife, willingly tolerated the pangs of prison, and readily endured the devastation of the dungeon for the simple reason that he had a mental picture of himself in the palace; he could see in his mind's eye the sun, the moon, and the eleven stars bowing down before him (Genesis 37:9–10). Vision is essentially a God-given revelation of one's purpose in life. It is the ability or faculty of perceiving the future with the eye of faith. It is a divine impression of one's purpose that is vividly conjured up in the imagination and which generates self-control, discipline, and restraint of its own accord.

Someone might ask, "How do I get a vision?" or "How do I get an understanding or revelation of my purpose in life?" The question of who we are is an age-old one. Because you were created by God, only in God can you truly discover your purpose. In much the same way that you need to ask the manufacturer if you want to understand the purpose of an automobile, you need to ask God to reveal your purpose. You also need to exercise the power of your imagination. Learn to dream big dreams!

What do you do with vision? You write it down.

> *And the Lord answered me, and said, Write the vision, and make it plain upon tables, that he may run that readeth it.*
>
> HABAKKUK 2:2, KJV

You write down a vision because it is for a future time. A vision describes something which is yet to happen and which will eventually be fulfilled. If the fulfillment seems slow in coming, wait patiently, because it will surely take place. It will not be unduly delayed.

One of the greatest visionaries of modern times, who is described as "a pioneer and innovator and the possessor of one of the most fertile imaginations the world has ever known,"[1] Walt Disney, documented his vision of a Disney World of entertainment; he had an artist's impression of Disney World. And so, although he died before the vision could be realized, his older brother and business partner Roy Disney was able to return from retirement and accomplish the vision with the opening of Walt Disney World in Orlando on October 1, 1971, more than five years after Walt Disney had passed away. Today, Walt Disney World in Orlando, Florida, is the number-one tourist attraction in the world.

- Demonstrate vigor.

Vigor speaks of strength, desire, passion, and zeal. God expects you to demonstrate energy and vitality in the things of God and to display a yearning for him, a longing for his presence, a hunger for his righteousness, and a craving for his Word. To be violent in your spirit, you must have vigor. There is a call for us to praise him with all our might and all our strength. In the words of the popular song by an unknown author:

> The zeal of God has consumed me
> It burns in my soul
> A driving force that cannot be stopped
> A fire that cannot be quenched

## I STANDS FOR IGNITE, IMPACT, AND IMPOSE

- Ignite your surroundings.

You are special. Not only are you fearfully and wonderfully made, but you are unique in that there is no one quite like you in the whole wide world. At your birth, you were loaded with everything you would need to make the world a better place. This is regardless of the circumstances of your birth. In the same way, at the time of the new birth, when you became a part of God's kingdom, he deposited within you everything you need to live as a child of God. When you became a child of God, you were prewired with all you need to be victorious in spiritual warfare. God has invested a lot in you, and so it is no surprise that he expects you to set the world alight. In Isaiah 60:1, the Bible says "Arise, shine; for your light has come!"

- Make an impact.

An impact occurs when one object collides with another. God created *you* to make an impact wherever you are located. You were created for such a time as this. As we said earlier, the whole of creation is groaning and crying for the manifestation of the sons of God. This is your time! A city set on a hill cannot be hidden, nor do men light a candle and hide it under a bushel. The Lord says in Matthew 5:16, "Let your light so shine before men, that they may see your good works and glorify your Father in heaven."

- Impose God's values on your environment.

Man's original mandate is clear from Genesis 1:26: "God spoke: 'Let us make human beings in our image, make them reflecting our nature so they can be responsible for the fish in the sea, the birds in the air, the cattle, and, yes, Earth itself, and every animal that moves on the face of Earth" (MSG).

As a Christian who has been redeemed from the Adamic curse, you still have a responsibility to look after the earth while on this side of eternity. This is at two levels. The first is what you might call your spiritual oversight over the earth. Do everything within your power to impose righteousness around you, because righteousness exalts a people, but sin is a reproach. In the words of the Lord's Prayer, recorded in Matthew 6:10, "Your kingdom come. Your will be done on earth as it is in heaven."

Secondly, you also have an environmental responsibility to ensure that the earth is preserved for future generations, if the Lord tarries. You have a duty to reduce your carbon footprints, to recycle more, and to avoid waste.

## O IS FOR OBSESSED

- Be obsessed with Jesus.

Be completely, totally, and unashamedly sold out for Christ! Are you a child of God? Are you proud of what God has achieved in you? Are you prepared to stand up for your faith even if it means paying the ultimate price?

King Solomon tells us to be fixated and preoccupied with the Lord. Hear him in this passage taken from Proverbs 4:20–23:

*Dear friend, listen well to my words; tune your ears to my voice. Keep my message in plain view at all times. Concentrate! Learn it by heart! Those who discover these words live, really live; body and soul, they're bursting with health. Keep vigilant watch over your heart; that's where life starts.*

MSG

Be obsessed with Jesus. Breathe, sleep, eat, dream, and live Jesus! The apostle Paul could not have put it any better when he said in Philippians 1:21 that "for to me, to live is Christ, and to die is gain." The same passage is translated in *The Message* as follows: "Alive, I'm Christ's messenger; dead, I'm his bounty. Life versus even more life! I can't lose."

## L IS FOR LOYAL

- Be loyal and true.

Your calling as a Christian is to be loyal to God and true to your vocation as someone who has been redeemed by the precious blood of the Lord Jesus Christ. Loyalty includes faithfulness, reliability, and steadfastness. More than anything else, loyalty is a state of the heart and includes the motives behind any action. In other words, it is only God who can truly say whether or not a person is loyal and true to him, since it is only God who sees and knows the state of the heart.

Having been redeemed, you are required to do your utmost to make your calling and election sure. Having become a born-again child of God, do your level best, as much as it lies within you, to make your life a *living* sacrifice that is both holy and pleasing to God as we are admonished to do in Romans 12:1. God is always seeking those who are loyal to him. In 2 Chronicles 16:9, we are told that "the eyes of the LORD run to and fro throughout the whole earth, to show Himself strong on behalf of those whose heart is loyal to Him."

## E IS FOR WHEN YOU HAVE HAD ENOUGH

- Enough is enough…is enough?

From the story of Esau and Jacob, we learn a very important lesson in spiritual warfare. In the twenty-seventh chapter of the Old Testament book of Genesis, Jacob stole his older brother Esau's blessing with the active connivance of his mother, Rebekah. We are told that when Esau discovered that Jacob had stolen his blessing, he pleaded with Isaac, his father, saying, "But do you have only one blessing? Oh my father, bless me too."

In reply, his father said to him, "You will live by your sword and serve your brother. *But when you decide to break free, you will shake his yoke from your neck*" (NLT, emphasis supplied).

Sometimes, all you need is to be sick and tired of being sick and tired—of a besetting sin, an addiction, a recurring problem, or a bad habit. Once you decide that enough is enough and make a quality decision that you will accept no more, God backs your decision, and you receive the unction to function and enter your breakthrough.

## N MEANS NOURISH

- Nourish your faith.

Give attention to building up your most holy faith, as we are told in Jude 1:20. The word "faith" as used here means our belief in the Lord Jesus. Make every effort to grow in grace and in the knowledge of the Lord. Lay up treasures for yourself in heaven. It is not enough to be born again. You need to grow in intimacy with the Lord. You need to understand God's principles, not just his miracles!

God has given you a foundation upon which he expects you to add value. The imagery is that of building works, one block at a time. Let us take a look at 2 Peter 1:3–10:

*Everything that goes into a life of pleasing God has been miraculously given to us by getting to know, personally and intimately, the One who invited us to God. The best invitation we ever received! We were also given absolutely terrific promises to pass on to you—your tickets to participation in the life of God after you turned your back on a world corrupted by lust. So don't lose a minute in building on what you've been given, complementing your basic faith with good character, spiritual understanding, alert discipline, passionate patience, reverent wonder, warm friendliness, and generous love, each dimension fitting into and developing the others. With these qualities active and growing in your lives, no grass will grow under your feet, no day will pass without its reward as you mature in your experience of our Master Jesus. Without these qualities you can't see what's right before you, oblivious that your old sinful life has been wiped off the books. So, friends, confirm God's invitation to you, his choice of you. Don't put it off; do it now. Do this, and you'll have your life on a firm footing.*

MSG

T MEANS TO TAKE CHARGE, TAKE OVER, TAKE CONTROL, AND BE TENACIOUS

- Take charge, take over, take control.

   As we said earlier, man was born to rule and reign. So wherever you find yourself, assume control, take ownership, occupy! There is a sense in which God is saying to you, like he told Joshua, "I'm giving you every square inch of the land you set your foot on—just as I promised Moses" (Joshua 1:3, MSG). Now, I am not advocating that you can go to the White House or Buckingham Palace and claim them for yourself just because you set foot on them! What I am saying here is that you can take spiritual control of your neighborhood, your locality, your city, your county, your state, or even your country and determine that the devil will have a difficult time operating there. You can do this in the place of prayer.

- Be tenacious.

   Be persistent, unrelenting, and consistent in your walk with the Lord. When it comes to your relationship with him, be steadfast, dogged, determined. Never quit. Never take no for an answer. Jesus put it beautifully in Luke's gospel when he taught his disciples to persist in prayer.

*Jesus told them a story showing that it was necessary for them to pray consistently and* never quit.

LUKE 18:1, MSG, EMPHASIS SUPPLIED

## HEROES AND HEROINES OF SPIRITUAL VIOLENCE

As we saw earlier in this chapter, Jesus said, "And from the days of John the Baptist until now the kingdom of heaven suffers violence, and the violent take it by force."

The watershed is clearly *the days of John the Baptist.* It would appear that prior to the birth of John the Baptist, people did not take the kingdom of heaven by force. We are not told how they received the kingdom—maybe they begged for it, we don't know. However, from the time of John the Baptist, there was a change. Folk no longer pleaded for the kingdom; they simply took it by force.

Let us now take a look at a few examples of people who took the kingdom of heaven by force.

## The Syrophoenician woman

This woman's amazing story is found in Mark 7:24–30. She overcame three difficult obstacles in her bid to enter the kingdom. And with the aid of her extraordinary faith, she basically *gatecrashed* her way into the kingdom!

How did she do it? Well, let us read her remarkable story from *The Message* translation of the Bible:

> *From there Jesus set out for the vicinity of Tyre. He entered a house there where he didn't think he would be found, but he couldn't escape notice. He was barely inside when a woman who had a disturbed daughter heard where he was. She came and knelt at his feet, begging for help. The woman was Greek, Syro-Phoenician by birth. She asked him to cure her daughter. He said, "Stand in line and take your turn. The children get fed first. If there's any left over, the dogs get it." She said, "Of course, Master. But don't dogs under the table get scraps dropped by the children?" Jesus was impressed. "You're right! On your way! Your daughter is no longer disturbed. The demonic affliction is gone." She went home and found her daughter relaxed on the bed, the torment gone for good.*

We can learn a few lessons from this mighty woman of faith. First, she was initially ignored by the Lord. However, this is did not put her off. What do you do when it seems the Lord is distant?

Second, the Lord Jesus told her that she was not yet invited to partake of the kingdom. She was told in no uncertain terms to bide her time. This was another form of rejection—but she had not come this far to be turned away. Nothing was going to stop her now! Did you know that the manuscript for *Animal Farm,* the iconic and international best seller, was rejected by five different publishers? However, George Orwell, the author, refused to be deterred. He kept plugging on until he found a publisher who was willing to publish his work.

Susan Boyle became an overnight superstar in April 2009. According to *The New York Times*, "Ms. Boyle, 48, was a frumpy unknown before appearing as a contestant on *Britain's Got Talent* in April [2009], stunning the judges and audience with a crystal-clear rendition of the song "I Dreamed a Dream" from the musical *Les Misérables*. A YouTube clip of that performance became an instant phenomenon. According to Visible Measures, an American company that computes viewership of Internet videos, it has been watched 310 million times in all of its forms."[2]

Boyle's first album, *I Dreamed a Dream,* which was released on November 23, 2009, became the best-selling album in the world for 2009, selling nine million copies. In September 2010, Boyle was officially recognized by Guinness World Records as having had the fastest selling debut album by a female artist in the UK and the most successful first-week sales of a debut album in the UK, and she was also awarded the record for being the oldest person to reach number one with a debut album in the UK.[3] Boyle performed for Pope Benedict XVI on his tour of Britain in 2010.

In an interview with Piers Morgan on *Piers Morgan's Life Stories,* aired by ITV1 in London on August 11, 2011, Boyle said that she had previously auditioned twelve times, and each time she was rejected and told she was not good enough. However, she said she did not want to give up on her dream of becoming a singer! So she continued to audition until she got her breakthrough. Let me ask you a question: how much do you want your breakthrough?

Finally, this lady refused to take offense at Jesus. Jesus compared her to a dog at its master's table—so you could say that she was called names! However, she was focused. She knew what she wanted and she refused to accept "no" for an answer. Are you prepared to go all the way, or are you easily deterred?

## THE WOMAN WITH THE ISSUE OF BLOOD

Regrettably, we do not know the name of this remarkable woman of faith. By the time she came on the biblical scene, she had spent all she had on doctors in an attempt to find a solution to her problem. Unfortunately, the doctors could not help her. Jesus was her only hope. She knew what she wanted and was certain that if only she could just touch Jesus's clothes, her problems would end. Let us read her remarkable story, found in Mark 5:25–34 in *The Message* translation of the Bible.

*A woman who had suffered a condition of hemorrhaging for twelve years—a long succession of physicians had treated her, and treated her badly, taking all her money and leaving her worse off than before—had heard about Jesus. She slipped in from behind and touched his robe. She was thinking to herself, "If I can put a finger on his robe, I can get well." The moment she did it, the flow of blood dried up. She could feel the change and knew her plague was over and done with.*

*At the same moment, Jesus felt energy discharging from him. He turned around to the crowd and asked, "Who touched my robe?" His disciples said, "What are you talking about? With this crowd pushing and jostling you, you're asking, 'Who touched me?' Dozens have touched you!" But he went on asking, looking around to see who had done it. The woman, knowing what had happened, knowing she was the one, stepped up in fear and trembling, knelt before him, and gave him the whole story. Jesus said to her, "Daughter, you took a risk of faith, and now you're healed and whole. Live well, live blessed! Be healed of your plague."*

There is a lot to learn from this remarkable woman—not least the fact that she was single-minded. The crowd around Jesus did not deter her. The fact that she had a problem which made her ceremonially unclean in her society and therefore unable to mix with normal people did not discourage her either. She forced her way through the crowd, received her healing, and came to the attention of the Lord! What a woman!

## BLIND BARTIMAEUS

Another hero who was not discouraged or put off by the crowd was Bartimaeus. He was a poor blind man who appears to have known about Jesus. The crowd tried to suppress his plea for help, but he would have none of it. He basically forced his way into the kingdom of heaven.

Let us read his wonderful and inspiring story from Mark 10:46–54, using The New Living Translation of the Bible:

*Then they reached Jericho, and as Jesus and his disciples left town, a large crowd followed him. A blind beggar named Bartimaeus (son of Timaeus) was sitting beside the road. When Bartimaeus heard that Jesus of Nazareth was nearby, he began to shout, "Jesus, Son of David, have mercy on me!" "Be quiet!" many of the people yelled at him. But he only shouted louder, "Son of David, have mercy on me!"*

*When Jesus heard him, he stopped and said, "Tell him to come here." So they called the blind man. "Cheer up," they said. "Come on, he's calling you!" Bartimaeus threw aside his coat, jumped up, and came to Jesus. "What do you want me to do for you?" Jesus asked. "My rabbi," the blind man said, "I want to see!" And Jesus said to him, "Go, for your faith has healed you." Instantly the man could see, and he followed Jesus down the road.*

Not only did Bartimaeus want help, but when he got the Lord's attention, he cast off his coat so that there was nothing weighing him down. The writer of Hebrews could not have expressed it better when he said in Hebrews 12:1, "Let us strip off every weight that slows us down, especially the sin that so easily trips us up. And let us run with endurance the race God has set before us" (NLT). Are you still being weighed down by sin? To run the race effectively, you need to travel light.

These all took the kingdom of heaven not by soliciting for it, but by violence. And so should you!

## YOU ARE A THERMOSTAT, NOT A THERMOMETER

A thermometer reflects the temperature around it. A thermometer contains liquid, typically mercury or colored alcohol that expands and rises in the tube as the temperature increases and then contracts and drops as the temperature decreases. A thermostat, on the other hand, maintains the temperature of a system at a constant *preset* level, regardless of the temperature around it. As a child of God, you are not a thermometer but a thermostat.

In spiritual warfare, you are not like the thermometer, which goes up and down depending on the temperature around it. Instead, you should be constant, immoveable, and unshakeable—like the thermostat. You should not be moved by what you see or how you feel; you should only be moved by the Word of God. In any and every situation, you should be able to say like the psalmist in Psalm 27:13, "I would have lost heart, unless I had believed that I would see the goodness of the LORD in the land of the living."

Any marriage where the couple's love for each other is based on the way they feel at any particular time is doomed. In marriage, love is really a commitment to each other. In the same way, any Christian whose spiritual life goes up and down like a yo-yo whenever things go up or down around them will be at the mercy of the Enemy. This reminds me of the nursery rhyme, "The Grand Old Duke of York":

> Oh, the grand old Duke of York
> He had ten thousand men
> He marched them up to the top of the hill
> And he marched them down again.
> And when they were up they were up
> And when they were down they were down
> And when they were only halfway up
> They were neither up nor down.

## FOOD FOR REFLECTION

- How do we devise strategy in spiritual warfare?
- What is your understanding of the call to spiritual violence?
- Can you recall any time when you took by force something spiritual that was rightfully yours?
- When we bind the strong man (who is, of course, Satan) what goods of his can we plunder?
- As a Christian, if you are not like a thermometer, what instrument can you liken yourself to?

## PRAYER FEATURES

- Dear Lord Jesus, your Word says that we are not unaware of the devices of the devil. Please open my eyes to see and understand the strategy and plans of the Enemy.
- Help me, Lord, to be violent in spirit and to take hold of every provision which you have made available for me.
- I pray, Lord, for the grace to depend on the Holy Spirit for divine strategy in my dealings with the Enemy.
- I pray, Lord, that in my walk with you, you would enable me to be constant, immoveable, and unshakeable like a thermostat.
- Teach me, Lord, to be consistent.

ACTION POINTS

- Get hold of both a thermometer and any device which uses a thermostat. Examine them both carefully. Write down in your journal the differences which you notice between these interesting instruments.
- Study the life of Tamar, Judah's daughter-in-law, as it is recorded in Genesis 38. Ask yourself whether Tamar was right in pretending to be a prostitute in order to obtain what was rightfully hers.
- Make a list of the provisions which you believe are rightfully yours as a child of God and which the Enemy tries to take from you from time to time.

Chapter Five

# YOUR AUTHORITY OVER THE ENEMY

———⟨ΩⁿΩ⟩———

*Behold, I give you the authority to trample on serpents and scorpions, and over all the*
*power of the enemy, and nothing shall by any means hurt you.*

LUKE 10:19

A s a child of God, you have the authority to trample, crush, and walk over
*all* the power of the Enemy. Your authority is not just over some of the
Enemy's powers: you can exercise influence over every sphere of his oper-
ations and over every single one of his powers. You have complete, absolute, and
total authority over the Enemy. However, before we unpack the word *authority*, we
need to fully understand who the Enemy is.

Who is the Enemy? Revelation 20:2 tells us that he is the dragon, that serpent of old, the devil, who is also called Satan. But who is he? And why is he
the Enemy? How did he *become* the Enemy?

We find the answers to these questions in Isaiah 14:12–15 and Ezekiel
28:12–19. Satan was created Lucifer, son of the morning. He was the embodiment of wisdom and beauty. He was the personification of splendor, magnificence, and exquisite loveliness. He was in Eden, the garden of God, even before
man was created. His clothing was chrysolite, white moonstone, beryl, onyx,
jasper, sapphire, turquoise, and emerald—all beautifully personalized and set in
the finest handpicked gold.

Lucifer was one of at least three archangels created by God. The others were
Gabriel and Michael. Gabriel was the angel who was sent to announce the birth
of Jesus to Mary in Luke 1:26. Gabriel had been sent to give Daniel skill and
understanding in Daniel 8:15–26. Although he is not specifically called an
archangel in the Bible, I believe he is one because of his testimony to Mary in
Luke 1:19, when he said: "I am Gabriel! I stand *in the very presence* of God"

(NLT). Michael is the archangel who waged war on the devil when the angel sent to answer Daniel's prayer was held up by the evil and demonic prince of Persia in Daniel 10:13. See also Jude 1:9, where we are told that the archangel Michael contended with the devil over Moses's body.

God ordained and anointed Lucifer as the mighty archangel who led worship in heaven. He had access to the holy mountain of God and walked among the stones of fire. It is believed that his body was crafted with all varieties of musical instruments. He was the quintessence of celestial music, melody, and worship.

Lucifer was blameless in all he did from the day he was created until a certain day, the *evil day*, when evil was found in him. His heart became filled with pride because of his beauty. He thought to himself that he would ascend to heaven and set his throne above God's stars. He would climb to the highest heavens and be like the Most High God. He would dethrone God and enthrone himself as god almighty. He corrupted his wisdom for the sake of his splendor. In effect, Lucifer committed sin.

As God cannot tolerate or even behold sin, he decided to banish Lucifer from his holy mountain, the mountain of God, forever. However, Lucifer was not going to go quietly without a fight! From Revelation 12:3–4 and 7–9, we understand that the devil called up all the angels he had control over, approximately one third of the angels in heaven, and decided to go to war against the Most High God, the Lord of Lords and the Ancient of Days. There was war in heaven! The forces of God, represented by the archangel Michael and his angels, fought the forces of evil, represented by Lucifer and his angels. Lucifer lost this battle, and God expelled him from his place among the stones of fire. As Lucifer fell, he took with him all the angels who had supported his cause, dragging them along with his tail as he tumbled from heaven. These fallen angels became his demon spirits. Their punishment will be to eventually spend eternity in hellfire—an appalling, dreadful place where, in the words of the Lord Jesus in Mark 9:48, "their worm does not die, and the fire is not quenched."

## HOW DID SATAN ORCHESTRATE MAN'S FALL?

After that epic battle in heaven, Lucifer became Satan, the devil, God's enemy, and as we are told in John 10:10, set himself up to steal, kill, and destroy anything and everything created by God. When man was created, Satan became man's archenemy. Although we cannot know for sure, it seems that Satan fell just before man was created. It is therefore not surprising that he immediately set about trying everything within his power to destroy man.

When he fell, Satan must have felt that it would be a major *coup d'état* if he could destroy Adam and Eve by making them disobey God's commandment not to eat the fruit of the Tree of the Knowledge of Good and Evil. Satan knew that if he could compel Adam and Eve to violate God's instruction, man would lose his authority over the earth, and Satan would be able to take over from them as the god of this world. Furthermore, if man disobeyed God, sin would be automatically introduced into the human race, and every person born of a woman would invariably become a sinner without Satan having to lift a finger. The devil was confident that if he could introduce man to sin, it would inevitably and ultimately lead to death and destruction.

It's not hard to imagine what was going on behind the scenes in Eden. Perhaps Satan called a meeting of his war cabinet, made up of himself as supreme ruler and chairperson, his principalities, and his powers. This was their greatest battle since their humiliating and ignominious eviction from heaven like a bunch of common criminals. I can visualize Satan outlining the prize that was up for grabs at the outset of the meeting: This was their opportunity to seek revenge and make God pay for their shameful expulsion from heaven. This was their blessed and providential break. This kind of lucky break only came once every trillion years! There was no guarantee that there would ever be another. This was their moment, their opportunity! They could not let this chance slip through their fingers. They had to grab it with both hands. The prospect of destroying God's creation and taking man along with them to hell would have made the devil and his cohorts salivate. Satan would have warned them not to be carried away. They had to be very, very careful…there was no margin for error.

It seems to me that in the end, Satan's war cabinet decided that it would be unwise to approach Adam directly, because he appeared to be closer to God. Adam was the one who was first created and was more unlikely than Eve to succumb to their lure. They would go after the woman instead.

Their seven-point plan was simple:

*Step 1:* Familiarize yourselves with God's instructions to Adam and Eve to see if there is anything in them that can be exploited. As they studied God's words to Adam and Eve, they would have become aware that there was a specific instruction not to eat of the Tree of the Knowledge of Good and

Evil. If the humans were to disobey this law, the penalty would be death. *This shouldn't be too difficult,* the dark forces thought to themselves. *All we have to do is make both the man and his wife willfully disobey God's direct instruction to them.*

*Step 2:* Go through Eve. They probably reasoned that if they could make Eve fall, it was only a matter of time before Adam would also go down. She was extremely beautiful and charming, and Adam was head over heels in love with her. He wouldn't be able to resist anything she asked him to do. On the other hand, if they went through Adam, he was unlikely to have the same effect on her.

*Step 3:* Recruit the serpent. The serpent was a shrewd, wise, and beautiful animal. He had four legs just like the other animals. He was delightful and had a wry sense of humor. Eve seemed to like him—they were always chatting and playing around in the garden. Satan's cohorts determined to aid him in becoming Eve's very good friend and encourage him to become her confidant.

*Step 4:* Make the serpent vulnerable to demonic oppression and possession. Open up his spirit through demonic influences. Then enter into the serpent's body, take over his faculties, and communicate through him. Make the transformation seamless, and let the serpent approach Eve as usual. Eve would think she was talking to her friend and not know that Satan had taken over.

*Step 5:* Create doubt in Eve's mind by distorting the instruction God gave: "You are free to eat from any tree in the garden; but you must not eat from the Tree of the Knowledge of Good and Evil, for when you eat from it you will certainly die." Ask her, "Did God really say that you must not eat the fruit of *any of the trees* in the garden?"

*Step 6:* Appeal to Eve's natural inclinations and desires. Make her see that the fruit looks attractive and is very desirable. Assure her that she will not die if she eats the fruit. Emphasize to her that *God* knows that the moment she eats the fruit, her eyes will open, she will become like God, and she will know the difference between good and evil; that is the reason why the tree is called the Tree of the Knowledge of Good and Evil. Make her think that the fruit is what she needs.

*Step 7:* Suggest that she takes a bite from the fruit of the tree—she has nothing to lose, but everything to gain. Doesn't she want to be like God and know the difference between good and evil? Remind her to give some of the fruit to her husband as well, because it would be unthinkable for her to keep this "blessing" to herself.

Unfortunately for mankind, Satan's plot worked to plan. It was executed with military precision and led to the fall of man and his eventual banishment from the garden of Eden.

Now, back to the devil.

Following his fall, Satan's destiny is eternal separation from God. Having done his crime, he must spend his time…in hell. Hell was created by God as a place of punishment for Satan and his demons. (I don't think Satan's fallen angels fully grasped what they were getting themselves into when they took sides with Satan. However, it is too late for them now—serving as little more than Satan's errand boys, they are doomed to spend eternity with their master in hell. For now, Satan has a very complex and highly organized network of demon spirits who can communicate with each other at the speed of light, giving the false impression that he is omnipresent, like God.)

Hell is a horrible, awful place. It is a place of eternal, perpetual, never-ending suffering, anguish, torture, and torment. In hell, fire and brimstone constantly burn. *Satan does not want to go to hell alone.* Along with his demons, he desires to take as many people as he can with him. For this reason he appeared to Eve in the garden of Eden in the form of a serpent. He deceived Eve and led both her and her husband into sin, and with them, the whole of humanity. He continues to deceive millions of people today.

## THE ENEMY'S NAMES

Satan is known by many different names in both the Old and New Testaments. Each of these names has a distinct significance, providing us with a good idea of who Satan really is and giving us an inkling of his mission and purpose. I have set out below a table of Satan's various names and their significance, all arranged in alphabetical order. To help with your personal study, I have also included the Scripture references to which they relate. The list is by no means exhaustive. It is written from my individual perspective and from my personal understanding of Scripture.

| SATAN'S NAME | SIGNIFICANCE | SCRIPTURE REFERENCE |
|---|---|---|
| Abaddon | The angel of the abyss or the bottomless pit, known as *Abaddon* in Hebrew and *Apollyon* in Greek. These words mean "a destroying angel" or "a destroyer." Here we see Satan at his lethal best. He wants to completely destroy and totally extinguish man from the face of the earth. He abhors man as the most important part of God's creation and wants him thoroughly demolished and vanquished. | Revelation 9:11 |
| Accuser of the Brethren | In this passage in Revelation, Satan is called the "the accuser of our brethren" who accused them before our God day and night. The word "accuser" is used in the sense of a prosecutor who seeks to condemn a defendant in criminal proceedings. The devil is not letting us off at all! He is working flat out, accusing the brethren (the children of God) before God "day and night." Thank God for Jesus our Advocate, who is at the right hand of the Father pleading our case and justifying us! The Enemy is also an accuser in making people feel wretched, perpetually guilt-ridden and unable to forgive themselves even when God has forgiven them. | Revelation 12:10 |
| Adversary | Satan is the greatest adversary of the children of God. He is an opponent, he is a foe, he is a challenger, he is our antagonist, and he is the enemy of our faith. To properly handle Satan in his | 1 Peter 5:8 |

| | | |
|---|---|---|
| Adversary, cont. | role of adversary, Christians are enjoined to be sober and vigilant. | |
| Angel of Light | Satan is able to transform himself into an angel of light. He often pretends to be what he is not. But why would he do this? He does this in order to mislead people into thinking that he is actually an angel, and once he gains their trust he is able to lead them astray. For instance, why do you think people say that the devil you know is better than the angel you don't know? | 2 Corinthians 11:14 |
| Apollyon | The angel of the bottomless pit or abyss, known as *Apollyon* in the Greek and *Abaddon* in Hebrew. The words mean a destroying angel or a destroyer. (Please see notes on *Abaddon* above). | Revelation 9:11 |
| Beelzebub | Beelzebub is the chief of evil spirits or, as we are told in the Synoptic Gospels, the ruler of demons. This shows Satan as the head of his evil hierarchy, with complete overall responsibility for the actions of his demon spirits. As their chief or ruler, he can do with his evil spirits and demons as he pleases. | Matthew 12:24 Mark 3:22 Luke 11:15 |
| Belial | Belial is a person or something that is worthless, useless, and of no value whatsoever. Satan is the personification of Belial because he has no value either now or in the world to come. | 2 Corinthians 6:15 |
| Deceiver | The devil is the great deceiver. He misleads, hoodwinks, and lies to people in an attempt to lead them off track. He deceives by either concealing the truth or by misrepresenting the truth. | Revelation 12:9 |
| Devil | *The devil* is the main name by which Satan is known today. It comes from the Greek word *diabolos*,[1] from which we also have the modern English word "diabolical." *Diabolos* means a traducer, a false accuser, and a | Matthew 4:1, 5, 9 Ephesians 4:27 Revelation 12:9, 20:2 |

| | | |
|---|---|---|
| Devil, cont. | slanderer. This is Satan the devil at his diabolical best: falsely accusing, slandering, and being the supreme embodiment of evil. | |
| Enemy | *The Enemy* is from the Greek *echtros,* which itself is from the primary verb *echtho* (to hate) and means hateful (passive odious and active hostile). It is usually used as a noun: an adversary (especially Satan), enemy, and foe.[2] Satan is our enemy. He is the enemy of our salvation, and he will do anything to try to destroy the children of God. | Matthew 13:39 |
| Evil One | This name shows Satan as the personification of evil. The name is from the Greek *poneros,*[3] which shows the devil as a bad devil, the embodiment of evil. The devil is portrayed as grievous, harmful, lewd, malicious, and the epitomization of wickedness. The devil takes no prisoners. | John 17:15 |
| Father of All Lies | Satan gave birth to lies; he originated lies. There is no truth whatsoever in him. When he speaks a lie, he is at home and speaks from his own resources, because he is a liar and the father of it. As the father of lies, he falsifies the truth. | John 8:44 |
| God of This Age | When Adam and Eve fell, they gave their birthright to the Enemy, and from that moment the Enemy became the god of this world. However, in Christ Jesus you can be restored to your original position of dominion and rulership over the rest of God's creation. | 2 Corinthians 4:4 |
| King of Babylon | *Babylon* is a derivative of the Hebrew word *babel,*[4] which means confusion. In effect, the devil is the king and instigator of confusion, unlike God, who, according to 1 Corinthians 14:33, is not the author of confusion. Whenever there is confusion in the world today, you can be sure that Satan is at work. | Isaiah 14:4 |

| King of Tyrus | From the Hebrew *tsor,*[5] meaning a sharp stone, a rock. Satan is a sharp stone, capable of ripping people apart and destroying lives. Unlike Jesus who is the Rock of Ages, Satan is a false rock, giving false hope to millions of people in the world today. | Ezekiel 28:12 |
| --- | --- | --- |
| Leviathan | The Leviathan is a large sea monster. Here, the Enemy is called "Leviathan the fleeing serpent" and "Leviathan that twisted serpent." Clearly these are references to Satan as a sly, scheming serpent. | Isaiah 27:1 |
| Liar | Satan is not only the father of lies, but he is also a liar. Obviously, to be the father and originator of lies, he would have to be a pretty good liar himself! | John 8:44 |
| Little Horn | In the dream by Daniel in this Scripture, Satan is the little horn which grew so big and became so powerful that he exalted himself to the host of heaven; "and it cast down some of the host and some of the stars to the ground, and trampled them." The Scripture is probably referring to the time when Lucifer was filled with pride and decided to fight the host of heaven, led by the archangel Michael. | Daniel 7:8 Daniel 8:9–10 |
| Lucifer | This is Satan before his fall in all his magnificence, glory, splendor, and beauty, when as Lucifer he was the morning star and the son of the morning. | Isaiah 14:12 |
| Murderer | Satan is a murderer. He kills. He wants to drag as many people as he can with him to hell. | John 8:44 |
| Old Serpent | *The Old Serpent* refers to Satan from his time in the garden of Eden when he took over the faculties of the serpent in his bid to make Eve fall. He is crafty, cunning, and conniving. | Revelation 12:29 Revelation 20:2 |
| Power or Dominion of Darkness | Satan epitomizes all that the forces of darkness represent. He stands for everything that is evil, dark, gloomy, and wicked. | Colossians 1:13 |

| Prince of the Power of the Air | The devil is described by Paul the apostle here as the "prince of the power of the air" who controls the unbelieving world and the world system. Here we see the devil as the spirit at work in the hearts of those who refuse to obey God, and who follow the passionate desires and inclinations of their sinful nature. | Ephesians 2:1–3 |
|---|---|---|
| Roaring Lion | Satan is not exactly called a "roaring lion" in the Bible. He is likened to one. We are told in this passage that the devil walks about like a roaring lion. Here he is seeking people to devour, demolish, and destroy. | 1 Peter 5:8 |
| Ruler of Demons | This is another name for Beelzebub. (Please see the notes on Beelzebub above.) | Luke 11:15 |
| Satan | As we have seen earlier in this chapter, Lucifer became "Satan" when he sinned and was thrown out of heaven. The name means "adversary." Satan is without doubt the greatest opponent and foe of God's children on this side of eternity. | Job 1:6–9 Matthew 4:10 |
| Serpent | Satan is not just referred to as "that old serpent" in the Scriptures, but he is in fact also called the Serpent. | Genesis 3:1 Revelation 12:9 |
| Tempter | The devil is the tempter. He tempts by dropping thoughts and ideas into your mind in an attempt to make you disobey God. | Matthew 4:3 Thessalonians 3:5 |
| Thief | The devil is not just a thief but in point of fact is the original thief. He tries to steal from God's children, and lots of the time he succeeds. He steals their joy and the seed of the Word of God from their hearts. He also steals their health and their God-given ideas. | John 10:10 |

| Wicked One | Here the devil is the characterization, image, and personification of wickedness, vice, sin, immorality, evil, iniquity, and malfeasance. He is not merely wicked; he is the wicked one. | Matthew 13:19 |
|---|---|---|

## SATAN'S PRIMARY PURPOSE

Notwithstanding what Satan's various names tell us about his mission, Jesus made it clear in John 10:10 that Satan's primary purpose is to steal, kill, and destroy. That is his chief calling, his main mission, his principal vocation, his prime ministry. He is a thief, always looking for ways to steal from God's children. He steals stability from governments and peace from our communities. He also steals ideas. He is a murderer: he kills visions, self-confidence, people, and more. He is a destroyer: he destroys homes, marriages, relationships, and careers.

To his primary purpose, you may also add Satan's role as the accuser of the brethren. As we saw in the table above, in Revelation 12:10 he is called the "the accuser of our brethren," who accused them before our God day and night. The enemy specializes in making people feel wretched, perpetually guilt-ridden, and unable to forgive themselves even when God has forgiven them.

Satan manifests and reveals himself to different people in diverse ways. To some he manifests himself through the bondage of sin. For others the manifestation of Satan in life may be an addiction. It can be poverty or lack. It may be barrenness or unfruitfulness in whatever form. It can also be debt. It may even be an illness or fear. It may be relationship problems, or even death. Each of these is an expression of the devil's threefold ministry of stealing, killing, and destroying.

## THE AUTHORITY OF THE BELIEVER

In whatever way Satan chooses to operate in our lives, as a born-again child of God, you have absolute authority over him through Jesus Christ. The authority that God has given you over Satan, the Enemy, is comprehensive: it is ample, wide-ranging, thorough, far-reaching, sweeping, all-embracing. It is not *just* authority over Satan, but also authority over all of Satan's cohorts, assistants, and associates, as well as over all his powers. Through his death and resurrection, Jesus conquered the devil, disarmed him, and obtained a name that is superior to and mightier than any other name, whether in heaven, on the earth, or underneath the earth. On account of this, Paul tells us in Philippians 2:9–10 that at the mere mention of the name of Jesus, every knee must bow and every tongue declare, proclaim, pronounce, and announce that Jesus Christ is indeed Lord!

Jesus's resurrection is not just a fact of history: it is a present reality in our lives today. The authority that we have comes from Jesus's triumph over the Enemy and is only available to us in Christ Jesus. It is one of our privileges as children of God. It's our right, our entitlement, our privilege, and our prerogative. We simply need to exercise it for our benefit.

> *Behold, I give you the authority to trample on serpents and scorpions, and over all the power of the enemy, and nothing shall by any means hurt you.*

> LUKE 10:19

What is authority? The word translated "authority" is from the Greek word *exŏusia* (pronounced ex-oo-see-ah),[6] the same root word that gives us *right*, which we examined in chapter 1. In relation to authority, it means *the power to do as one pleases*. It includes physical and mental power, authority, and the power of government, that is, the power of someone whose will and command must be obeyed and submitted to. It is "the power or right to give orders, make decisions, and enforce obedience."[7]

## WHAT CAN YOU ORDER SATAN TO DO?

Effectively, as a child of God, you have the right to order Satan to carry out your lawful instructions. But what is a lawful instruction? *It is a command which you give to the Enemy based on the Word of God.* Your order to Satan to do or refrain from doing something can only be a lawful instruction *if it is framed within the parameters of the delegated authority which you have in Christ Jesus.*

Your directive to the devil must have the following characteristics for it to be a lawful instruction:

*First, you must be a child of God.* This is a condition precedent, because your authority over the devil is derived from Jesus Christ; it is only available to you if you are a believer in Christ. The Bible tells us in Mark 16:17 that the power to cast out demons is one of the signs that will follow *those who believe.* If you are not born again and known by the name of the Lord, any instruction you issue to the devil is an *unlawful* instruction. The story of the seven sons of Sceva in Acts 19:13–16 shows that if you are not a child of God, you order Satan around at your own peril. According to the *New Living Translation:*

> *A group of Jews was traveling from town to town casting out evil spirits. They tried to use the name of the Lord Jesus in their incantation, saying, "I command you in the name of Jesus, whom Paul preaches, to come out!" Seven sons of Sceva, a leading priest, were doing this. But one time when they tried it, the evil spirit replied, "I know Jesus, and I know Paul, but who are you?" Then the man with the evil spirit leaped on them, overpowered them, and attacked them with such violence that they fled from the house, naked and battered.*

*Second, you must address the devil or demonic spirit in the name of Jesus.* In Mark 16:17, the Bible says, "And these signs shall follow those that have believed: *in my name* they shall cast out demons; they shall speak with new tongues" (DBT). The God's Word Translation puts it this way: "These are the miraculous signs that will accompany believers: They will use *the power and authority of my name* to force demons out of people. They will speak new languages" (emphasis supplied).

When you address the devil in the name of Jesus, he obeys for three reasons:

1. Colossians 2:15 tells us that Jesus disarmed the devil on the cross of Calvary. The God's Word Translation says Jesus stripped him of his power.
2. Following his death and resurrection, Jesus declared to his disciples in Matthew 28:18 that all authority has been given to him in heaven and on earth.
3. The Bible tells us in Philippians 2:9–11, that "God exalted him to the highest place and gave him the name that is above every name, that at the name of Jesus every knee should bow, in heaven and on earth and under the earth, and every tongue acknowledge that Jesus Christ is Lord, to the glory of God the Father" (NIV).

*Third, your instruction to the devil must be rooted in the Word of God.* You cannot, for instance, order Satan to self-destruct because that would be contrary to the Word of God in Revelation 20:1–10 and in Matthew 8:29, where the demons asked Jesus, "Why are you interfering with us, Son of God? Have you come here to torture us before God's appointed time?" (NLT). You have to be aware that the devil knows the Bible. Remember that he quoted from the Bible when he tempted Jesus at the beginning of the Lord's ministry in Matthew 4:6. The devil doesn't take any prisoners; he will resist you if you give him an unlawful instruction!

However, provided that you fulfill the three conditions set out above, you can do with Satan as you please. You can command him and expect him to obey you.

Scripture gives us many examples of lawful instructions you can issue to the devil:

- You can bind him (Mark 3:27).
- You can restrain him (Isaiah 54:17).
- You can resist him (James 4:7; 1 Peter 5:9).
- You can rebuke him (Luke 9:42; Zechariah 3:2).
- You can plunder his goods (Matthew 12:29).
- You can cast out his evil and demonic spirits (Mark 16:17; Acts 8:7).
- You can undo his work (1 John 3:8).
- You can disarm him (Colossians 2:15).
- You can frustrate his counsel (2 Samuel 15:31).
- You can nullify his power (Luke 10:19).
- You can destroy his plans (Isaiah 8:10).
- You can destroy his yoke and lift his burdens (Isaiah 10:27).
- You can disrupt his meetings (Isaiah 54:15).
- You can uproot any seed or tree which he has planted (Matthew 15:13).
- You can demolish and tear down his strongholds (2 Corinthians 10:4).
- You can send him to the waterless places (Matthew 12:43).
- You can command him to stop meddling or interfering (1 Peter 5:8–9; Jude 1:9).

As a child of God, you have the authority to give Satan orders as well as the power to enforce his obedience. You have total and complete authority over Satan! In other words, Satan has no alternative but to submit to your will and obey your command. If you address him in the name of Jesus Christ, he must obey and do as he is told. He has no choice. All you have to do is to *simply* speak the word.

# HOW AUTHORITY WORKS IN PRACTICE

## AN OFFICER AND A MAN OF AUTHORITY

In the eighth chapter of Matthew's gospel, we read an amazing and wonderful story which beautifully illustrates the practical outworking of authority. An officer of the Roman army came to see Jesus in a place called Capernaum. He was a centurion, meaning that he was a commanding officer with oversight of one hundred soldiers. He told Jesus that his young servant lay at home paralyzed and in unimaginable suffering, and he pleaded with Jesus to help him. Jesus then informed him that he would go to his home and heal the servant. However, in reply the soldier said that he was not worthy to have Jesus visit his home. "Just say the word," he told Jesus, "and my servant will be healed. For I myself I am a man under authority, with soldiers under me. I tell this one 'Go,' and he goes; and that one, 'Come,' and he comes. I say to my servant, 'Do this,' and he does it" (Matthew 8:5–10, NIV).

The man was right. Jesus spoke the word, and the centurion's servant was healed. In exercising authority over the Enemy, God expects you to speak the word in faith. Whether the Enemy likes it or not, he will have no option but to obey.

## THE ORDER OF A JUDGE OF HER MAJESTY'S HIGH COURT

In the summer of 2006 in my role as an attorney, I acted for a client who was scheduled to be removed from the United Kingdom to a popular Caribbean country. She had been arrested by the United Kingdom Border Agency as an illegal immigrant and detained under the immigration rules. This was happening on a Saturday, and the courts were closed. The only way to stop her removal was to apply to a duty judge at the high court for an injunction restraining the secretary of state for the Home Department from removing her. This would require a telephone application *without notice* to the United Kingdom Border Agency, and so would only be granted by a judge in the most pressing, urgent, and exceptional cases.

Looking at the documents before me, I could see that the removal of this lady to her country would be unreasonable and perverse—it had all the hallmarks of man's inhumanity to man as well as the abuse of power. I therefore decided to seek a telephone injunction from the duty judge at the Administrative Court, Queen's Bench Division of the High Court of Justice, at the Strand in London. At the request of the judge, I faxed some papers to his clerk, after which the judge telephoned me, and I then made my application to his lordship over the telephone.

The judge granted my application and restrained anyone from removing my client from the United Kingdom. By the time the order was made, my client was already at the airport on her way out of the United Kingdom. However, as soon as the United Kingdom Border Agency was made aware of the order of the high court judge, the removal was immediately canceled. My client was taken back to the detention center, was subsequently released from detention, and was eventually granted discretionary leave to remain in the United Kingdom.

I remind you, all of this happened on a weekend. There was no hearing in open court, and the judge did not have to put on his wig and gown, yet he was able to stop the removal of this young lady from the United Kingdom. All he did on that lovely summer's day was to issue a restraining order, and the United Kingdom Border Agency, influential and powerful as it is, had no choice but to comply. As a Justice of Her Majesty's Court Service, the judge had tremendous authority, and he exercised it to huge effect for the benefit of my client.

In the same way, as true believers, our authority over the Enemy flows from our relationship with God. We are God's children, his heirs, and the vessels of his Spirit. God therefore expects you to exercise that authority to maximum result.

## EXERCISING AUTHORITY IN THE AREAS OF BONDAGE TO SIN, POVERTY, ILLNESS, AND ADVERSITY

How do we deal with the Enemy's manifestations in the areas of bondage to sin, addiction, poverty or lack, barrenness or unfruitfulness in whatever form, debt, illness, fear, relationship problems, and death? There are five things to keep at the forefront of our minds:

FIRST, KEEP IN MIND THAT IT IS FINISHED.

Constantly, remind yourself that Jesus took care of the root cause of the problem on the cross of Calvary. When Jesus declared that "it is finished," he meant every single word. The Bible tells us in 1 John 3:8b that Jesus came to destroy, do away with, demolish, extinguish, annihilate, and put an end to every work of darkness. Having done so, we are told in Colossians 2:15 that he publicly humiliated the Enemy, triumphed over him, overcame him, and prevailed over him in all things. We must understand and appreciate the fact that if Jesus has truly set us free, then we are *free* indeed. In Christ Jesus, we are free from any and every bondage or addiction; we are liberated from fear; we are healed of every sickness, disease, or infirmity; we are emancipated from the Adamic curse; and we are redeemed from spiritual death.

## Second, speak the Word into the situation

As we saw in chapter 3, the Word of God is the sword of the Spirit. We need to be fully armed with the Word. We must drench ourselves in the Word of God, saturating in it in such a way that, as Paul admonishes in Colossians 3:16, the Word actually dwells in us richly, thoroughly, fully, completely, deeply, and totally. We have to know the teachings and truths of Scripture that are right and appropriate for our particular situations. This comes as you allow the Word to become flesh to you, as you make it a part of your daily routine. You must study, meditate, and ruminate over it. You must store it in the deep recesses of your heart. You need to make it a part of your everyday life. If you do these things, then in the time of need, the right word for your circumstance will come out of your spirit.

## Third, take corresponding action

Faith on its own, without an appropriate step on our part, amounts to nothing (James called it "dead" in James 2:17). It is a waste of time, and it is futile. You must take a step that demonstrates that you believe that what you have prayed about has in reality taken place in the realm of the spirit. As you step out in faith, you will see the physical manifestation of your deliverance, breakthrough, provision, healing, or victory, as the case may be. Like Abraham's servant, you have to "be in the way" for the Lord to help you (see below). As you know, it takes two! God is willing and able; are you willing to take his hands and step out in faith?

> *And he said, Blessed be the Lord God of my master Abraham, who hath not left destitute my master of his mercy and his truth: I being in the way, the Lord led me to the house of my master's brethren.*
>
> GENESIS 24:27, KJV

This must be said: part of taking corresponding action and stepping out in faith is avoiding *any and every* appearance of evil. If God has set you free from alcoholism, for instance, then it would be sensible to stay away from every place where alcohol appears or is celebrated, including places where alcohol will be freely available such as bars, taverns, pubs, and even office parties. The same would apply to other habits and addictions.

## FOURTH, PRAY MORE THAN EVER BEFORE

Prayer is the key which moves God's hands, which in turn moves the universe. If Jesus needed to pray, then you cannot do without prayer. Pray, pray, pray, pray, pray, pray, and pray yet more. You can never pray enough. Pray in the name of Jesus. Pray all types and manners of prayer. Pray at all times. Pray without ceasing. Prayer is a master key. It is the key of David, referred to in Revelation 3:7, which opens a door which cannot be locked and locks a door which cannot be opened. Those who know the secret of prayer will use it to unlock the unfathomable riches of salvation in Christ Jesus.

## FIFTH, REMEMBER THAT PRAISE IS COMELY

Learn to give thanks to God in *all* things. We need to learn to praise God when things are good and when things don't look so good! Most people will give thanks when things are going well. The real challenge is to give praise to God when evil things happen to you or when things don't go the way you expect. But that is where the real blessing is! Praise God for *who* he is—the Creator of all things. Praise him for *what he is to you*—your Savior, Redeemer, Healer, Advocate, Protector, and Provider. In all situations and in every circumstance, praise him because he is able to make every situation work out for your benefit, even if it is difficult or painful for a time. Praise him when you feel like it. Even when you do *not* feel like it, praise him anyway. There is power in praise: God loves our praises so much so that the Bible tells us in Psalm 22:3 that he actually dwells in our praises.

## FOOD FOR REFLECTION

- What is your understanding of who Lucifer is?
- In what ways has Satan manifested himself in your life?
- Have Satan's names given you a better understanding of his mission?
- What is authority?
- In what ways have you exercised your authority over Satan?
- Is it realistic to give thanks to God in all circumstances?
- Can you ever pray too much?

### PRAYER FEATURES

- Lord, open my eyes to understand and know the schemes and devices of the Enemy.
- Lord, help me to recover whatever the Enemy has stolen from me, to repair whatever he has destroyed in my life, and to resurrect whatever he may have killed in me.
- Lord, I receive boldness through the power of the Holy Spirit to exercise authority over the Enemy in all things.
- Lord, help me to pray without ceasing.
- Lord, teach me to give thanks in all things.

### ACTION POINTS

- Identify the areas of your life where you need to exercise authority over the Enemy.
- Make a decision to give thanks to God at all times for the next week, no matter what comes your way.
- Make a decision to pray more often.
- Identify the things which the Enemy may have stolen from you, those things that he may have destroyed in your life, and whatever he may have killed in your life. Using your authority over the Enemy, begin to seek a restoration of those things which have been stolen, a repair of what has been destroyed, and a resurrection of what has been killed.

Chapter Six

# Demonic Schemes and Methods

—⟨ℰℰ⟩—

*So that Satan will not outsmart us. For we are very familiar with his evil schemes.*

2 CORINTHIANS 2:11, NLT

Although the birth of Jesus had been widely prophesied all through the Old Testament Scriptures, Satan did not know the precise circumstances under which he was to be born. And so the moment Satan became aware of the royal birth, he tried to get rid of the baby Jesus. He made several attempts to kill him. First, King Herod was provoked by Satan to ruthlessly slaughter all the boys aged two and under in Bethlehem and the surrounding areas. However, having been warned in a dream, Joseph took the infant Jesus and Mary to Egypt by night to avoid being killed by King Herod. The attacks continued in Jesus's adult life: on a number of occasions during his earthly ministry the Jews attempted to stone Jesus to death, but he escaped. Jesus was always one step ahead of the devil—until he was ready to die.

When it was time for him to die, Jesus intentionally, willingly, and voluntarily gave himself up in the garden of Gethsemane. This was calculated, premeditated, and deliberate on the part of Jesus. However, I believe that the devil did not know this—*he* probably thought the reason he was able to have Jesus arrested was because Judas agreed to betray him for thirty pieces of silver.

*He came back a third time and said [to his disciples, who were sleeping in the garden as Jesus prayed on the night of his arrest], "Are you going to sleep all night? No—you've slept long enough. Time's up. The Son of Man is about to be betrayed into the hands of sinners. Get up. Let's get going. My betrayer has arrived."*

MARK 14:41–42, MSG

*No sooner were the words out of his mouth when Judas, the one out of the Twelve, showed up, and with him a gang of ruffians, sent by the high priests, religion scholars, and leaders, brandishing swords and clubs. The betrayer had worked out a signal with them: "The one I kiss, that's the one—seize him. Make sure he doesn't get away." He went straight to Jesus and said, "Rabbi!" and kissed him. The others then grabbed him and roughed him up.*

MARK 14: 43–46, MSG

By arranging Jesus's death like that of an ordinary villain on the cross of Calvary, Satan thought Jesus would remain in the grave and rot away like everybody else. He had no idea, no inkling whatsoever that by killing Jesus, he would be helping Jesus to fulfill his purpose for coming to the world. He did not know that Jesus was *born* to *die*.

*But we speak wisdom among the perfect; but wisdom not of this world, nor of the rulers of this world, who come to nought. But we speak God's wisdom in [a] mystery, that hidden [wisdom] which God had predetermined before the ages for our glory: which none of the princes of this age knew, (for had they known, they would not have crucified the Lord of glory).*

1 CORINTHIANS 2:6–8, DBT, EMPHASIS SUPPLIED

When Jesus died on the cross of Calvary, the Enemy would have thought that was his end. There must have been one huge party in the camp of the Enemy, with wild and unimaginable celebrations.

The devil was probably celebrating his greatest trophy yet in his war with God Almighty. To make Adam and Eve sin against God in the beginning was something, but to actually be the mastermind and architect behind the brutal execution of the Son of God, putting him to death on a cross like a criminal—that would rank among the greatest victories ever won. He must have given his cohorts a week off work and brought them all together to celebrate this mind-boggling victory over God's own Son. "What a revenge!" he must have thought to himself. "Now everybody born of a woman will end up in hellfire like me…"

The imagery I have of Satan's rowdy celebrations following the death of Jesus is that of the wild celebrations of the Amalekites who raided Ziklag, David's village at the time. We find the story in 1 Samuel 30. We are told that they tore Ziklag to pieces and then burned it down. They captured all the women, young and old, and drove them like a herd of cattle. By the time David and his men returned to the village, it had been burned to the ground, and their wives, sons, and daughters had all been taken as prisoners of war. The Bible records that David and his men burst out into loud wailing. They wept, wept, wept, and wept until they were exhausted with weeping and could cry no more.

In 1 Samuel 30:8, we are told that David prayed to the Lord and asked, "Shall I go after these raiders? Can I catch them?" and the answer came, "Go after them! Yes, you'll catch them! Yes, you'll make the rescue [and recover everything the Amalekites have taken]" (MSG). Verse 16 tells us that when David and his men arrived in the camp of the Amalekites, "There they were, *spread over all the land, eating and drinking and dancing,* because of all the great spoil that they had taken from the land of the Philistines and from the land of Judah" (emphasis supplied). *The Message* says, "They were scattered all over the place, eating and drinking, gorging themselves on all the loot they had plundered from Philistia and Judah."

At that time, Satan must have thought that the phenomenon, the marvel, and the enigma that was Jesus of Nazareth had ended…forever. He believed he had destroyed God's plan to redeem mankind from his grip. At last, he could concentrate on his own plot to lead all mankind into hell. If Jesus, who was God's ace and God's most prized weapon, could not defeat him, surely now God would give up his plan to rescue man from Satan's hold!

A lot of thoughts and ideas must have raced through the devil's evil mind. He would have asked himself, *How will God react to the death of his beloved Son?* Peradventure, he could even use his newfound notoriety as the brains behind Jesus's crucifixion as leverage to negotiate with God. He would have to play hardball if he wanted to get any substantial indulgence from God—but what concession would God give? What could he expect from God? Would God agree to reinstate him to his original position as Lucifer?

"Would God allow me to…" Satan would have been jolted into reality from his daydreams with a colossal *bang,* because all of a sudden there was an underground eruption, an earthquake of gargantuan proportions, and the building where Satan and his cohorts were having their merrymaking was shaken violently. "What the hell is going on here?" Satan would have screamed to his bodyguards.

He did not have to wait long for an answer: it was time for him to receive the greatest upset and the rudest shock of his entire life. Suddenly, unexpectedly, miraculously, and spectacularly, Jesus turned up before him.

"I…I…I…I…thought you…you…you…were dead," the devil would have stammered in fright. Jesus would have answered, "I was dead but I now am alive. I give up my life and take it again. Now, give me the keys of death and life."

The story of the Amalekite raid on Ziklag ends when David caught the raiders unawares and slaughtered them—much the same way that Jesus caught the devil unawares when he arrived with his resurrection body on that glorious Easter morning. I can imagine the terror, the embarrassment, and the astonishment on Satan's face as Jesus stood before him like a jolt from the blue.

Through his death and resurrection, Jesus defeated, overpowered, conquered, crushed, routed, trounced, disarmed, and completely annihilated the power of the devil and his cohorts once and for all! In his death, Jesus destroyed the power of sin, overcame the fear of death, and retrieved the paradise that Adam had lost in the garden of Eden. If Satan had known that Jesus's death would lead to his own defeat and conquest, he would not have killed Jesus. Thank God for that Friday when Jesus died. No wonder it is called Good Friday!

## LIKE A LION

Although a defeated foe, Satan the Enemy still goes about the world like a roaring lion seeking whom to demolish, destroy, and devour.

> *Stay alert! Watch out for your great enemy, the devil. He prowls around like a roaring lion, looking for someone to devour.*
>
> 1 PETER 5:8, NLT

Note that the Bible does not say that the devil *is* a roaring lion, but that he prowls around *like* a roaring lion. In other words, he presents and behaves like a lion. "Why is this important to know?" you may ask. To answer that question, perhaps we ought to find out why lions roar. According to Jon Grinnell, Associate Professor of Biology at Gustavus Adolphus College, in an article entitled "The Lion's Roar: More than Just Hot Air": "On a still night the sound of lions roaring can carry five miles or more and can serve as an acoustic signpost, proclaiming for all who would hear that these lions are owners of this land."[1] In other words, one of the reasons lions roar to is to send fear into others.

It would appear that in like manner, Satan pretends to be a roaring lion just to frighten people and keep them in bondage! Fear leads to bondage—in reality, fear and bondage go hand in hand. For the most part, the devil uses the fear of the unknown and the fear of death as tools to keep people enslaved to him. He may roar, but he can no longer bite. The sting has been taken out of him. However, as long as people are in bondage to the fears he provokes, he has power over them. He can control them, and he can ultimately destroy them. Remember that over the millennia since Adam and Eve, the fear of death has been one of the greatest weapons used by Satan to keep human beings in captivity. That is, of course, prior to Jesus's victory over him at Calvary:

*Forasmuch then as the children are partakers of flesh and blood, he also himself likewise took part of the same; that through death he might destroy him that had the power of death, that is, the devil. And deliver them who through fear of death were all their lifetime subject to bondage.*

HEBREWS 2:14–15, KJV

So how do we combat the fears inspired by Satan's roars? With the power of the truth that clears away lies and leaves fear without legs to stand on!

To be able to properly handle Satan, you need to know your God, and you need to know who you are in Jesus. That is the starting point: being a child of God and knowing who you are. From that, you must understand your authority as a believer over the Enemy. Finally, you also need to be familiar with the Enemy's schemes and devices. You cannot afford to be unaware, ignorant, or uninformed of his methods and modes of operation.

## DEMONIC HIERARCHY

When I was a freshman at university, I joined a group called Selective Evangelism (SE). SE was a small, intimate group which preached the gospel of Jesus Christ exclusively to Satanists, gangsters, and members of cults and other secret societies on the university campus. We also brought healing and deliverance in the name of Jesus to people who were demon possessed. The group was headed by a former Satanist who had come to know Jesus and who gave us a lot of insight into the sinister world of darkness from his personal experience. What I share in this section comes from what I learned during my membership in SE, my personal encounters with demonic spirits in my ministry, and my reading and understanding of Ephesians

6:12, Colossians 2:15, and Daniel 10:10–21.

To assist the devil in carrying out his primary purpose of stealing, killing, and destroying, I believe he heads a complex and highly organized evil network. As indicated earlier, unlike God, the devil is *not* omnipresent. However, he does sometimes appear ubiquitous because of his ability to communicate within his network faster than even the speed of light.

The devil appears to have a hierarchy, which in my view is similar to this:

Satan is the supreme master and lord of his evil demonic network, and he sits pretty at the pinnacle as the commander in chief. His word is law in this brutal and vicious setup. There seems to be a territorial prince or principality in every major strategic region of the world. The "prince of Persia" referred to in Daniel 10:12–13 is an example. These principalities are next to the devil in hierarchy and report directly to Satan. They in turn line manage the national rulers.

Each country has a national ruler (also known as a "power") who rules over the country's airspace and reports to the territorial prince in charge of the region where the country is located. The "prince of Greece" mentioned in Daniel 10:20–21 is thought to be an example of a national ruler.

Every city also has a city governor or ruler of darkness placed over it.

The national rulers supervise and have oversight over the city governors, who in turn rule over cities and have control over the neighborhood watchmen—demonic spirits, luciferous spirits, satanic spirits, familiar spirits, foul spirits, and elemental spirits—whose duty is to cause spiritual wickedness and havoc in high and low places.

Understanding this hierarchy can help you battle against Satan's forces more intelligently.

## USEFUL TIPS FOR SPIRITUAL WARFARE

In spiritual warfare, you can isolate the particular demonic agent you are dealing with. You can ring an impregnable fence around it with the blood of Jesus and cut off any reinforcement from the camp of the Enemy. This can be a useful strategy when conducting deliverance for somebody who is demon possessed.

Another important tactic is to pray grace ahead of you in anticipation of difficult times. The Bible tells us in Hebrews 4:16 to approach the throne of grace with confidence and boldness so as to obtain mercy and find grace for our help in times of need. In your mountaintop experiences with God, remember not just to enjoy the moment but also to pray grace, mercy, and strength in advance of those inevitable valley experiences when you may not be as strong.

When you cast a demonic spirit out of a possessed person, it is essential to make sure that the person's heart is not left empty; otherwise, as Jesus said in Matthew 12:43–45, the demonic spirit will return with seven more deadly spirits, and the person will become worse off than before. You can ensure that the heart is not left unoccupied by:

- Leading the delivered person to salvation and asking him or her to invite Jesus in as Savior and Lord. Lead the delivered person to pray the sinner's prayer: "Lord Jesus, I acknowledge that I am a sinner. I believe with my heart that you died for my sin and that you were raised from the dead for my justification. Your Word says in Romans 10:9 that 'if you confess with your mouth the Lord Jesus and believe in your heart that God has raised Him from the dead, you will be saved.' I confess with my mouth that you are my Savior and my Lord. I invite you to come into my heart and make me a new creation. Thank you, Lord Jesus, for saving me. Please write my name in your Book of Life. In Jesus's name I pray. Amen."

- Leading the newly saved person to ask the Lord to baptize them by and in the Holy Spirit.
- Teaching the newly saved person to read the Bible and pray daily.
- Ensuring that the newly saved person joins the membership of a local Bible-believing church, where his or her new faith can be nurtured.

## HOW DOES THE ENEMY OPERATE?

Satan's strategies are not new—and understanding them will enable you to take authority with greater confidence and effectiveness. For the rest of this chapter, we'll look at some of Satan's most common strategies and weapons.

### SIN

Sin is perhaps the most powerful weapon in the Enemy's arsenal against the Christian. This is not surprising, because Satan was the first sinner. He gave birth to sin when pride was found in his heart, and he introduced sin into the world through his temptation of Adam and Eve. Sin is disobedience to God. Sin creates a gulf and a chasm between God and us. How does the Enemy get us to commit sin? He does it through his temptations. To make it easier for you to fall, the devil adapts his temptations to suit your natural inclinations and desires. He will vary his enticements to match your lifestyle.

The Bible assures us in 1 Corinthians 10:12–13 that God has made provision for you on two fronts. He will not allow you to be tempted beyond what you can bear, and with each temptation, God will make a way of escape to ensure that you do not need to succumb to its lure—so you should not sin, even if Satan's temptations are strong. On the other hand, if you do commit sin, you need to repent immediately and seek God's forgiveness. To repent is to make a U-turn; it is to recognize your error, confess your sins to God, and not go back to them. Proverbs 28:13 says, "People who conceal their sins will not prosper, but if they confess and turn from them, they will receive mercy" (NLT).

Some people become so disappointed with themselves if they commit sin that they run away from God instead of repenting. If you repent immediately, your fellowship with God is unlikely to be broken. We are told in 1 John 1:8–10 that "If we say that we have no sin, we deceive ourselves, and the truth is not in us. [However] if we confess our sins, He is faithful and just to forgive us our sins and to cleanse us from all unrighteousness. If we say that we have not sinned, we make Him a liar, and His word is not in us."

If you try to hide from God or run away, not only will your fellowship be broken, but you will make yourself vulnerable to the attacks of the Enemy. It is bad enough to break the hedge of protection which God has put in place over your life; but it is suicidal not to have the hedge repaired. Ecclesiastes 10:8 tells us that "whoso breaketh down a hedge, a serpent biteth him" (DBT).

## IDOLATRY

God is a very jealous God. In Exodus 20:5 he tells us that he is "a jealous God who will not tolerate your affection for any other gods" (NLT). He insists that he must occupy first place in our lives on all occasions and at all times. He must have priority and be number one. He doesn't want to share your love and devotion with anyone or anything else.

This is all a question of priority. Because of that, whatever takes first place in your life other than God is an idol, whether it is family, business, a career, or anything else. Idolatry is a sin which God detests. The stories of Scripture make it clear that it is very easy to fall into idol worship. This is a subtle weapon which the Enemy uses to great advantage. You must be alert and on your guard at all times.

## SATANIC OPPRESSION

The devil oppresses people in at least three different ways. The first is by indwelling them through one of his demon spirits and possessing their faculties. The demoniac in the country of the Gadarenes, whom we read about in Mark 5, is an extreme example of this type of demonic oppression. The Bible tells us that he "lived among the tombs; and no one could bind him anymore, even with a chain; for he had often been bound with fetters and chains, but the chains he wrenched apart, and the fetters he broke in pieces; and no one had the strength to subdue him. Night and day among the tombs and on the mountains he was always crying out, and bruising himself with stones" (RSV).

Secondly, the devil oppresses people by taking control of their minds and making them do things which a rational human being would not do. Examples abound all around us. In April 2011, a New York mother who had just been involved in a domestic dispute loaded her four children into a minivan before driving them into the Hudson River, killing herself and three of the children—two boys, ages five and two, and an eleven-month-old girl—after her ten-year-old son escaped through the window of the minivan. In 1994, Susan Smith, a South Carolina woman, drowned her young sons, three-year-old Michael and fourteen-month-old Alex, by strapping them into their car seats and driving the car into a pond. She is currently serving a life sentence for the killings.

Thirdly, the devil subjects people to actual (sometimes almost tangible) domination when they are asleep. These are people who become semiconscious and feel an evil force trying to squeeze life out of them. They attempt to speak, but the words just don't come out.

In addition, I believe that madness, schizophrenia, and manic depression can all be forms of demonic oppression.

## FIERY DARTS

That the Enemy attacks us is a fact. As Paul tells us in Ephesians 6:16, the Evil One sometimes strikes through the use of fiery darts and spiritual arrows, which we can stop with the "shield of faith." Psalm 91 is a good Scripture to personalize and pray for yourself and your loved ones on a regular basis, as a way of building up your shield of faith.[2]

These flaming arrows can manifest in various ways in the natural:

- ILLNESSES: Some illnesses and diseases are not natural, but are the direct result of demonic arrows and satanic activity. This is hardly surprising because we live in a fallen world where the devil operates as a god. I am not saying that all sicknesses are the result of the Enemy's flaming arrows; however, some diseases definitely have their origin in hell. How do you tell if a particular illness is an attack of the devil? Well, ask the Lord for insight. During his earthly ministry, we see Jesus healing a variety of illnesses caused by demonic activity. For instance, in Mark 9:17–21, he healed a man who was made epileptic by the devil, and in Luke 13:10–13 (MSG), he healed a woman so twisted and bent over with arthritis by a spirit of infirmity that she couldn't even look up. Also, in Mark 9:17–29 we are told about a man whose son was possessed of an evil spirit. The demon spirit made the boy deaf and dumb and caused him to have fits. The Lord knows what illness stems from demonic activity, and you have direct access to him in prayer. Ask him to show you what lies at the root of diseases you encounter.

- ACCIDENTS: Certain accidents occur at home, at work, on the road, and even in the air which have no logical explanation. They happen when everything is in order and there is no reason why there should be a malfunction or things should go wrong. Some of these are orchestrated in the pit of hell and are the result of satanic attacks.

- INEXPLICABLE LOSSES: There are times when you lose items of jewelry or even clothing. It may be a wristwatch, a ring, a tie, a book, anything. You remember placing the missing item somewhere in your home. You are sure that nobody has actually taken it. However, you can't find it. It is as if it has just vanished into thin air. Has that ever happened to you? It may be an attack of the Enemy. Why would the Enemy attack in this way? To create fear and make you feel suspicious. To make you feel vulnerable. Remember, fear is the greatest weapon this "roaring lion" has.

- TERRORIST ATTACKS: Since September 11, 2001, when the Twin Towers of New York City were destroyed in a series of coordinated terror attacks, the world has witnessed an unprecedented increase in the number of terrorist attacks. A lot of these acts of violence have been carried out by suicide bombers, who have been brainwashed by religious extremists into believing that they are working for God. Without a doubt, such attacks are planned and executed at the behest of the adversary.

- NIGHTMARES: A nightmare is a dream that can cause a strong negative emotional response from the sleeper, typically fear and/or horror. The dream may contain situations of danger, discomfort, or psychological or physical terror. Sufferers usually awaken in a state of distress and may be unable to return to sleep for a prolonged period of time.[3] There are people who are scared of going to bed at night because they usually have all kinds of frightening experiences in their sleep. Such people are under attack from the Enemy.

- PANIC ATTACKS: A panic attack, according to Merriam-Webster, is an episode of intense fear or apprehension that is of sudden onset. Panic attacks are extremely frightening. They seem to come out of the blue, strike at random, and make people feel powerless, out of control, and as if they are about to die or go mad.[4]

## PERSECUTION IN THE FAMILY, AT WORK, OR IN THE PUBLIC SQUARE

Persecution is harassment or maltreatment on account of your faith as a child of God. In Hebrews 11:35–38, the Bible tells us about heroes of faith who were persecuted for their faith in the Lord. It says, "Others were tortured and refused to accept their freedom so they could be raised from the dead to a better life. Some were laughed at and beaten. Others were put in chains and thrown into prison. They were stoned to death, they were cut in half, and they were killed with swords. Some wore the skins of sheep and goats. They were poor, abused, and treated badly. The world was not good enough for them! They wandered in deserts and mountains, living in caves and holes in the earth" (NCV).

There are two promises associated with persecution in the New Testament. In Mark 10:29–30, Jesus, in answer to a question by Simon Peter, promises that whoever has forsaken mother, father, children, spouse, houses, basically anything for him, will receive a hundredfold in this world *with* persecution. The other is in 2 Timothy 3:12, where the apostle Paul states that "everyone who wants to live a godly life in Christ Jesus will suffer persecution" (NLT). In other words, anyone who lives as a child of God in this world *will* invariably suffer one form of persecution or another.

Persecution is an attack of the Enemy. The goal of persecution is to make us compromise or even renounce our faith. However, if you don't fall or give up on account of persecution, there is a reward for you. Jesus said in Matthew 5:10, "Blessed are those who are persecuted for doing what God approves of. The kingdom of heaven belongs to them" (GW).

### IGNORANCE

We saw in chapter 1 that one of the major ways in which the Enemy prevents people from walking in the victory they have in Jesus is through ignorance. We cannot take hold of what we do not know belongs to us. Neither can we exercise authority over the Enemy if we are not aware in the first place that we have authority over him.

The Enemy keeps people ignorant by preventing them from accessing the Word of God—or simply by distracting them from doing so. In the Western world where the Bible is readily available, people just do not study the Scriptures: they read the newspapers, undertake continuing professional development in their careers, read novels, and spend hours in front of the television, but do not have time for the Word—and this describes people who would identify themselves as

Christians! A lot of people read the Bible only in church on Sundays. Most do not have a structured pattern of personal study of the Word of God. Some people begin to nod off the moment they pick up the Bible to read at night. No doubt the Enemy is at work.

One of the things we said in chapter 1 is that knowledge comes by revelation through the study of the Scriptures. As you give yourself to God, he gives of himself to you. It is those who seek him wholeheartedly, fervently, and passionately who find him. From the days of John the Baptist until now, the kingdom of heaven has suffered violence, and it those people who are violent and passionate in their hearts who take it by force. Can God see passion in your heart? Can he see fervor in your eyes? Is there fire in your bones? Can you say that the zeal of the house of the Lord has consumed you, becoming a fire that cannot be quenched, a driving force that cannot be stopped?

There can be no substitute for a personal study of the Word of God! Daily devotionals, Bible commentaries, and recorded messages by anointed preachers and teachers are wonderful and useful. However, they cannot take the place of the Word of God. They must not replace a time of personal study of the Word. *Every* Christian individual must study and meditate upon the Word for him or herself. Nobody can do that for anyone else.

## DECEIT

In fulfilling his ministry of stealing, killing, and wreaking destruction, the devil employs deceit and trickery. He is the father of lies, and deceit is Satan's territory! He is at home when he lies to people and misleads them. He started deceiving and misleading from the beginning. Remember his encounter with Eve in the garden of Eden? Satan twisted God's Word and manipulated Eve into believing that if she ate the fruit of the Tree of the Knowledge of Good and Evil, she would become like God.

There are all types of false prophets and deceiving spirits out in the world today who work under the guidance and inspiration of the devil. They teach and propagate erroneous doctrines concocted from the very pit of hell. Their goal is to lure people into a false sense of security, to make them, in the words of Amos 6:1, at ease or complacent in Zion. But please beware! To combat deceit and false teachings, you *must* search the Scriptures *for yourself.* You must adopt the attitude of the Jews in Berea in Acts 17:11, who after listening to the most moving and inspirational sermon from the apostle Paul, said to themselves, "That was a powerful word from God. But we'd better open the scrolls and spend some time searching the Scriptures just to be sure that everything the man of God has taught us is true."

## FALSE ACCUSATION

False accusation is a specialty of the devil. As the accuser of the brethren, the devil is constantly making false accusations against Christians. He is either telling God about a sin somebody has just committed or reminding them of how filthy and unworthy they are. A lot of folks buy into this and go about with what has been called a "sin consciousness." These people are forever repenting of sins—their sins of commission and omission; the sins committed in their sleep.

They even repent of the sins that God has forgiven, which, quite frankly, God is sometimes no longer even aware of! In Psalm 103:12, we read that as far as the east is from the west, so far has he removed our transgressions from us. I believe that the Bible deliberately uses "east and west" as opposed to "north and south" because the distance between east and west appears limitless, unlike the distance between the north and south which are not limitless because of the North and the South Poles. God uses this imagery to show that unlike us humans, when he forgives, he forgets.

As a child of God, you should never deliberately commit sin. However, the apostle John tells us in 1 John 2:1–2 that if you do fall into sin, God has made provision to help you. You have an advocate with God in the person of the Lord Jesus, who pleads your case for you. You need to repent immediately and ask God for forgiveness. The Bible says in 1 John 1:9 that if we confess our sins, God is faithful and just to forgive us and to cleanse us from all unrighteousness. Let us take him at his word and refuse to believe the devil instead of God.

## MUSIC

Music originated from God and was created solely for his worship, his glory, and his pleasure. However, the Enemy also has a passion for music. This is not surprising, and three reasons immediately come to mind for his passion:

- *His origin as the archangel who led worship in heaven.* As we said in chapter 5, God ordained and anointed Lucifer (who became the devil when he fell) for this role. Although he is now fallen, music still flows in his veins.

- *He sees music as a means to an end.* Music is generally regarded as the gateway to the soul. Music is therefore a way by which Satan takes hold of the minds and hearts of unsuspecting multitudes of people, leading them astray.

- *As God's enemy, he tries to destroy whatever God has created.* We have seen that God originated music for his own worship, glory, and pleasure. What the Enemy has done in relation to music is to corrupt it and make it unfit for God's original purposes.

When it comes to music, we need to be very careful, because some of the lyrics of the albums and singles that grace the music charts are written and devised from the pit of hell. The idea is to lure as many unsuspecting people as possible into devil worship. Of course, some worldly music is of mere human inspiration. However, quite a few such songs—even those that sit at number one on the charts—are demonic.

Let us take a look at "Hallelujah," the 2008 Christmas number-one single in the UK. (The positions of all songs are based on weekend sale totals, from Sunday to Saturday. Usually, the number-one Christmas single is the song at the top of the UK Singles Chart on the Sunday before Christmas Day.) The song "Hallelujah" was written by Canadian singer-songwriter Leonard Cohen and originally released on his 1984 studio album *Various Positions*. Cohen was born into a middle-class Jewish family of Polish ancestry in Montreal, Quebec, on September 21, 1934.

Like many other Jews named Cohen, Katz, Kagan, etc., his family made a proud claim of descent from the Kohanim: "I had a very Messianic childhood," he told Richard Goldstein in 1967. "I was told I was a descendant of Aaron, the high priest."[5]

He later became a Buddhist and in 1996 was ordained as a Buddhist monk. He is said to have taken the Dharma name *Jikan*, which means "silence."

The word *hallelujah* means "praise the Lord," and it is a common feature of countless Christian hymns, praise songs, and gospel songs, from Handel's majestic *Messiah* to the little-known song "Hallelujah Anyhow." A lot of Christians will sing along to Leonard Cohen's "Hallelujah" without knowing that some of the lyrics may actually be profane! The first verse starts very well, making you think that this is probably a gospel song. But close listening reveals otherwise: astonishingly, the second verse appears to refer to both David and Samson in their moments of adultery. The metaphor is that both David and Samson are singing hallelujah with their mistresses, Bathsheba and Delilah, while in the very *act* of adultery!

Now, I don't know how many Christians would want to sing along to those lyrics if they paid attention—but because the chorus is so melodious and easy on the ear, and because *hallelujah* means "praise the Lord," you may actually find yourself humming along to the melody without knowing what you are singing. As always, you must be careful what songs you listen and sing along to, because through music you can very easily and inadvertently open up your soul to the devil and be lured unwittingly into devil worship.

## OCCULTISM AND FALSE RELIGIONS

Occultism and false religions have been around for hundreds if not thousands of years. Occultist groups present in various guises, including sometimes branding themselves as religious groups. These sects all have two things in common:

- *They are false religions.* The Bible teaches very clearly in John 14:6 that Jesus is the only way to God. He is the way, the truth, and the life, and no one can go to God except through him. Therefore, any religious group which presents any other route through which man can go to God is a false religion, no matter how spiritual or sanctimonious their teachings may appear to be.

- *They are incompatible with biblical Christianity.* Each sect either attacks an area of the life of Jesus or condemns a core teaching of the Bible so that if you are a member of that group, it becomes impossible for you to be a born-again child of God. Membership in any such group is incompatible with your status as a Christian.

For example, Islam teaches in Sura 23:91 and Sura 19:88–89 that God neither begets nor is he begotten, and in Sura 4:154–158 that Jesus (known as *Isa*) was a prophet who was neither killed nor suffered death. This is a direct attack on Jesus as the Son of God who died to save the world. John 3:16 tells us, "For God so loved the world that He gave His only begotten Son, that whoever believes in Him should not perish but have everlasting life." The Bahá'í Faith teaches that God is transcendent, unknowable, and inaccessible; therefore God cannot incarnate himself to be present among men. This attacks the incarnation of Jesus. The Jehovah's Witnesses believe in a one-person God, called Jehovah. There is no Trinity. Jesus is the first and greatest thing Jehovah created. Before his life on earth, he was the archangel Michael. This teaching is contrary to the teachings of the Bible on the Trinity and the fact that Jesus is God, as is clearly laid out in John 1.

These two criteria remain true for all of the groups we encounter today: the Ancient Mystic Order of Rosæ Crucis (AMORC), also called the Rosicrucian Order, the Grail Movement, Eckankar (the Religion of the Light and Sound of God), Buddhism, Hinduism, Christian Science, the Church of Jesus Christ of the Latter Day Saints (Mormons),The Unification Church (Moonies), and others.

Many of these groups also reject the divine authorship of the Bible and thus deny the authority of Scripture: the Bible teaches clearly in 2 Timothy 3:16 that all Scripture is God-inspired. Some even worship other gods, an attack on God's instruction in Exodus 20: 3 that we should not worship any other god beside him.

In the West at least, the Enemy is undertaking a major recruitment drive into the occult and false religions in these last days. His trick is to make them very attractive and chic. He does this by enlisting the help of A-list stars in the world of music, sports, and movies, as well as world leaders, as they publicly declare their allegiance to these faiths and/or their practices. Cases in point are the popularity of yoga[6] and many Eastern religious practices which are now being presented in Europe and America as trendy, fashionable, and stylish.

## FEAR

Fear is a scheme that the devil uses to great effect. From my personal study, the words "do not be afraid" or "fear thee not" (depending on the Bible translation) appear over one hundred times in the Bible! The message from God is quite clear: we need not be afraid!

Why would God go to such extraordinary lengths to admonish us not to be fearful? The reason is because fear can cripple you; it can distort the mind and shrivel the spirit. Most times, fear is wholly unreasonable and irrational. In reality, fear is a spirit, one which prevents you from exercising the power of rational thought. Somebody once said that fear is *false evidence appearing real.* How spot on!

Taken to extremes, fears can become phobias. A phobia is a type of fear which, in the main, is irrational. It can be described as an obsessive and persistent fear of a specific object or situation.[7] There are so many phobias that we do not have enough room in this book to mention all of them. However, here are a few of the more common phobias:

- Aerophobia: the fear of air or draughts
- Agoraphobia: the fear of open spaces
- Aichmophobia: the fear of knives
- Algophobia: the fear of pain
- Anthropophobia: the fear of people
- Arachnophobia: the fear of spiders
- Aviophobia: the fear of flying
- Belonephobia: the fear of needles
- Claustrophobia: the fear of confined spaces
- Dromophobia: the fear of crossing a street
- Haemophobia: the fear of blood
- Monophobia: the fear of being alone
- Mysophobia: the fear of contamination or dirt
- Nyctophobia: the fear of the night or darkness
- Pantophobia: the fear of everything
- Phobophobia: the fear of being afraid
- Photophobia: the fear of light
- Ponophobia: the fear of work
- Scopophobia: the fear of being looked at
- Scotophobia: the fear of the dark
- Sitophobia: the fear of food or eating
- Spectrophobia: the fear of mirrors
- Toxiphobia: the fear of poisoning
- Triskaidekaphobia: the fear of the number thirteen
- Zoophobia: the fear of animals

Some phobias are symptomatic of an anxiety disorder. Through phobias, the Enemy is able to hold people captive. However, by the anointing of the Holy Spirit, anybody who is afflicted by any phobia can be set free. The Bible tells us in 1 John 3:8 that Jesus came into this world to destroy all the work of the Enemy.

## STAGNATION

One tactic of the adversary in his fight against God's creation is to attempt to make people stagnant, motionless, and still. This can be in their relationships, their spiritual lives, their careers, their finances, and even their ministries. Satan picks on an individual and decides to oppose, resist, and stand against him or her. No matter how hard they work or try, there seems to be a glass ceiling they cannot go beyond. They become perpetually stuck on the same level.

At work, while people who qualified after them and whom they inducted into the company as new employees become directors, people under this form of attack are still at the level of supervisors. Their spiritual life is even worse: it is static, still, stationary, stagnant. There is no semblance of growth whatsoever. Instead of being teachers, as we are told in Hebrews 5:12–14, they are still babies who need to be bottle-fed with milk. In fact, looking back over the years, they can clearly identify a time when they were closer to God than they are today.

Stagnation is a powerful tool of the Enemy because it leads to a feeling of inadequacy, low self-esteem, and disappointment. The sufferer feels as though the whole world is against him. To deal with stagnation, you need to resist and stand against the devil in the name of Jesus, and he will back off. If not dealt with, stagnation can lead to extreme frustration and the temptation to give up.

## FRUSTRATION

Another scheme of the Enemy is to frustrate people. He knows that if he can perpetually keep people from achieving their goals, they will eventually give up and give in. He does this, among other ways, by:

- *Preventing you from achieving your goal.* You get so close to it. You see it, but just when you are about to take hold, you lose it. You are never able to close a deal or achieve anything. Something always happens to frustrate you. It is always so close, yet so far away.
- *Blocking your progress.* You know what to do. When you tell others, you

see the results in their lives. But it does not seem to work for you. It feels as if there a ceiling over you beyond which you cannot never get.

- *Thwarting your plans.* Satan can destabilize your plans. The plans look good on paper, but they never seem to work out in reality, no matter how hard you work.

Frustration prevents you from entering your breakthrough. It is an irritation that goes beyond the natural. It is evil. It comes from the pit of hell. The solution is to destroy the Enemy's yokes and his burdens in your life by, through, and in the name of Jesus.

## UNFORGIVENESS

Unforgiveness, resentment, or bitterness is a poisoned chalice which Satan uses to destroy lives. In the words of Proverbs 14:12, it is a way that seems right to a person, but which ends up in death and destruction. On the face of it, bitterness appears to be a good way of getting even with a person who has hurt you; however, in reality, by not forgiving others, you harm yourself instead. Unforgiveness is a cancer which not only hinders spiritual growth but can also have a devastating effect on physical health. It nibbles away at the relationship between man and God, causing deterioration in fellowship with God. It eats up the human immune system, causing a variety of diseases and medical conditions. If you want God's forgiveness, not only must you forgive those who hurt you, you must also pray for them and bless them, as the Lord instructs in Luke 6:28.

## UNBELIEF

Unbelief is essentially any form of prevailing skepticism shown toward spiritual things. It is not just a lack of faith, but some sort of rebellion against God's truth. Wherever there is unbelief, it will not be possible to please God. As we are told in Hebrews 11:6, to please God, we must approach him in faith, believing that he exists and that he cares enough to respond to those who seek him.

In the time of Elisha the prophet in ancient Israel, a certain King Ben-Hadad of Aram launched a siege on Samaria, the capital of Israel. This pushed the Samaritan economy into a terrible recession, with food prices soaring astronomically. Hyperinflation put most food items beyond the reach of most people. It was so bad that a couple of women decided to take turns to killing, cooking, and eating their children!

According to the story, which can be found in 2 Kings 7, at the height of the crisis, when the forecasts by both the Bank of Samaria and the Samaritan Federal Reserve were at their bleakest, the man of God, the prophet Elisha, declared that within twenty-four hours, the prices of essential food items would drop to what they were before the crisis began. Elisha's prophecy was completely contrary to all the economic data available to the government—it didn't make any sense at all! The economic adviser to the king of Samaria told Elisha that even if the windows of heaven were opened, it could still not happen. In other words, the level of his unbelief was such that he could not bring himself to believe that even if *God* decided to perform a miracle, it could happen. He was sure that the situation could not change overnight, God or no God. This is the height of unbelief. It does not get any worse than this! The man displayed such an extraordinary level of incredulity about God's ability to do what he had promised to do that the prophet had no choice but to pronounce a curse on him. Elisha told him that he would see the miracle happen with his two eyes, but he would not eat of it.

Elisha's prophecy came to pass. Through the direct intervention and provision of God, the following day, the prices of essential food items dropped to what they had been before the crisis. The king then appointed his economic adviser to supervise the sale and distribution of the foodstuff to the members of the public. This man did indeed see the miracle happen, but he did not partake of it, because as the people rushed to buy these essential items, they trampled him to death.

## THE LOVE OF MONEY

On its own, there is nothing wrong with money. In fact, money is a good thing. After all, the Scriptures say in Ecclesiastes 10:19 that money answers all things! However, as Paul warns in 1 Timothy 6:10, the *love* of money is not only a sin, but it is in fact the root of all evil. Show me a person who loves money, and I will show you somebody who is enslaved to Mammon, the god of money. Show me a person who loves money, and I will show you a person who will do anything to acquire money: steal, cheat, bend the rules, and even kill! To love money is to serve Mammon. Jesus's words in Matthew 6:24 are the truth of reality: you cannot serve God and Mammon. Because of its relative power in our lives, one of the easiest ways by which the Enemy stops people from being part of God's kingdom is to enslave them to Mammon.

## SOWING TARES AMONG THE WHEAT

Another strategy of the devil is to sow tares among the wheat. Jesus describes this in the Parable of the Tares and Wheat in Matthew 13:24–30. The *tares* are a type of weed which grow in a cornfield. They look very much like wheat, and it is usually very difficult to tell the two apart until the time of the harvest. In Jesus's parable, the wheat represents the Christians, and the tares represent the children of the devil. The Darby Bible Translation uses the word "darnel," a kind of seed hardly identifiable from wheat seeds, which strongly resembles wheat in its immature stage. It says that the Enemy "sowed darnel amongst the wheat." As they grow together, the tares tend to choke the wheat.

In practical terms, I believe that the devil sows tares among the wheat in three primary ways.

*First, he does it by infiltration.* Satan plants imitators in the church. These are essentially demonic agents who look like born-again Christians but whose mission is to either sap the anointing of God and make the ministers ineffective or in some cases even destroy the minister through sin. They fit in perfectly, looking the part and speaking the language. In some cases they may not even be aware that Satan is using them. This is one of the reasons why we need continuous self-examination to see if we are still in the faith. (See chapter 10 for a more detailed look at self-examination.)

*Second, he does it by introducing erroneous and false doctrines.* Satan finds a minister with an audience and seeks to corrupt their reasoning on critical doctrinal issues, thereby leading many into error. A classic example is that of the Reverend Jim Jones, who founded The Peoples Temple, which was initially structured as an interracial mission for the sick, homeless, and jobless but eventually became a cult. When a government investigation began into his cures for cancer, heart disease, and arthritis, Jones decided to move the group to Ukiah in Northern California.

Jim Jones's teachings grew stranger. He preached the imminent end of the world in a nuclear war, and the group later moved to San Francisco and Los Angeles. After an exposé during the mid 1970s in the magazine *New West* raised suspicions of illegal activities within the Temple, Jones moved some of the Temple membership to Jonestown, Guyana, where the Temple had leased almost four thousand acres of dense jungle from the government. They established an agricultural cooperative there, called The Peoples Temple Agricultural

Project. They raised animals for food, as well as assorted tropical fruits and vegetables for consumption and sale.

In the meantime, Jones developed a belief called *Translation,* in which he and his followers would all die together and would move to another planet for a life of bliss. Mass suicides were practiced. The saga ended in tragedy with the death of 914 members—638 adults and 276 children—in November 1978.

*Third, Satan plants tares by disguising himself as an angel of light.* In the poem "Satan, You're Under Arrest!" I made the point that the devil is conniving, sly, devious, and brimming with evil. He is able to disguise himself in an attempt to mislead the gullible. The Bible states in 2 Corinthians 11:14, "And no wonder! For Satan himself transforms himself into an angel of light." *The Message* expresses it this way: "Satan does it all the time, dressing up as a beautiful angel of light."

Nowhere is this more prevalent than in the so-called apparitions of the "virgin Mary" commonly reported by the Catholic Church. In reality, these apparitions are nothing but the devil camouflaging and dressing up as a beautiful angel of light! Mary, the mother of Jesus, didn't remain a virgin after his birth, because she had other children with her husband Joseph. In Mark 6:3, we read as follows: "Then they scoffed, 'He's just a carpenter, the son of Mary and the brother of James, Joseph, Judas, and Simon. And his sisters live right here among us.' They were deeply offended and refused to believe in him" (NLT). It is therefore incorrect to continue to refer to her as the "virgin Mary."

Moreover, there is no basis in Scripture for either praying in the name of Mary or asking Mary (or indeed, any of the saints) to pray for you. The words of Jesus in John 14:6 are crystal clear: "I am the way, the truth, and the life. No one can come to the Father except through me" (NLT). Furthermore, as a child of God, you have direct access to God through Jesus. First Timothy 2:5 states clearly that Jesus is the only mediator between God and man. You don't need *any other* go-between or intermediary. The Bible clarifies this position in Hebrews 4:15–16: "Now that we know what we have—Jesus, this great High Priest with ready access to God—let's not let it slip through our fingers. We don't have a priest who is out of touch with our reality. He's been through weakness and testing, experienced it all—all but the sin. So let's walk right up to him and get what he is so ready to give. Take the mercy, accept the help" (MSG).

In his intriguing book *Almost Midnight,* Richard David Thompson shares the following remarkable story:

In May 2005 the current Pope Benedict XVI was consecrated to Our Lady (The Virgin Mary) who had appeared to three children in Fatima, Portugal, in 1917. An incident exposing the deceptive manifestations of Mary to the biblically aware was experienced by an evangelist I know. He came across a shrine to an apparition of her near his outreach venue in Europe. In his afternoon prayertime the Lord showed him to pray against this shrine. He was confronted in his bedroom by the face of "Mary" asking him why he was speaking against her, imploring him to leave her alone and saying that she was doing no harm to the people. He could feel a manipulative, drawing power trying to seduce him to accept her words and become tolerant of her hold over the area. He spoke firmly and said, "You are not Mary but the false queen of heaven", and commanded the spirit to leave in the name of Jesus. Remarkably, the face was suddenly removed, as if a mask had been peeled off, to reveal a grotesque beast that roared at him and then disappeared! There was a tremendous sense of break-through in the spiritual realm and that night nearly everyone at his meeting, about 200 people, gave their lives to Christ with many healed and delivered from evil spirits. Indeed, Satan can appear as an angel of light.[8]

Don't be bamboozled by the devil. Remember that all that glitters is not gold. If you receive an "angelic" visit, test it against the Scriptures. That is just what God expects you to do. First John 4:1 states, "Beloved, do not believe every spirit, but test the spirits, whether they are of God; because many false prophets have gone out into the world."

FOOD FOR REFLECTION

- Have you ever felt crippled by fear?
- How have you dealt with fear in the past?
- Why do you think the Enemy goes about like a roaring lion?
- Have you ever had difficulty forgiving anybody?
- Do you regularly suffer from panic attacks? Do you have recurring nightmares?

## PRAYER FEATURES

- Lord, open my eyes to see the provision you have made in your Word to enable me to deal with fear.
- Lord, I resist the Enemy in the area of fear. You spirit of fear, I bind you and destroy your hold over my life in Jesus's name.
- Lord, grant me the spirit of discernment to enable me to understand the methods of the Enemy.
- Lord, create in me a hunger for your Word and a thirst for righteousness.

## ACTION POINTS

- Determine to know God through a consistent study of the Bible.
- If you are harboring unforgiveness against anybody, decide to forgive them and pray that God would bless them.
- Make up a confession against fear, based on the Word of God, which you can recite to yourself on a regular basis.
- Make a conscious effort to take more interest in gospel-based music as opposed to worldly music.

Chapter Seven

# HOW DOES THE ENEMY DISOBEY?

——◦◦◦——

*For the weapons of our warfare are not carnal but mighty
in God for pulling down strongholds.*

2 CORINTHIANS 10:4

When a person becomes a born-again child of God—that is, a Christian—many different things happen in the sphere of the spirit. I believe from the witness of Scripture that one of those things is that the Lord places his seal of redemption upon that person. This stamp is invisible to the naked eye but noticeable in the realm of the spirit, and so Satan and his demon spirits can perceive it. The apostle Paul put it succinctly when he reminded the church in Ephesus of this seal in the following words:

*And grieve not the Holy Spirit of God, whereby ye are sealed unto the day of
redemption.*

EPHESIANS 4:30, KJV

The imagery is that of a wealthy or influential Jewish person who goes to the marketplace to purchase something that is too large for him to carry home by himself. He buys an item, places his seal upon it, but returns home without it. When he gets home, he sends his servant to the market to pick up the item for him. The servant is able to identify the item bought by his master because he can recognize his seal. In the same way, Jesus has redeemed us with his precious blood that was shed on the cross of Calvary and placed his seal upon us. On the day of redemption, this seal will identify us when the Lord returns to take his people home.

In other words, it would appear that there is some evidence on me, on my *physical, mortal* body, which shows that I as a Christian belong to Christ. Clearly, this seal is not visible to the naked eye.

As we have seen, Satan is a spirit. Even if we do not wish to admit it, the fact remains that Satan has been around much longer than any of us human beings. It is therefore not rocket science to figure out that Satan is in a position to know whether or not you as an individual have authority over him. In other words, he knows whether or not you are a child of God.

As we saw in in chapter 5, the devil knew that the seven sons of Sceva (Acts 19:13–16) were not Christians! They did not know Jesus as Lord and Savior but were exorcists who saw the Christians preaching, healing the sick, and exercising authority over Satan. They were so impressed that they decided to have a go themselves. They told a demon-possessed man, "We exorcise you by the Jesus whom Paul preaches." The evil spirit answered them, "Jesus I know, and Paul I know; but who are you?" Then the man who had the evil spirit jumped on them and overpowered them all.

In your journey through life as a Christian, there are times when Satan will try to disobey your lawful instructions. This sometimes happens even when you are in right standing and right living with God (although Satan will usually tell you that you are not, and that any difficulties you face are your fault—remember his strategy of creating "guilt consciousness"!). There are simply times when he wants to try something on. He may want to push the boundaries to see if you as a Christian know your birthright as a child of God.

If Satan disobeys your instructions or opposes you as a Christian, you should be able to oppose him, chastise him, and avenge his insubordination. God has made provision to enable you as a child of God to discipline Satan should he refuse to obey your lawful orders. But what is disobedience? Within the context of this discussion, *disobedience* means to ignore, to resist, to defy, to flout, to refuse to comply with, to go against, to challenge, or to contravene. In other words, Satan disobeys the Christian if any of the following happens:

- If he ignores you
- If he resists or withstands you
- If he flouts your lawful instruction
- If he defies or refuses to obey you
- If he decides to go against you in any form

- If he refuses to comply with your command
- If he attacks you or rises up against you in any way
- If he decides to challenge or to contravene your prayers

How does Satan manifest his insubordination against the Christian? How does he display his noncompliance to our lawful instructions? Let us look at some biblical examples.

## SATAN'S INSUBORDINATION- SCRIPTURAL EXAMPLES

### THE ENEMY OPPOSES THE DISCIPLES

In Matthew 14:22–24, we read about how the Enemy withstood the disciples of Jesus and tried to stop them from carrying out the Lord's instructions. Jesus had just ministered to a great crowd of people. It was now early evening, and he instructed his disciples to row across the lake in a boat. However, as the disciples tried to get across the Sea of Galilee in obedience to the Lord's instruction, they encountered the most difficult, vociferous, and strident opposition imaginable.

The wind was contrary, and there was such a massive gale that by about three or four in the morning, when Jesus returned to them, they had only managed three or so miles! The disciples had a specific instruction to cross the lake in a boat. They were carrying out the Lord's order. But there was such a massive backlash and hostile response from the Enemy that they could neither carry out their assignment nor fulfill their calling at that moment in time. Clearly, the Enemy was at work.

How did they deal with the Enemy's opposition? Well, they invited the presence of the Lord, who came to them walking on the water. We are told that when Jesus came into the boat, the wind ceased. Are you in his presence? Do you practice his presence? Are you conscious of his presence?

### PETER AND HIS BUDDIES TOIL ALL NIGHT WITHOUT A RESULT

In John 21:3–7, following Jesus's crucifixion, Peter decided to return to his old profession of fishing. His buddies, James and John, as well as Nathanael and two other disciples, opted to go with him.

Peter and his associates had the following in their favor:

- *Experience and expertise.* These were professionals—people who had fished for a living before Jesus met them at the beginning of his ministry. In the case of James and John, their father Zebedee was also a fisherman. They had probably learned their trade from their father. It is plausible that fishing had been in the family for generations. In fact, when Jesus met James and John, they were with their father and mending their nets. So not only were they good at what they did, they were also self-sufficient in that they could make and mend their own fishing nets and possibly their own boats and other equipment.

- *Resources.* They had enormous resources at their disposal. They had the benefit of the tools of their trade—the boats, the nets, etc. They had a partnership, with the synergy that comes with that. They were a team, and they worked as a TEAM—Together Each Achieves More. They also had time as a resource. They could fish all night long if they chose to. Indeed, they worked all night! But perhaps the greatest resource of all was the sea full of fish, which they had to themselves. Whatever catch they could take was all theirs.
- *Resolve.* They were diligent. They were not shy of hard work. We are told that they "toiled all night" in the account in Luke 5:5. Not only were they good at what they did, but they were also willing and able to give whatever it took for them to achieve their goal, even if it meant staying up all night. And work hard they did. They put their expertise and their years of experience to good use. They toiled. They worked like elephants.

Notwithstanding everything at their disposal—their skills, their resources, and the diligent application of their expertise to their work—they achieved nothing. They were unfruitful. There was stagnation. They worked like elephants but could only manage to eat like ants. Surely the Enemy must have been at work!

How did they deal with the Enemy's resistance? They acted on a specific word from God. Jesus told them to cast their net on a particular side of the boat. This was God's revealed word for their situation. They received it, it generated faith within them, and they acted on it. The result was a catch that was so huge that the net almost broke. Sometimes, all we need is a specific word from God, a spoken word, a *rhema*, which when acted upon will lead to a breakthrough. The Lord speaks all the time. When was the last time you heard the Lord speak to you?

## THE ENEMY BLOCKS THE ANSWER TO DANIEL'S PRAYER

In Daniel 10 we read that in the third year of Cyrus, king of Persia, a message was revealed to Daniel, who then fasted and prayed for three full weeks. Now on the twenty-fourth day of the first month, an angel appeared to him and told him that from the first day that he set his heart to understand, to humble himself before his God, and to pray, his prayers were heard; and the angel was dispatched to him in answer to his prayers.

However, the prince of the kingdom of Persia withstood and fought the angel for twenty-one days until the archangel Michael, one of the chiefs of God's princes, was sent to rescue the angel. The prince of Persia is generally accepted to be a demonic spirit: a principality. How did Daniel deal with the Enemy's resistance? He persisted in prayer until he received his answer.

## THE DISCIPLES ARE UNABLE TO CAST OUT AN EVIL SPIRIT

In Mark 9:17–29 we are told about a man whose son was possessed of an evil spirit. The demon spirit made the boy deaf and dumb and caused him to have fits. This man took his son to the disciples of Jesus so that they would deliver the boy and set him free. The disciples did their best, but unfortunately, they could not cast out the evil spirit.

When Jesus arrived shortly afterwards, he cast out the deaf and dumb spirit from the boy. What did Jesus teach his disciples about how to deal with the Enemy's refusal to obey their lawful instruction? Jesus's disciples later asked him privately why they could not cast out the evil spirit. So he said to them, "This kind can come out by nothing but prayer and fasting."

Not just fasting, but prayer and fasting. Sometimes, to birth your breakthrough or deliverance, you will need to travail in prayer and fasting. When was the last time you fasted and prayed? As a Christian, you need to fast on a regular basis. Fasting is powerful and should be a regular part of your spiritual routine.

## IF THE ENEMY COMES IN LIKE A FLOOD

There are times when the Enemy seeks to overwhelm you. He floods you with wave after wave of all kinds of problems, difficulties, and challenges, with the aim of derailing or even drowning you. Have you ever felt so overpowered and overcome by the vicissitudes of life that you became suicidal? Like they say, it does not rain, it pours. If and when this happens, the Lord by his Spirit will lift up a standard against the Enemy. The Lord raises you to a higher platform where the Enemy's deluge cannot affect you.

> *When the enemy comes in like a flood, the Spirit of the Lord will lift up a standard against him.*

ISAIAH 59:19

If you feel so overwhelmed, engulfed, and inundated by your problems and difficulties that you want to give up, stop and think. It may be the Enemy at work. Ask the Lord to raise a standard against the flood of the Enemy in your life. It was Sir Winston Churchill, one of the greatest prime ministers the United Kingdom has ever had, who said on October 29, 1941:

> Never give in, never give in, never; never; never; never—in nothing, great or small, large or petty—never give in except to convictions of honor and good sense.[1]

When you give up on your dream or give in to your challenges, you abort your dream and give the devil something to rejoice over! You also disappoint the Lord Jesus, who is waiting for you to enforce the victory he won on your behalf at Calvary. Remember that Isaiah 53:11 tells us that Jesus "shall see of [the fruit of] the travail of his soul, [and] shall be satisfied" (DBT). The fruit of Jesus's travail is the outworking of grace in *your* life. So hang in there!

## THE ENEMY INTRODUCES SIN INTO THE CAMP OF THE LORD

Satan knows that God cannot tolerate sin. Sometimes, he attempts to introduce sin into the camp of the Lord so that he can have his way. The story is told in the seventh chapter of Joshua about a man named Achan. When Israel defeated Jericho, God gave the Israelites specific instructions: the city and everything in it was to be completely destroyed as an offering to the LORD. Only Rahab the prostitute and the others in her house were to be spared, because she had protected the Israeli spies. They were instructed not to take any of the things set apart for destruction, or they themselves would be completely destroyed and bring trouble on all Israel. Furthermore, God instructed that everything made from silver, gold, bronze, or iron was sacred to the LORD and was to be brought into his treasury.

Achan violated these direct instructions from the Lord and took some of "the accursed things" from Jericho. He took a beautiful Shinar robe, two hundred shekels of silver, and a fifty-shekel bar of gold, which he hid among his things. God became angry with the people of Israel. When next they went to war, with a relatively tiny city called Ai, the Israelites were soundly defeated.

Eventually, God revealed what had happened to Joshua, who destroyed both Achan and the accursed things in response. The answer to the problem was to deal with the sin. There was repentance in the camp, and God's blessing returned.

## THE ENEMY SOWS A SEED OF DOUBT INTO THE MIND OF JOHN THE BAPTIST

When he was in prison, just before he was brutally beheaded by King Herod, John the Baptist started to have doubts as to whether Jesus was indeed the Messiah, the Son of the Most High God. The story is told in Luke 7:19–23. At this time, John's expectations and desires were most likely not in accordance with God's plan. He probably expected Jesus to set him free from prison. When that didn't happen, the Enemy began to introduce seeds of doubt into his mind. So John sent two of his disciples to Jesus to find out from him if he was in fact the Messiah, or whether he should look for another. Jesus dealt with the situation by asking John's disciples to tell John about the miracles they saw Jesus performing: the blind seeing, the lame walking, the deaf hearing, and the dead being raised to life. This was both a recounting of God's miracles and a reference to ancient prophecies in Scripture regarding the Messiah. Jesus showed that the best panacea to doubt and unbelief is the Word of God, confirmed with signs and wonders following.

## THE ENEMY ATTACKS THE EARLY CHURCH

In Acts 3 and 4, we read that not long after the early apostles received the baptism of the Holy Spirit, Peter and John went up together to the temple at three o'clock, the set time for the afternoon prayer meeting. According to John Gill:

> This was one of their hours of prayer; it was customary with the Jews to pray three times a day, Daniel 6:10 which, according to the Psalmist in Psalm 55:17 were evening, morning, and at noon; to which seems to answer the three times that are taken notice of by Luke in this history:

that in the morning was at the third hour, as in Acts 2:15 or nine o'clock in the morning; that at noon was at the sixth hour, as in Acts 10:9 or twelve o'clock at noon; and that in the evening at the ninth hour, as here, or three o'clock in the afternoon.[2]

On this particular day, as they went into the temple, they saw a man who had been born lame. He was laid at the gate of the temple called Beautiful every day to beg alms from those going into the temple. When he saw Peter and John, he begged them for money. Peter then told him to look at them.

Thinking that Peter and John were about to give him money, he looked at them with anticipation. Having gotten his attention, Peter told him, "Silver and gold I do not have, but what I do have I give you: in the name of Jesus Christ of Nazareth, rise up and walk." Peter then took him by the right hand and lifted him up, and immediately he was healed. The man who was lame began to praise God and shout, and everybody knew he was the lame man who had begged at the gate Beautiful. He held on to Peter and John and followed them around, walking, leaping, and praising God. People began to gather.

As the crowds gathered, Peter saw an opportunity to preach the gospel of salvation, and through his message, about five thousand people received Jesus. The priests and the Sadducees were not happy about this, and they decided to arrest Peter and John. The disciples were held in custody overnight. The following day, they were brought before the elders, rulers, and scribes, who commanded them not to speak or teach in the name of Jesus. There is no doubt that the Enemy was working behind the scenes to orchestrate these threats in an attempt to stifle and suppress the gospel.

Peter and John, having an understanding of the methods and schemes of the Enemy, immediately recognized that Satan was at work. So they reported what had happened to the church. The church began to pray and to call upon God for boldness to preach the Word of God. After they had prayed, the place where they were gathered shook, and they were filled afresh with the Holy Spirit. After this experience, the apostles and the rest of the church began to speak the Word of God with audacity, boldness, and great courage. This was an instance of being opposed by the Enemy. On this occasion, the early apostles used prayer as the weapon to deal with the Enemy's recalcitrance.

# AN ARRAY OF WEAPONS TO FIGHT WITH

As you can see from the above illustrations, the Christian has an array of weapons, an assortment of spiritual apparatus in his armory, with which to discipline Satan should he fail to follow the believer's lawful commands or stand against him. We will look at these weapons and the conditions for using them in the next three chapters.

## FOOD FOR REFLECTION

- In what ways have you experienced Satan's disobedience?
- How did you deal with the situation?
- How should we deal with Satan's disobedience?
- Why do you think Satan sometimes pushes the boundaries?
- How easy do you think it is for Satan to introduce sin into the Lord's camp?

## PRAYER FEATURES

- Lord, teach me to persevere in prayer.
- Lord, teach me to be conscious of your presence.
- Lord, whenever the Enemy overwhelms me like a flood, please let your Spirit raise up a standard against him.
- Lord, teach me to listen for your voice.
- Lord, as I hear you speak to me, I pray that you will build up my faith.

## ACTION POINTS

- Make a note of the last time you heard God speak and what he said to you.
- If you have never heard God speak, invite him to speak to you today in a way you can understand. Ask him to anoint your heart and your ears so you can hear him clearly.
- Determine to carry out every instruction the Lord gives to you as an individual.

# Chapter Eight

# FULFILLING YOUR OBEDIENCE

—◆◇◆—

*And being ready to punish all disobedience when your obedience is fulfilled.*

2 CORINTHIANS 10:6

The Most High God is almighty, all-powerful. To make use of the familiar phrase often used in church, God is "omnipotent, omnipresent, and omniscient." In other words, God is not just all-knowing and all-powerful, he is also able to be present everywhere at the same time. He is eternal and not bound by time. Not only did he exist before the beginning began, he actually began the beginning! He will continue to be even when time comes to an end. He is undying, unending, perpetual, enduring, and everlasting. He transcends time.

Jesus told the Jewish religious leaders in John 8:58, "Most assuredly, I say to you, before Abraham was, *I AM,* "meaning, in effect, that he is interminable, timeless, and unchanging. He is the only potentate, the only true sovereign. The monarchs of this world whom we venerate—our kings, queens, princes, and princesses—are mere mortals. They came from dust, and unto dust they most certainly will return at the end of their days.

> Dust to dust, end to lust
> Sand to land
> Naked and bare at birth
> Nude and undressed at death
> Dirt to dirt, ashes to ashes
> Mud to muck
> All rejoice at birth
> All cry when breath turns to death to earth.

God is the Ancient of Days, the unchanging changer. He was, he is, and he will ever be. "I am that I am" is his name (Exodus 3:14). He is an adept, adroit, and skillful master planner. He knows the end of a thing even before it starts. Nothing takes him by surprise. He knows all things, understands all things, and sees all things. There is nothing hidden from him. Even darkness is plain before him. The psalmist captures these attributes of God beautifully in the 139th Psalm:

*O Lord, you have examined my heart and know everything about me. You know when I sit down or stand up. You know my thoughts even when I'm far away. You see me when I travel and when I rest at home. You know everything I do. You know what I am going to say even before I say it, Lord. You go before me and follow me. You place your hand of blessing on my head. Such knowledge is too wonderful for me, too great for me to understand! I can never escape from your Spirit! I can never get away from your presence! If I go up to heaven, you are there; if I go down to the grave, you are there. If I ride the wings of the morning, if I dwell by the farthest oceans, even there your hand will guide me, and your strength will support me. I could ask the darkness to hide me and the light around me to become night—but even in darkness I cannot hide from you. To you the night shines as bright as day. Darkness and light are the same to you.*

PSALM 139:1–12, NLT

It is therefore not surprising that the Lord has made adequate arrangements for those times when the adversary chooses to disobey our lawful instructions as born-again children of God. He has covered and taken care of every eventuality. There is sufficient provision to take care of the Enemy's provocation. There is ample ammunition to quench any noncompliance. And there are more than enough supplies to tackle any defiance by the Enemy!

## THE NEED TO DO OUR PART

However, we must do our part. Paul urged the Corinthians to be "ready to punish every disobedience" in 2 Corinthians 10:6. This was not just in relation to Satan, *but in relation to our own lives.*

To be able to punish the Enemy's disobedience, *your own* obedience to God must *first* be complete. You must first submit and subject yourself to God before you can tackle the Enemy's recalcitrance. In other words, you must *walk* the *talk*. But what does that mean? Let us look at this passage in context.

> *For though we walk in the flesh, we do not war according to the flesh. For the weapons of our warfare are not carnal but mighty in God for pulling down strongholds, casting down arguments and every high thing that exalts itself against the knowledge of God, bringing every thought into captivity to the obedience of Christ, and being ready to punish all disobedience when your obedience is fulfilled.*

2 CORINTHIANS 10:3–6

In the battle against Satan, the enemy and opponent of our faith, we are nothing on our own. However, in Christ Jesus, we have ability, strength, power, and authority over Satan. As Paul declared in Acts 17:28, "For in Him we live and move and have our being." In spiritual warfare, our obedience to God is a condition *precedent* to fighting the Enemy. It must come first. Without complete and total obedience to God, as well as absolute submission to God's will on our part, we cannot even begin to think about dealing with the devil's disobedience.

By "obedience to God" I am not in any way talking about *sinless* perfection. You don't have to be morally perfect to battle Satan. However, you do require a heart that is fully after God. In the words of 2 Chronicles 16:9, your heart needs to be "fully committed" to God (NIV) for you to be able to combat the devil. This can only be achieved by the power of the Holy Spirit at work within you because, as we are told in Zechariah 4:6, "'You will not succeed by your own strength or by your own power, but by my Spirit,' says the Lord All-Powerful" (NCV). I believe that is why the Bible instructs us in James 4: 7, "Therefore submit to God. Resist the devil and he will flee from you." To be able to battle Satan, you must first be fully submitted and yielded to God.

So the all-important question is, how do we complete our own obedience? How do we become truly submitted to God? How do we *walk* the *talk*?

## YOU MUST BE SAVED

Salvation is the prerequisite to obeying God. To obey God, you must first be saved. You must know Jesus as your personal Savior and Lord. In the words of Jesus in

John 3:7, "you must be born again." You cannot be a "born Christian"—that is, you cannot become a Christian *simply* by being born into a Christian family.

The Bible lays out four steps to salvation:

- Conviction. To be saved, there must be conviction for sin, for righteousness, and for judgment in your heart. John 16:7–8 makes it clear that it is the Holy Spirit who convicts, and nobody else, not even the preacher. In the words of 2 Corinthians 7:10, you must feel "godly sorrow" for sin. You must come to a point where you realize that you are a sinner and that you cannot help yourself. This should lead to confession.

- Confession. Having realized that you are sinner, you now confess, acknowledge, and proclaim with your lips that you are a sinner and acknowledge that Jesus died for your sins and rose from the dead for your justification, as the Bible tells us in Romans 10:9. After that, you invite him into your life as your personal Savior and Lord. This should lead to a transformation in your life (Romans 10:10).

- Conversion. When you have invited the Lord into your life, the Holy Spirit converts and transforms you. You turn into a new creation in Christ Jesus, as Paul tells us in 2 Corinthians 5:17. Conversion takes place on the inside, in your spirit. Your spirit is transformed and is now able to communicate with God. You become born again. As a new creation, the old is gone, and you become a new baby who needs the sincere milk of the Word of God to grow, as apostle Peter tells us in 1 Peter 2:2.

- Commitment. Commitment helps you to grow as a child of God. You surrender your life to God and to the teachings of Christ. Jesus becomes enthroned as Lord in your life. You become his disciple by submitting yourself to the discipline of his teachings. You do not pick and choose which Scriptures to accept and obey; instead you accept all Scripture as the inspired Word of God as the Bible tells us in 2 Timothy 3:16–17. You begin to bear fruit—both the fruit of the Spirit in terms of Christian character and becoming more and more Christlike, which Paul talks about in Galatians 5:22–23, and the fruit of souls by telling others about Jesus and leading them to Christ, as Jesus teaches us to do in Matthew 28:19.

FULFILLING YOUR OBEDIENCE

## YOU MUST KNOW THE LORD FOR YOURSELF

In order for you to fulfill your obedience, your name must be written in the Lamb's Book of Life, which the Bible talks about in Revelation 21:27. You need to have a personal relationship with Jesus Christ. This is an individual thing between you as a person and God. God does not have grandchildren, and so it does not matter if you were—or weren't—born into a Christian family! The fact that your parents are Christians is simply irrelevant. You must decide for yourself and acknowledge that you are a helpless sinner, after which you must personally accept the sacrificial death of Jesus on the cross. You must then invite Jesus into your heart as your personal Savior and Lord.

## YOU MUST BE IN RIGHT STANDING WITH GOD

To be righteous is to be in right standing with God, to lead a live that is pleasing to God. Proverbs 16:7 says that when your ways are pleasing to God, he promises to make even your enemies live at peace with you. Remember what God said about Jesus? On more than one occasion, God the Father said, "This is My beloved Son, in whom I am well pleased" (Matthew 3:17; Matthew 17:5). Is God well pleased with you?

If God had to give you a character reference, what would he say? Would it be similar to his testimony to Satan concerning Job? In Job 1:8, God said to Satan, "Have you noticed my friend Job? There's no one quite like him—honest and true to his word, totally devoted to God and hating evil" (MSG).

## YOU MUST BE IN RIGHT LIVING WITH GOD

To be in right living with God is to seek to align who you are in reality with your positional standing in Christ Jesus. It is not enough to proclaim that you are holy because of what Jesus accomplished on the cross of Calvary, wonderful as that is. There is a need to *actually* live a holy life. Your day-to-day life must mirror and reflect your position in Jesus. This is a lifelong process. It comes through putting the Word of God in the driver's seat of your life and becoming a doer of the Word as James instructs in James 1:22.

## YOU MUST KNOW WHO YOU ARE IN CHRIST JESUS

You must have a revelation of who you are in Christ Jesus. Unfortunately, mere head knowledge is not enough. For instance, you understand that as a child of

God, all the resources of heaven are at your disposal. This is because Ephesians 1:3 declares that in Christ Jesus, God blesses you with all spiritual blessings in the heavenly places. In Jesus, you overcome all. As Romans 8:37 tells us, you are more than a conqueror, not because of who you are, but because of what Jesus accomplished on your behalf at Calvary.

You must be persuaded that as a Christian, you were conceived and brought into life by God. You are born of the Spirit of God. You were ransomed by the precious blood of Jesus, and the Spirit of God who dwells within you is greater than the devil in the world. The divine seed dwells within you.

As a born-again child of God, you have been given the Holy Spirit to empower you to live for Christ. You should enjoy the fullness of his ministry in your life as the *paracletus,* the Greek word for the Holy Spirit, which is translated *advocate, defender, protector, helper, comforter, intercessor, counselor, assistant,* and *teacher.* The Holy Spirit is all of these things for *you.*

## You Must Know God, Be Strong, and Do Exploits

It is not just enough to know about God. You need to know God, to understand his ways, fathom his character, and know his principles. The Bible says in Daniel 11:32 that the people that know their God shall be strong and do exploits. According to Albert Barnes:

> The word "exploits"…is supplied by the translators, but not improperly. The meaning is, that they would show great prowess, and perform illustrious deeds in battle."[1]

To do "exploits," in the words of missionary William Carey, is to "Expect great things from God. Attempt great things for God."[2]

All the Israelites of Moses's day knew were the miracles of God, his acts and deeds; they had no real concept or perception of who God really was. No wonder they showed such petulance during their wilderness journey! In Psalm 103:7 the Bible tells us that God made known his ways to Moses, his acts to the children of Israel. The New Living Translation says that God "revealed his character to Moses and his deeds to the people of Israel." However, unlike the Israelites, Moses knew God's ways, his character and principles. This must have been an answer to prayer, because earlier, Moses had prayed to God in Exodus 33:13, saying, "If it is true that you look favorably on me, let me know your ways so I may understand you more fully and continue to enjoy your favor. And remember that this nation is your very own people" (NLT).

How much of God do *you* know? Paul sums this up brilliantly in Philippians 3:10, where he writes:

*[For my determined purpose is] that I may know Him [that I may progressively become more deeply and intimately acquainted with Him, perceiving and recognizing and understanding the wonders of His Person more strongly and more clearly], and that I may in that same way come to know the power out-flowing from His resurrection [which it exerts over believers], and that I may so share His sufferings as to be continually transformed [in spirit into His likeness even] to His death, [in the hope]...*

AB

## YOU MUST AVOID CARELESSNESS AND NONCHALANCE

In your walk with God, there is a requirement to avoid complacency and a nonchalant attitude toward God. The Bible says in Amos 6:1, "Woe to you who are at ease in Zion, and trust in Mount Samaria." To be at ease in Zion is to forget that you are in spiritual warfare and become entangled in civilian pursuits. Paul warns against this in 2 Timothy 2:4, when he tells Timothy that "Soldiers don't get tied up in the affairs of civilian life, for then they cannot please the officer who enlisted them" (NLT). To be at ease is also to take your focus off the Lord. In Matthew 14:30, Peter, who had been walking on water, began to sink when he took his eyes off the Lord and saw that the wind was boisterous.

According to Barnes:

Woe to them that are at ease—The word always means such as are recklessly at their ease, "the careless ones," such as those whom Isaiah bids [in] Isaiah 32:9–11, "rise up, tremble, be troubled, for many days and years shall ye be troubled." It is that luxury and ease, which sensualize the soul, and make it dull, stupid, hard-hearted. By one earnest, passing word, the prophet warns his own land, that present sinful ease ends in future woe. "Woe unto them that laugh now: for they shall mourn and weep." Luke 6:25[1]

## YOU MUST CONTINUE UNTIL THE END

Although I realize that this is a controversial issue, I do not personally believe in the doctrine of *eternal security*—that is, "once saved, forever saved." I believe that having become a child of God, it is possible to backslide, lose your faith, and go back to your old ways. My reasoning is simply that if there were eternal security, Paul the apostle would not have said that he disciplines himself so as to avoid being a castaway after preaching to others! Listen to his words in his first epistle to the Corinthians:

> *Don't you realize that in a race everyone runs, but only one person gets the prize? So run to win! All athletes are disciplined in their training. They do it to win a prize that will fade away, but we do it for an eternal prize. So I run with purpose in every step. I am not just shadowboxing. I discipline my body like an athlete, training it to do what it should. Otherwise, I fear that after preaching to others I myself might be disqualified.*

1 CORINTHIANS 9:24–27, NLT

I love the way verses 26 and 27 are translated in *The Message*. It says:

> *I don't know about you, but I'm running hard for the finish line. I'm giving it everything I've got. No sloppy living for me! I'm staying alert and in top condition. I'm not going to get caught napping, telling everyone else all about it and then missing out myself.*

To my mind, salvation is in three parts: *past, present,* and *continuous*. We are saved when we accept Jesus into our hearts as Savior and Lord. This is but the beginning. We are *being* saved as we go through life, becoming true disciples, living our lives for God, and allowing the Word of God to become a reality in our lives. Finally, we *will be* saved if we continue until the very end. It is not how we start the race that is important, but how we finish it. First John 3:2 advises us that when Jesus returns, it is those who are still in the faith who will see him as he is and become just like him.

## YOU MUST ABIDE IN THE LORD'S PRESENCE

This entails practicing the Lord's presence: i.e., being conscious of his presence at all times. It requires spending quality time in daily communion and fellowship with

God in private prayer and in quiet meditation upon the Word of God. It requires daily devotion. Do not be like those of God's children who remember him occasionally when they have a need, but forget all about God when it is well with them.

To put it differently, God does not delight in sporadic and infrequent visitors who come to his presence with visitors' visas. He seeks those who would permanently reside in his presence. God delights in those of his children who love him for *who* he is and not just for *what* he is, because they are the ones most likely to abide in him. And it is those who make their home permanently in his presence whose obedience is truly complete.

## IDENTIFYING AREAS WHERE YOU CAN BE MORE FULLY OBEDIENT

In addition to the foregoing, there are several common areas where many of us need to be obedient or perhaps more *fully* obedient as Christians. As you read the rest of this chapter, ask yourself if you are truly walking in obedience in each of these areas. If not, you are not yet experiencing the fullness of obedience in your life—and you are handicapped for spiritual warfare.

### TITHING

I know some folks may not want me to go into this. It is contentious and controversial, and you may not like me afterwards, but I will deal with it anyway! The *tithe* is a tenth part of one's monthly or annual income or produce, and it is an ancient form of worship. The first record of giving the tithes is found in Genesis 14:17–20, and was when Abram (before God changed his name to Abraham) offered a tenth of the spoils of war to Melchizedek, the priest of the Most High, on his victorious return from war. *Tithing therefore predates the Law of Moses.* This is very important because it shows us that the tithe is not an "Old Testament thing" with which we can do away under the New Covenant, as is sometimes claimed.

The tithe belongs to God. It must be given to him regularly as an integral part of your worship. To do otherwise is to rob God. Now, who would want to steal from God? Certainly the devil will not want to obey anyone who *cheats* God: I can tell you that for free!

> *"Should people cheat God? Yet you have cheated me! But you ask, 'What do you mean? When did we ever cheat you?'" "You have cheated me of the tithes*

*and offerings due to me. You are under a curse, for your whole nation has been cheating me. Bring all the tithes into the storehouse so there will be enough food in my Temple. If you do," says the Lord of Heaven's Armies, "I will open the windows of heaven for you. I will pour out a blessing so great you won't have enough room to take it in! Try it! Put me to the test! Your crops will be abundant, for I will guard them from insects and disease. Your grapes will not fall from the vine before they are ripe," says the Lord of Heaven's Armies. "Then all nations will call you blessed, for your land will be such a delight," says the Lord of Heaven's Armies.*

MALACHI 3:8–12, NLT

## SWEARING TO YOUR HURT

How often do you make a promise only to discover that you cannot fulfill it? You must think very carefully before making any promises. In spiritual warfare, your word must be your bond. Once you give your word, then you must do what you have promised—even if it hurts. Satan will not respect anyone who is not reliable. You must take yourself seriously. You must be dependable. You must respect the words that you speak. If you do, God will honor you and Satan will obey you.

*Who may worship in your sanctuary, Lord? Who may enter your presence on your holy hill? Those who lead blameless lives and do what is right, speaking the truth from sincere hearts. Those who refuse to gossip or harm their neighbors or speak evil of their friends. Those who despise flagrant sinners, and honor the faithful followers of the Lord,* and keep their promises even when it hurts. *Those who lend money without charging interest, and who cannot be bribed to lie about the innocent. Such people will stand firm forever.*

PSALM 15, NLT, EMPHASIS SUPPLIED

In Judges 11 we read the heartrending story of Jephthah. This true story illustrates the essence of what it means to swear to one's hurt. Jephthah was a judge and ruler over Israel. He was going into battle with the Ammonites, who had terrorized the country for eighteen years. In a solemn vow, he told God that if he were given a clear victory over the Ammonites, he would offer to God as a sacrificial burnt offering whatever was the first to come out of the door of his house to meet him when he returned in one piece from the battle.

It is not clear why Jephthah made such a solemn promise to God. Could it be that he did not expect to return from the battle in one piece? Possibly; after all, the Ammonites had laid siege on his people for nearly two decades. On the other hand, it is also probable that he expected a servant to be the first to meet him. One thing is clear: *he does not appear to have thought through the possible effects of keeping his vow.* In any event, God gave him total victory. He completely annihilated the Ammonites and plundered their goods.

Jephthah returned from the battlefield with great rejoicing. However, his happiness was about to be shattered. On his return, his daughter, his only child, ran from the house to welcome him home, dancing to the sound of music. She was the first to come out of his front door to meet him.

When he realized who it was, he ripped his clothes and cried out in anguish, "Ah, my darling, my dearest daughter, my only begotten, you have completely destroyed me. I'm despicable. My heart is torn to pieces. I made a solemn vow to God and I can't take it back! This is going to really hurt, but I can't help it." She said, "Oh, Daddy, if you made a vow to God, do to me what you vowed; God did his part and saved you from your Ammonite enemies."

Then this remarkable young woman said to her father, "But let this one thing be done for me. Give me two months to wander through the hills and lament since I will never marry, I and my dear friends."

"Oh yes, go," he said. He sent her off for two months. She and her dear girlfriends went among the hills, lamenting that she would never marry. At the end of the two months, she came back to her father. He fulfilled the vow that he had made.

Although there is some question about how Jephthah fulfilled his vow, it appears from a close reading of the passage that he actually offered her as a burnt offering to God. Lord, have mercy!

## EVANGELISM

Every Christian has a mandate to preach the good news of Jesus. The Holy Spirit makes it possible for you to be a witness of Jesus Christ as he empowers and enables you to testify to what Jesus has done in your life (Acts 1:8). The empowerment of the Holy Spirit is not just to help you to speak in tongues or be blessed in your own life. It is to transform you into an operative eyewitness for Jesus. All you are required to do is to attest to what he has done for you. Like the blind man who was healed by Jesus, you are to tell the world of the transformation he has made in your life: "Once I was blind, but now I see" (John 9:25).

Every child of God has a responsibility to preach the good news of salvation. There are no exceptions. God expects you to reconcile the world to him, in the same way that you were reconciled to God.

> *Telling the Good News does not give me any reason for bragging. Telling the Good News is my duty—something I must do. And how terrible it will be for me if I do not tell the Good News.*
>
> 1 CORINTHIANS 9:16, NCV

## FAITHFULNESS

As a child of God, you are a steward of God's grace. In Ephesians 6:7 the Bible instructs servants and slaves to "work with enthusiasm, as though you were working for the Lord rather than for people" (NLT). This passage applies to you and me because a steward is essentially a present-day servant, or slave; we are basically God's servants and slaves. As a steward, God has not called you to be successful, but to be faithful. In all things, he expects you to be trustworthy, dependable, accountable, reliable, and responsible.

> *Moreover it is required in stewards that one be found faithful.*
>
> 1 CORINTHIANS 4:2

Faithfulness often entails loyalty and a diligent application of oneself to a vision. Success, on the other hand, is a by-product of faithfulness. God told Joshua in Joshua 1:8 that if the book of the law did not depart from his mouth, if he meditated upon it day and night and carefully carried out what was written in it, he would become prosperous and have good success. In effect, Joshua's faithfulness would invariably and inevitably result in success and prosperity.

## PRACTICAL LOVE

You cannot say you love God, who is invisible, if you do not show love to your fellow human beings who you can see (1 John 4:20). You must demonstrate love to those around you. If you see somebody in need, don't just pray for him or her if you can satisfy the need. See yourself as the answer to that person's prayer. Meet that need. Whatever you do for anybody in the name of the Lord will not go unrewarded. Remember, too, that when you give to a poor person who is not in a position to repay you, you are actually lending to the Lord.

> *When you help the poor you are lending to the Lord—and he pays wonderful interest on your loan!*
>
> PROVERBS 19:17, TLB

He will definitely repay you. You can be sure of that, because God is not a debtor to anyone!

## YOUR CONFESSION

The tongue is very powerful: Proverbs 18:21 tells us the power of life and death actually resides therein. The things you say about yourself invariably come to pass, whether you believe them or not. The same is true of those over whom you have authority, like your children. It is therefore important that you do not say anything negative about yourself and about those in your care. If you make a negative confession, you are effectively undoing your prayers. Equally, if someone speaks a word against you or speaks something negative into your life—"You will never amount to anything in life," "You idiot," "You bastard"—you have a duty to reject it immediately; for instance, you can either say back to that person or mutter under your breath, "I reject that in Jesus's name."

There is a difference between *the fact* and *the truth*. The *fact* is what you may be experiencing at any particular point in time in your life, the day-to-day reality of life, the struggles, the challenges, the issues and the problems that you face on a daily basis. On the other hand, the *truth* is what God's Word says about the particular situation you are going through or the challenges you currently face—for instance that "God will liberally supply (fill to the full) your every need according to His riches in glory in Christ Jesus" (Philippians 4:19, AB) or "Is anything too difficult for the LORD?" (Genesis 18:14, NASB).

God expects you to confess and proclaim the truth of his Word, not the fact of your daily struggles!

## SPECIFIC INSTRUCTION FROM GOD

Instructions are to be carried out. They are not given for the fun of it. Of particular importance are instructions given by God. The fact of the matter is that God expects you to carry out his instructions—he is a good trustee of his own words, and he does not waste them! What have you done with the instructions that God has given *you* in the past? If you refuse or neglect to carry out God's instructions, then you are living in disobedience, and you need to repent and ask the Lord for forgiveness and mercy.

Thereafter, determine whether or not the directive can still be carried out. If it can, go ahead and do what God asked you to do. God is unlikely to give any new directives until you have carried out the previous ones. On the other hand, if for any reason the instruction can no longer be carried out, then you should wait for further instructions from God.

The story is told of a young prophet from Judah who was sent by God to King Jeroboam in Bethel. We are not told the name of the prophet, but the story can be found in 1 Kings 13. God specifically instructed the prophet not to eat or drink in Bethel and to take a different route on his way home. When he finished his assignment, he met an old prophet who told him that an angel had appeared to him and told him to take the prophet to his home and give him a good meal. The prophet had no idea that the old prophet was lying, so he went along to the old prophet's house. He had a good meal, but shortly afterwards, the prophet was killed by a lion for disobeying God.

Remember what God told King Saul through the prophet Samuel in 1 Samuel 15:22: your obedience is more important to God than any sacrifices that you may offer to him.

## THE MARITAL RELATIONSHIP

Husbands and wives are enjoined to submit to each other in Ephesians 5:21–30. For husbands, this means that they should love their wives and be prepared to die for them as Christ loved the church and gave himself for her. For wives, it means to submit to their husbands in all things as unto the Lord. In addition, the apostle Peter tells us in 1 Peter 3:7 that husbands need to honor their wives, understand them, and treat them with consideration and thoughtfulness.

I often hear men ask, "How do I honor my wife?" Well, to honor somebody is to esteem and venerate that person. Do you want to know what this means in practical terms? Let's put it this way: if you received a letter saying that the president or prime minister of your country was coming to your house for tea in a week's time, what would you do to receive such an august visitor? Whatever you would do to receive such a guest is what it means to give honor to another person.

For the husband, the Bible makes it quite clear in 1 Peter 3:7 that your prayers could be hindered if you maltreat your wife. So if you are finding your desired breakthrough elusive, perhaps you need to look inward at your relationship on the home front. On the other hand, if a wife does not accept the authority of her husband, her witness within her own family will be hampered (this is especially true if the husband is not a Christian. See 1 Peter 3:1). Secondly, it would appear from 1 Peter 3:5–6 that a wife who does not accept the authority of her husband is not a true daughter of Sarah. But what is a "true daughter of Sarah"? The answer seems to be a true believer. Adam Clarke tells us:

> As Abraham is represented the father of all his male believing descendants, so Sara is represented as the mother of all her believing female posterity. A son of Abraham is a true believer; a daughter of Sarah is the same.[3]

## LOOKING AFTER YOUR RELATIVES

God expects you as a believer to take care of your family—those belonging to your household or family unit. These are the people who are related to you by blood. To care for them is to help them financially, support them emotionally, and pray for them regularly.

> *But those who won't care for their relatives, especially those in their own household, have denied the true faith. Such people are worse than unbelievers.*
>
> 1 TIMOTHY 5:8, NLT

The question arises naturally: "How far does this go? Do I have to look after every member of my extended family no matter how remotely connected with me?" My answer would be that you have an obligation to help such relatives of yours who are so close to you that it would be inappropriate for you not to look after them.

Each case will be different. God expects you to look out for your spouse, your children, your parents and parents-in-law, and your brothers and sisters. If you belong to a close-knit family, then I believe God will expect you to also consider your nephews, your nieces, your brothers-in-law, your sisters-in-law, and your first cousins.

## SEVEN DAYS WITHOUT PRAYER MAKES ONE WEAK

Your times of prayer and devotion are an integral part of your life as a Christian. These are your moments of personal communion and fellowship with God. Their importance is accentuated by the fact that you receive nourishment and nutrition for your spirit during periods of prayer and devotion. Personal prayer and devotion should not be a weekly affair on Sundays, or even just a daily affair. It should be much more than that.

The Bible teaches us to have constant and continuing fellowship with God. In 1 Thessalonians 5:17, the apostle Paul admonished the Christians in Thessalonica to "pray without ceasing." The God's Word Translation uses the phrase "never stop praying." In Luke 18:1–8, Jesus told his disciples a story to illustrate the fact that Christians ought to pray all the time and not lose heart.

In effect, your quiet time (the time when you study the Bible, praise and pray, and listen for God's voice) should not just be a once-daily ritual. Over and above that, you should be in constant communion and intimacy with the Lord.

## DO NOT LET YOUR LEFT HAND KNOW WHAT
## YOUR RIGHT HAND IS DOING

As much as possible, your giving *to those who are in need* should not be a means for you to show off. Giving should be borne out of a deep conviction that without God, you are nothing, and it should form an integral part of your worship. It should therefore be done as unto God and in private, so that God who sees in secret may reward you openly.

> *Therefore, when you do a charitable deed, do not sound a trumpet before you as the hypocrites do in the synagogues and in the streets, that they may have glory from men. Assuredly, I say to you, they have their reward. But when you do a charitable deed, do not let your left hand know what your right hand is doing, that your charitable deed may be in secret; and your Father who sees in secret will Himself reward you openly.*

MATTHEW 6:2–4

*When you do something for someone else, don't call attention to yourself. You've seen them in action, I'm sure—"playactors" I call them—treating prayer meeting and street corner alike as a stage, acting compassionate as long as someone is watching, playing to the crowds. They get applause, true, but that's all they get. When you help someone out, don't think about how it looks. Just do it—quietly and unobtrusively. That is the way your God, who conceived you in love, working behind the scenes, helps you out.*

MATTHEW 6:2–4, MSG

## TREAT YOUR CHILDREN AS A LIMITED-TIME LOAN

Those of you who have children must recognize that your kids are a gift from God. Children are given to parents by God to look after *for a time*. Proverbs 22:6 tells us that God expects you to train them up in the right way, that is, in the way of the Lord, so that when they are older they will not depart from the way of the Lord. The New Living Translation puts it this way: "Direct your children onto the right path, and when they are older, they will not leave it."

You direct your children both by training and teaching them and by being good examples for them. Children are essentially copycats and will do what they see you do, even if you tell them to do otherwise. God expects you, like a skillful warrior, to *shoot* them like arrows toward their destiny in such a way that, from a young age, they know their purpose and are able to discover the reason for their existence. As a steward, you will someday appear before God to give an account of what you did with these children.

*And the Lord said, Shall I hide from Abraham that thing which I do; seeing that Abraham shall surely become a great and mighty nation, and all the nations of the earth shall be blessed in him? For I know him, that he will command his children and his household after him, and they shall keep the way of the Lord, to do justice and judgment; that the Lord may bring upon Abraham that which he hath spoken of him.*

GENESIS 18:17–19, KJV

God had confidence that Abraham would teach his children to keep the way of the Lord. What has your experience been with your kids? Can God say the same thing about you?

## FOOD FOR REFLECTION

- Are there areas of your life where you have been less than fully obedient?
- Have you ever sworn to your hurt? What would you have done if you were Jephthah?
- How do you walk the talk?
- When was the last time you led somebody to Christ?
- How much of the fruit of the Spirit do you reflect in your character?
- Why does the Bible refer to Christians as witnesses?
- If you are married, do you honor your spouse?
- If you have children, do you treat them as a limited-time loan from the Lord?

## PRAYER FEATURES

- Lord, teach me to realize that obedience is better than sacrifice.
- Lord, help me to be willing and fully obedient to you in all things.
- Lord, please help me to be a faithful witness, and make me bold enough to testify to others about what Jesus has done for me.
- Lord, help me to be more like Jesus. Let my life reflect the character of Christ.
- Lord, have your own way in my life. You are the potter and I am the clay. Mold and make me after your will.
- Lord, please help me, like a skillful warrior, to shoot my children like arrows toward their destiny.

## ACTION POINTS

- List the areas of your life where you have been less than fully obedient. Repent and ask the Lord for forgiveness.
- Do you have friends and family who have yet to know the Lord and who are in danger of dying without Jesus? Determine to pray for their salvation on a regular basis.
- Determine with God's help to lead at least one person to Christ in the next week. Be ready to provide effective follow-up for this person.
- If you have young children, begin to think of how you can direct them into the right path. Turn your thoughts into an action plan. Then write your plans in your journal.

Chapter Nine

# Preparation for Battle: The A-Z of Spiritual Warfare

—◦∾◦—

*Blessed be the LORD, my rock, who trains my hands for war, and
my fingers for battle.*

Psalm 144:1, NASB

The realm of the spirit is very real. It is as authentic as the earth and the
seasons we see around us. The things we see in the physical are controlled
by what we don't see. In reality, the spiritual controls the physical. This
should not come as a surprise because, as a human being, you are made up of three
parts: namely, spirit, soul, and body. You are a spirit, you have a soul, and you live
in a body. We do not see the real you, your spirit man, which controls the "you"
that we see. The Bible confirms the tripartite nature of man in 1 Thessalonians
5:23 when it says, "Now may the God of peace Himself sanctify you completely;
and may your whole spirit, soul, and body be preserved blameless at the coming of
our Lord Jesus Christ."

Your *spirit* is the part of you that makes contact with God and the realm of
the spirit. Proverbs 20:27 says that "the spirit of a man is the lamp of the LORD,
searching all the inner depths of his heart." You worship God and engage in spiritual
warfare through your spirit man. On the other hand, your *soul* includes your mind
and is the seat of your emotions and your will. Your *body* is the house for the real
you, and with your body you are able to live in this world and relate to other human
beings. When your body is destroyed for any reason or is no longer able to carry
you, you die, and your spirit man returns to God to face judgment because, as the
Bible tells us in Hebrews 9:27, "Each person is destined to die once and after that
comes judgment" (NLT).

The devil is no fable. He is real; he exists. Unfortunately, in the Western world a lot of people seem to think that the devil is a myth or fable. That is nothing short of an ironic lie from the pit of hell! The Enemy is at work every day. So should you be. In fact, because the Enemy knows that his time is fast running out, I believe he puts in extra hours every now and again.

> *So be glad, heavens, and those who live in them! How terrible it is for the earth and the sea, because the Devil has come down to you, filled with rage, knowing that his time is short!*

REVELATION 12:12, ISV

You also need to work extra hard because, as Jesus tells us in John 9:4, the day is far spent; night is drawing very close when no one can do any work. Carry out the hard work now with a strong heart, knowing that the Bible in Hebrews 4:9 promises a rest that awaits.

There are twenty-six basic issues to bear in mind when preparing for spiritual conflict. You might call these the "A to Z" of preparation for spiritual warfare.

### A: ABIDE. ABIDE IN CHRIST.

To succeed in spiritual warfare, you must be firmly rooted in Jesus. As John 15:5 puts it, he is the vine and we are just the branches. He must be your source and foundation. Everything you need to succeed on this side of eternity can be found in him. He requires you to draw your nutrition, nourishment, and sustenance from him. Without him we are nothing. When you are rooted in him, you become like trees that are planted by the riverside, whose leaves do not wither and who produce their fruit in season (Psalm 1:1–3).

To abide in Jesus is to seek first his kingdom and his righteousness. It is to seek him first in everything. It is to give him priority in all things. It is to trust him completely, to acknowledge him and seek his guidance and direction in all things. Remember that your victory is based on his victory over the devil on the cross of Calvary. Just like the branches are nothing without the tree, so you are nothing outside of Jesus Christ!

### B: BIBLE. LIVE IN THE WORD.

In this battle, you have to know the Word of God. You must spend quality time on it. As Paul tells us in 2 Timothy 3:16–17, the Word is God-inspired and beneficial for teaching what is true and correcting you when you go wrong. You ought to be able to accurately, appropriately, and correctly handle and divide the Word with the help, inspiration, and guidance of the Holy Spirit as we are required to do in 2 Timothy 2:15. As we saw in chapter 3, the Word is the sword of the Spirit, and it is quick, powerful, and sharper than any two-edged sword. When the Word is handled and managed properly, it brings life. However, if it is mishandled, it can destroy.

As you regularly and habitually spend quality time on the Word of God, you become purified and refined. The Word chips off the rough edges, impurities, and blemishes from your character to make you more and more Christlike, in the same way that water smooths the stones that lie in the bottom of a river. I believe that this reality is the reason why we are told in Ephesians 5:26–27 that Jesus washes the church with the water of the Word so that he can present her to himself "as a glorious Church without a single spot or wrinkle or any other blemish, being holy and without a single fault" (TLB).

## C: CHRIST. BE COMPLETELY CHRIST-CONTROLLED.

To be able to enforce the victory that Jesus won at Calvary, he must be sitting on the throne of your life. You must be sold completely to him. Like the apostle Paul said in Galatians 2:20, you must be able to say, "I have been crucified with Christ and I no longer live, but Christ lives in me. The life I now live in the body, I live by faith in the Son of God, who loved me and gave himself for me" (NIV). It is easy to make Jesus our Savior. But who is Lord of our lives? Jesus must be both Savior *and* Lord.

Once you become a child of God, your life is no longer yours. The life you live now belongs to Jesus Christ, the one who gave his life to ransom you. You must be able to say to the Lord, in the words of the famous hymn:

Take my life and let it be
Consecrated, Lord, to Thee;
Take my hands and let them move
At the impulse of Thy love.

Take my feet and let them be
Swift and beautiful for Thee;

Take my voice and let me sing,
Always, only for my King.

Take my lips and let them be
Filled with messages from Thee;
Take my silver and my gold,
Not a mite would I withhold.

Take my moments and my days,
Let them flow in endless praise;
Take my intellect and use
Every pow'r as Thou shalt choose.

Take my will and make it Thine,
It shall be no longer mine;
Take my heart, it is Thine own,
It shall be Thy royal throne.

Take my love, my Lord, I pour
At Thy feet its treasure store;
Take myself and I will be
Ever, only, all for Thee.[1]

Having become a child of God, there cannot be *any* area in your life that is a no-go to the Lord. You cannot say, for instance, "Well, Lord, you have control of everything except my finances." It is either all or nothing.

## D: Devil. Recognize that the Devil Is a Bad Devil!

Christians have no business playing around with ideas of the devil as a fun-loving, beer-swigging guy who just wants *you* to have a good time. The devil is a bad devil. The devil is full of evil. There is no good in him. He is the personification of evil. He is a liar and the father of lies. He is the enemy of our salvation. If he had the opportunity he would drag every child of God along with him to hell. He is crafty, cunning, and devious, and he will go to extraordinary lengths to derail you from your faith. If he sees any loophole, he will try to take advantage of it.

The good news is that in Christ Jesus, we overcome the devil. Following Jesus's victory at Calvary, God has highly exalted Jesus and given him the name above every other name, that at the mention of the name of Jesus every knee must bow in heaven, on earth, and underneath the earth (Philippians 2:9–11). That includes the devil's knees!

In the world, people say that "the devil you know is better than the angel you do not know." In spiritual warfare, however, the opposite is true: the devil (whether or not you know him) is far worse than the angel you do not know. You must take this seriously. You must depend completely on God and cover every eventuality. You cannot leave anything to chance.

## E: ENDURANCE. WALK IN THE FRUIT OF THE SPIRIT.

Endurance (also called *patience* or *stamina* or *staying power*) is one of the nine fruits of the Spirit. (The others are love, joy, peace, kindness, goodness, faithfulness, gentleness, and self-control.) Endurance enables you to stand in spiritual warfare—to see it through without falling. Endurance is not something you learn; it is a virtue which you cultivate and nurture with the help of the Holy Spirit as you walk closer to God. All the fruits of the Spirit come from the same "tree," the Holy Spirit being their source.

In spiritual warfare, there are times when you will be required to "endure hardship as a good soldier of Jesus Christ" (2 Timothy 2:3). Remember that the path is a straight and narrow one. In the journey of life, there will be moments when God will seem far away from you. At such times, you must be able to trust his Word, encourage yourself in the Lord, and continue to "run with patience the [Christian] race that God has set before [you]" (Hebrews 12:1, TLB).

## F: FELLOWSHIP. UPHOLD THE IMPORTANCE OF CHRISTIAN FELLOWSHIP.

To have fellowship essentially means that we are "fellows" in the same "ship." To have effective fellowship with somebody, you must have the following things in common: a shared identity, a common heritage, similar values, and the same destiny. As Christians, we have two levels of fellowship: fellowship with God in daily prayer and communion, and fellowship with other Christians through the ministry of the local church (1 John 1:3–4). We are not to undermine or neglect either of these.

*...not neglecting to meet together, as is the habit of some, but encouraging one another, and all the more as you see the Day approaching.*

HEBREWS 10:25, NRSV

Fellowship with God provides you with nutrition for the journey of life and strength for the battles you face on the way.

Fellowship within the setting of the local church provides a corporate anointing which is invaluable in spiritual warfare. From Deuteronomy 32:30, we understand that whereas an individual is able to chase one thousand, two people under a corporate anointing can put ten thousand to flight! This is hardly surprising because, as Jesus assures us in Matthew 18:20, wherever and whenever two or more children of God gather together to have fellowship in God's name, he is present among them.

## G: GOD. FEAR GOD WITH SINCERE REVERENCE.

In relation to God, your fear should be reverential, deferential fear. This fear makes you want to submit to God and obey him. It is this type of fear which we are told in Proverbs 1:7 is the beginning of all wisdom.

The fear of God affects every part of your life. It should make you want to please him in all things, at all times, and at all costs. It should make you abstain from all appearances of sin and evil. The fear of God is therefore a necessary tool for battling the devil.

Furthermore, to fear God is to trust him totally and completely. The fear of God should also make you want to lead as many people as you possibly can to the Lord because, as the apostle Paul puts it beautifully in 2 Corinthians 5: 11, "Knowing, therefore, the terror of the Lord, we persuade men." The *New International Version* is particularly enlightening here: "Since, then, we know what it is to fear the Lord, we try to persuade others." The preacher says in Ecclesiastes 12:13, "Let us hear the conclusion of the whole matter: Fear God and keep His commandments, for this is man's all."

## H: HOLINESS. RECOGNIZE THAT HOLINESS IS KEY.

Holiness is the outworking of our position in Christ Jesus as people who are in right standing with God. Put differently, holiness is right living. It is living a sinless life before God; that is, not committing sin *habitually* or *deliberately*, but repenting immediately if you fall into sin so that your fellowship with God is not broken. A Christian can fall into sin for a variety of reasons—principally through ignorance, by making a mistake, or through carelessness. However, as we are told in 1 John 3:9, "No one born (begotten) of God [*deliberately, knowingly, and habitually*] practices sin, for God's nature abides in him [His principle of life, the divine sperm, remains permanently within him]; and he cannot practice sinning because he is born (begotten) of God" (AB, emphasis supplied).

We are enjoined to be holy even as God is holy and perfect even as he is perfect. Why? Because, the Scriptures teach us that we cannot see God without being holy. See, for instance, Hebrews 12:14, which tells us to "make every effort to live in peace with everyone *and to be holy*; [because] without holiness no one will see the Lord" (NIV, emphasis supplied). To be holy you must depend on the Holy Spirit and the blood of Jesus, which cleanses from all impurities. However, you need to recognize that you also have a role to play in living a holy life.

In spiritual warfare, holiness is a master key. When you live a holy life, your life becomes a sweet-smelling aroma before the Lord. He delights in you. He takes pleasure in you. As with Job, he is able to show you off and say, "Have you seen my servant so-and-so? How there is none like him in all the earth?" Your battles become his battles. Your enemies become his enemies. With holiness, you have a master key with which you can unlock and open a variety of doors in spiritual warfare.

## I: INDUSTRY. BE INDUSTRIOUS AND DILIGENT IN WARFARE.

Be diligent. To be diligent is to be hardworking, thorough, meticulous, and scrupulous. It is applying yourself wholeheartedly to whatever your hands find to do. There is a blessing upon diligence and hard work. Proverbs 22:29 tells us, "Do you see a man diligent and skillful in his business? He will stand before kings; he will not stand before obscure men" (AB).

In spiritual warfare, there is no place for the mediocre, lazy, run-of-the-mill individual. Jesus himself left us an example of hard work. He never procrastinated, and neither should you. Jesus put it this way in John 9:4: "While it is daytime, we must continue doing the work of the One who sent me. Night is coming, when no one can work" (NCV). To underscore the fact that he was not shy of hard work, he said in John 5:17, "My Father never stops working, and so I keep working, too" (NCV). The Amplified Bible puts it this way: "My Father has worked even until now, he has never ceased working; he is still working and I, too, must be at divine work."

The Lord enjoins us in Luke 19:13 to "occupy" or "do business" until he returns in his second advent. The preacher tells in Ecclesiastes 9:10, "Whatever you do, do well. For when you go to the grave, there will be no work or planning or knowledge or wisdom" (NLT). Paul seems to agree with the preacher when he says in Colossians 3:23, "In all the work you are doing, work the best you can. Work as if you were doing it for the Lord, not for people" (NCV).

And just in case you think there are no rewards involved in this, the apostle Paul admonishes us in 1 Corinthians 15:58 as follows: "Therefore, my beloved brethren, be firm (steadfast), immovable, always abounding in the work of the Lord, always being superior, excelling, doing more than enough in the service of the Lord, knowing and being continually aware that your labor in the Lord is not futile, it is never wasted or to no purpose" (AB).

## J: Jesus. Make the Lord Your Example and Full Reliance.

You must depend totally and utterly upon Jesus. He's been there, seen it, and done it all—*but without sin.* He is the only one who can see you through. He gave you the authority with which to overcome the Enemy in the first place. You must rely completely on him. The weapons of our warfare are *only* effective insofar as they are employed through and in Christ. You rely on yourself to your peril, and you depend on man at your own risk. There is an anguish waiting for those whose trust is in man. Jeremiah 17:5 tells us, "This is what the Lord says: 'A curse is placed on those who trust other people, who depend on humans for strength, who have stopped trusting the Lord'" (NCV).

In agreeing to go through the pain and shame and dross of the cross because of the glory laid up for him, Jesus left an incredible example for us to follow. *The Message* puts it beautifully in Hebrews 12:1–3:

> *Do you see what this means—all these pioneers who blazed the way, all these veterans cheering us on? It means we'd better get on with it. Strip down, start running—and never quit! No extra spiritual fat, no parasitic sins. Keep your eyes on Jesus, who both began and finished this race we're in. Study how he did it. Because he never lost sight of where he was headed—that exhilarating finish in and with God—he could put up with anything along the way: Cross,*

*shame, whatever. And now he's there, in the place of honor, right alongside God. When you find yourselves flagging in your faith, go over that story again, item by item, that long litany of hostility he plowed through. That will shoot adrenaline into your souls!*

And what's more, the apostle Paul tells us in Romans 8:34 that Jesus is waiting right now at the right hand of God the Father in glory, interceding and pleading for you. He is also encouraging you, urging you not to give up or give in, but to go through the finish line. You can rely on him to empower you as you follow his example.

## K: KINGDOM. BE KINGDOM-MINDED.

Jesus instructs us in Matthew 6:33 to seek first God's kingdom and his righteousness. Interestingly enough, there are bags and bags of blessings associated with this admonition! We are told that when we obey this command, *all* the things for which people toil—such as money, clothes, food, and houses—will be added to us. *The Message* tells us, "Steep your life in God-reality, God-initiative, God-provisions. Don't worry about missing out. You'll find all your everyday human concerns will be met" (Matthew 6:33). In other words, these blessings will of their own accord locate you, pursue you, and overtake you when you prioritize God's kingdom! This happens as God grants you uncommon favor, makes room for you wherever you are located, blesses all the work of your hands, and enlarges your territory.

How do you seek first his kingdom? By actively desiring the manifestation of the principles of God's kingdom here on earth. You do this by earnestly praying, in the words of Matthew 6:10, "May your kingdom come and what you want be done, here on earth as it is in heaven" (NCV), and by living like a member of the kingdom and letting your light shine.

This really is a question of priority. God must have priority of place in your daily experience; he must come first. You must be kingdom-minded, because although we are in the world, we are not of the world (1 John 2:15–17).

## L: LOVE COVERS A MULTITUDE OF STUFF!

God commands us in Luke 10:27–28 to love the Lord our God and to love our neighbor as ourselves. But what is love? There are three Greek words that are translated "love": *agape, phileo,* and *eros.* Each is very different.

*Agape* is the God kind of love; it is sacrificial and unconditional love. This is the kind of love demonstrated by God when he gave his son Jesus Christ to die in order to redeem us unto himself. We didn't deserve it, nor is there a way of repaying him. *Phileo* is generosity or kindness or bigheartedness; it is from this word that we get the word *philanthropy.* It speaks of charity and benevolence. *Eros* has to do with romantic love, the kind of love between a man and a woman, and it is from this word that we get the word *erotic.*

The apostle Paul describes in great detail the God kind of love in 1 Corinthians 13:1–8:

> *If I [can] speak in the tongues of men and [even] of angels, but have not love (that reasoning, intentional, spiritual devotion such as is inspired by God's love for and in us), I am only a noisy gong or a clanging cymbal. And if I have prophetic powers (the gift of interpreting the divine will and purpose), and understand all the secret truths and mysteries and possess all knowledge, and if I have [sufficient] faith so that I can remove mountains, but have not love (God's love in me) I am nothing (a useless nobody). Even if I dole out all that I have [to the poor in providing] food, and if I surrender my body to be burned or in order that I may glory, but have not love (God's love in me), I gain nothing.*
>
> *Love endures long and is patient and kind; love never is envious nor boils over with jealousy, is not boastful or vainglorious, does not display itself haughtily. It is not conceited (arrogant and inflated with pride); it is not rude (unmannerly) and does not act unbecomingly. Love (God's love in us) does not insist on its own rights or its own way, for it is not self-seeking; it is not touchy or fretful or resentful; it takes no account of the evil done to it [it pays no attention to a suffered wrong]. It does not rejoice at injustice and unrighteousness, but rejoices when right and truth prevail. Love bears up under anything and everything that comes, is ever ready to believe the best of every person, its hopes are fadeless under all circumstances, and it endures everything [without weakening]. Love never fails [never fades out or becomes obsolete or comes to an end].*
>
> *As for prophecy (the gift of interpreting the divine will and purpose), it will be fulfilled and pass away; as for tongues, they will be destroyed and cease;*

*as for knowledge, it will pass away [it will lose its value and be superseded by truth].*

AB, EMPHASIS SUPPLIED

As a Christian, Jesus instructs you in John 13:35 to demonstrate this unconditional, sacrificial love—that is, *agape,* the God kind of love—because that is one way by which people will know that we are his disciples!

## M: MERCY. SHOW KINDNESS, COMPASSION, MERCY, AND JUSTICE.

As a Christian, you have a social responsibility to the world around you. Your immediate surroundings, your neighborhood, should be a better place because of you. As children of God, Jesus tells us in Matthew 5:13 that we are salt to the earth. In the same way that salt both produces flavor and is a preservative, God expects you to give flavor to the world around you and to protect, preserve, and safeguard righteousness and justice.

In addition, you must remember to show mercy and kindness to those around you. You should have the poor, the less fortunate, and the needy among you in regular contemplation, and you must help them as a matter of course. King Solomon puts it beautifully in Proverbs 28:27: "Whoever gives to the poor will have everything he needs, but the one who ignores the poor will receive many curses" (NCV).

William Shakespeare describes mercy this way in *The Merchant of Venice* in one of his most famous passages:

> The quality of mercy is not strain'd,
> It droppeth as the gentle rain from heaven
> Upon the place beneath. It is twice blest:
> It blesseth him that gives and him that takes.

> 'Tis mightiest in the mightiest, it becomes
> The thronèd monarch better than his crown.
> His scpetre shows the force of temporal power,
> The attribute to awe and majesty,
> Wherein doth sit the dread and fear of kings;

But mercy is above this sceptred sway;
It is enthroned in the hearts of kings,
It is an attribute to God himself,
And early power doth then show likest God's
When mercy seasons justice. Therefore . . .
Though justice be thy plea, consider this:
That in the course of justice, none of us
Should see salvation. We do pray for mercy,
And that same prayer doth teach us all to render
The deeds of mercy.[2]

In the Beatitudes of Matthew 5, we are told that those who show mercy will in turn receive mercy. The prophet Micah puts it this way in Micah 6:8: "O people, the LORD has already told you what is good, and this is what he requires of you: to do what is right, to love mercy, and to walk humbly with your God" (NLT).

## N: NIGHT. REMEMBER THAT NIGHTTIME IS A GOOD TIME TO FIGHT THE ENEMY!

Be prepared to do warfare at night. By "warfare" I mean exercising authority in the name of Jesus and demolishing demonic fortresses and satanic strongholds, destroying speculations and every lofty thing raised up against the knowledge of God, and taking the thoughts of men captive to the obedience of Christ. I mean uprooting trees which God has not planted in your family, neighborhood, and country, as well as establishing righteousness in your home, community, and country through declarations *in the place of prayer.* Warfare also includes binding the Enemy and frustrating his plans and machinations.

Jesus prayed all night before he made one of the most important decisions of his ministry. In Luke 6:12–13 we read, "Now during those days [Jesus] went out to the mountain to pray; and he spent the night in prayer to God. And when day came, he called his disciples and chose twelve of them, whom he also named apostles" (NRSV). He left us an example to follow.

Why do we particularly need to pray at night? The Bible tells us in 1 Thessalonians 5:17 to "never stop praying" (NLT), and in Ephesians 6:18, it instructs that we "with all prayer and petition pray at all times in the Spirit, and with this in view, be on the alert with all perseverance and petition for all the saints" (NASB). God expects you to pray at all times. *However, nighttime is a good time to pray not just because of the example of Jesus, but because it is a time when you can concentrate without any distractions.*

Furthermore, as we saw in chapter 5, one of the devil's names is the *power or dominion of darkness.* We said that "Satan epitomizes all that the forces of darkness represent. He stands for everything that is evil, dark, gloomy, and wicked." The Enemy loves darkness and hates light with a passion. Not surprisingly, a lot of his activities take place at night when most people are in bed, asleep. He likes to operate under the cover of darkness. Most cults and secret societies do the same thing: they function at nighttime under concealment of darkness. There is therefore scope for staying up late at night to engage in spiritual warfare.

In my experience, once you make up your mind to wake up at night to pray and do warfare, and you actually do it a few times, God takes over and it becomes habitual. The Holy Spirit wakes you up to pray. I believe that God is always seeking people who can stand in the gap and intercede (Ezekiel 22:30). So next time you find it difficult to sleep at night, instead of tossing up and down on your bed, wake up and spend some time in prayer.

## O: OPEN HEAVENS. OPERATE UNDER OPEN HEAVENS.

There is nothing so wonderful for a child of God who is engaged in spiritual warfare as to operate under open heavens! In Deuteronomy 28:12, the Bible tells us, "The LORD will open the heavens, his rich storehouse, for you. He will send rain on your land at the right time and bless everything you do. You will be able to make loans to many nations but won't need to borrow from any" (GW).

When the heavens are open to you, God automatically *embarrasses* you with his goodness and mercy. Jesus is the ultimate example of what it means to operate under open heavens.

When the heavens are open to an individual, the following inevitably happens:

- He or she receives God's seal of approval.
- He or she has access to the storehouse of God's bounty, his rich treasury in the heavens, his sky vaults, his good treasure, the heavens.
- He or she will enter breakthrough.
- Blessings will pursue and overtake him or her.
- He or she will experience uncommon favor before God and man.

- He or she will receive divine connections in business, career, or ministry. Such a person is miraculously linked with those who will help him or her move to the next level.
- He or she will be fruitful in season.
- God will supply all his or her needs.

The heavens are open when you walk in obedience to God (Deuteronomy 28:1). On the other hand, the heavens can be shut against you because of disobedience (Deuteronomy 28:15, 23).

## P: PRAYER. ACKNOWLEDGE THAT PRAYERLESSNESS IS A SIN—AND CHANGE YOUR HABITS!

Did you know that prayerlessness is a sin? In the book of 1 Samuel 12, we hear the man of God saying in verse 23 that "Moreover as for me, God forbid that I should *sin* against the LORD in ceasing to pray for you."

What then is prayerlessness? I believe it is one of three things:

- Not praying at all (Luke 18:1). There are Christians who don't pray at all. They do everything else except pray. Some don't pray because they don't know how to communicate with the Lord in prayer. Others don't pray because they've had a bad experience when they felt their prayer wasn't answered. In reality, God always answers the prayers of his children; however, the answer may not be what you are expecting. For every prayer made to the Lord by a Christian, God will answer in one of three ways: he will say yes, or no, or not yet.
- Not praying enough (1 Thessalonians 5:17). There are children of God who pray on only two occasions. First, they pray to God when in group fellowship, say in church. Second, they call upon God when they are in trouble or distress. However, they forget to pray when they don't have any challenges in their lives or when they are not participating in corporate worship.
- Not praying according to God's will (1 John 5:14). There are Christians who pray, but they might as well not bother because they are praying amiss. They are not praying according to God's will as revealed in the Scriptures. An example would be somebody who asks the Lord to give

him an automobile because he wants to show off to his friends. Another example would be somebody asking God to kill his spouse so he can marry somebody else.

If you fall into any of these three categories, you need to repent and ask the Lord for mercy. In spiritual warfare, you cannot afford not to pray. The weapons of our warfare, which we saw in some detail in chapter 3, can only be exercised in the place of prayer. Therefore, to effectively combat the devil, you need to pray.

Avoid the sin of prayerlessness at all costs. And remember that if you do not *pray*, you easily become a *prey*.

## Q: Quit. Quit Giving Excuses!

Determine not to give excuses unless absolutely unavoidable. Excuses are simply what they are: excuses, reasons for failure, explanations for defeat. If our Lord Jesus had wanted to give up on the cross, he had a million and one reasons to do so. He was not immune to the temptation to give up—he even prayed that the cup might pass over him. But crucially, he submitted himself to God's sovereign will and held on.

In chapter 3, we said that in spiritual warfare there is no room for turning back. You have to always be on the offensive. You have to keep attacking the Enemy; on account of this, your back is left bare.

Like Jesus, you must learn to have the mentality of an achiever. This starts with a quality decision not to quit no matter what and to be the best you can be in all things. Having put your hand to the plow of salvation, determine that you will never look back at the things you have left behind. If things go wrong, take responsibility and learn from your mistakes. Always remember that if properly harnessed, your mistakes can become miracles. Don't blame anyone else!

## R: Ready. Be Ready at All Times

> *Be prepared, whether the time is favorable or not.*
>
> 2 TIMOTHY 4:2, NLT

Being in spiritual warfare means you must equip yourself and be geared up for war at all times. You equip yourself by:

- Giving yourself to the ministry of the Word of God. The Word is able to build you up and give you an inheritance among the saints (Acts 20:32).
- Praying in the Holy Ghost (Jude 1:20).
- Disciplining your body (1 Corinthians 9:27).

You must always be prepared. But "prepared to do what?" you might ask. Let me give some ideas to assist you in your personal study:

- To exercise authority over the Enemy (Luke 10:19).
- To give an answer to anyone who asks you as to the reasons why you believe (1 Peter 3:15).
- To preach the gospel of salvation and testify about your faith (2 Timothy 4:2).
- For the rapture. You must be ready for the Lord's return and live each day as if it were your last (Matthew 24:42).

## S: SOBER. BE SOBER AND VIGILANT.

You need to be watchful because, as we are told in 1 Peter 5:8, your adversary the devil goes about seeking whom to destroy. The Scriptures tell us in Romans 8:14 that as many as are led by God's Spirit are God's children. You must be on your guard at all times.

To be sober is:

- To avoid debauchery, licentious living, and drunkenness (Galatians 5:19–21).
- To submit to God and be sensitive to the leading and direction of the Holy Spirit (Ephesians 4:30).
- To walk in the Spirit (Galatians 5:16).
- To practice God's presence (Psalm 16:11).
- To pray without ceasing (1 Thessalonians 5:17).

In spiritual warfare, you must be alert and sensitive to any and every leading, guidance, or direction which God gives you by the Holy Spirit. Spiritual sobriety and knowledge of the Word will enable you to discern God's voice.

T: TEMPTATION. EXPECT TEMPTATION—AND RESIST IT.

In this warfare with the enemy of our souls, expect to be tempted. Temptation comes with the territory. Temptation itself is not sin, but yielding to temptation is. In Hebrews 4:15, the Bible says of the Lord Jesus, "We don't have a priest who is out of touch with our reality. He's been through weakness and testing, experienced it all—all but the sin" (MSG). Whatever happens, do not yield to temptation. Remember that all the devil can do is to tempt you by dropping ideas into your mind. He can't actually make you sin. At the end of the day, it is up to you to either accept or reject his propositions, no matter how alluring and appealing they may be!

Let us get something straight: the goal of temptation is to make you fall. So it is the devil who tempts you, not God! No matter how difficult your temptation might seem, it is not new, for as King Solomon tells us in Ecclesiastes 1:9–10, there is nothing new under the sun. It has happened to somebody in the past and will most likely happen to somebody else in the future. In any event, as we saw earlier, in chapter 6 in our discussion on sin, God has made provision for you at two levels. Firstly, he will not let the Enemy tempt you beyond what you can handle. And secondly, he will always make a way for you to escape with each temptation. This is captured brilliantly by Paul in 1 Corinthians 10:13 when he says, "All you need to remember is that God will never let you down; he'll never let you be pushed past your limit; he'll always be there to help you come through it" (MSG). So you don't need to give in to temptation.

God does not tempt you; God *tests* you instead. He tries you, because trials burn out the dross in your life and bring out the best in you. Job 23:10 tells us that when we are tried in fire, we come forth as gold.

U: UNDERSTANDING. GET UNDERSTANDING.

Understanding is insight or perception or discernment. It is a form of revelation where God sheds light or grants insight into an issue or situation. It is much more than comprehension or knowledge. In a sense, understanding is a spiritual talent. It can be described as a mixture of the word of wisdom and the word of knowledge, two of the nine gifts of the Spirit (1 Corinthians 12:4–11). God is the source of all insight. We receive understanding through a deep personal relationship with God, because it comes by inspiration of the Holy Spirit.

In Acts 21:10–11, we see insight at work:

*After several days of visiting, a prophet from Judea by the name of Agabus came down to see us. He went right up to Paul, took Paul's belt, and, in a dramatic gesture, tied himself up, hands and feet. He said, "This is what the Holy Spirit says: The Jews in Jerusalem are going to tie up the man who owns this belt just like this and hand him over to godless unbelievers."*

MSG

If you read the rest of Acts 21, you see that Paul went to Jerusalem and was indeed arrested!

The really interesting thing is that you can ask God in prayer to give you revelation on an issue. And as long as you ask according to his Word, he will hear your prayer and grant your petition. So you do not need to be in the dark, particularly as you wage war on this enemy who is invisible to you and me.

## V: Vows. Keep Your Vows.

Vows are solemn promises made to God in which we tell him that if he does what we ask of him, we will do or refrain from doing a specified thing. A vow is usually conditional upon God answering a prayer. Vows are voluntary and need not be made; however, once made, they cannot *and should not usually* be broken. They must be carried out. So please fulfill your vows. Carry out your promises.

In Matthew 5:33–37, Jesus teaches that we don't need to make a vow:

*You have also heard that our ancestors were told, "You must not break your vows; you must carry out the vows you make to the Lord." But I say, do not make any vows! Do not say, "By heaven!" because heaven is God's throne. And do not say, "By the earth!" because the earth is his footstool. And do not say, "By Jerusalem!" for Jerusalem is the city of the great King. Do not even say, "By my head!" for you can't turn one hair white or black. Just say a simple, "Yes, I will," or "No, I won't." Anything beyond this is from the evil one.*

NLT

It may be a good exercise to ask the Holy Spirit to bring to your remembrance any unfulfilled vows which you may have forgotten about. If you are sincere, the Holy Spirit will normally bring any such matters to your remembrance. If he does, deal with them as quickly as you can.

## W: WILLINGNESS. BE WILLING AND OBEDIENT.

Willingness means to be willing, enthusiastic, ready, or eager. According to *Chambers 21ˢᵗ Century Dictionary*, to be willing is to be "eager and co-operative." Willingness is an attitude of the heart. Deep down within you, *are you really* enthusiastic about God? Does God excite you? Are you eager for the things of God? Are you ready to receive from God? Do you expect the miraculous? In your day-to-day business, are you expectant? How large is your receptacle? As Elisha told the widow in 2 Kings 4:3, are you able to "borrow thee vessels abroad of all thy neighbors, even empty vessels; *borrow not a few*" (KJV)? Or are you just going through the motions of life?

Obedience, on the other hand, is simply carrying out God's instructions. Put simply, it is to please God. Sometimes we have to learn obedience, just like Jesus, who, according to Hebrews 5:8, learned obedience by the things which he suffered. Jesus obviously had to learn how to obey because, being God himself, he had no need to obey anyone prior to the advent!

It is important to always bear in mind the fact that God always prefers obedience to any form of sacrifice. In this warfare, don't try to bargain with God: just obey him.

## X: X-RAY. EXAMINE YOURSELF CAREFULLY.

In spiritual warfare, you need to constantly search yourself to see if you are still on track for the ultimate prize: heaven. Is your name still in the Lamb's Book of Life, or has it been erased? Examine yourself in the light of God's Word, and be prepared to ask yourself some difficult and, if necessary, awkward questions (2 Corinthians 13:5).

Sometimes, the Word of God is like an X-ray machine. The Bible tells us in Hebrews 4:12 that "God's word is living and active. It is sharper than any two-edged sword and cuts as deep as the place where soul and spirit meet, the place where joints and marrow meet. *God's word judges a person's thoughts and intentions*" (GW, emphasis supplied). The Amplified Bible puts it this way: "For the Word that God speaks is alive and full of power [making it active, operative, energizing, and effective]; it is sharper than any two-edged sword, *penetrating to the dividing line of the [a] breath of life (soul) and [the immortal] spirit, and of joints and marrow [of the deepest parts of our nature], exposing and sifting and analyzing and judging the very thoughts and purposes of the heart"* (emphasis supplied).

Use the Word of God to explore your motives as you study and apply it to your life. The gift you gave to John or Marie the other day, what was the real motive behind it? And what was the reason behind the help you rendered in church last Sunday—was it given unto the Lord, or was it to catch somebody's attention and be noticed? Remember that as Paul tells us in 1 Corinthians 11:31, if you scrutinize and examine yourself, you are unlikely to be painfully scrutinized by someone else.

## Y: YIELD. GIVE YOURSELF FULLY TO THE LORD.

In the battle with the forces of hell, you want to give yourself over to the Lord completely. Do not hold anything back. The Lord expects total surrender and complete self-denial. He says those who wish to become his disciples must first deny themselves, take up the cross, and follow him. This is not surprising, because as Jesus told us in Matthew 7:13–14, the way that leads to eternal life is narrow and straight, whereas the path to hell is a highway. Surrender all, totally and completely, to the Lord.

The true meaning of surrender is superbly captured by the classic hymn, "I Surrender All":

All to Jesus I surrender,
All to Him I freely give;
I will ever love and trust Him,
In His presence daily live.

*Refrain*
I surrender all,
I surrender all.
All to Thee, my blessed Savior,
I surrender all.

All to Jesus I surrender,
Humbly at His feet I bow,

Worldly pleasures all forsaken;
Take me, Jesus, take me now.

All to Jesus I surrender,
Make me, Savior, wholly Thine;
Let me feel Thy Holy Spirit,
Truly know that Thou art mine.

All to Jesus I surrender,
Lord, I give myself to Thee;
Fill me with Thy love and power,
Let Thy blessing fall on me.

All to Jesus I surrender,
Now I feel the sacred flame.
Oh, the joy of full salvation!
Glory, glory to His name![3]

## Z: Zeal. Let the Zeal of the Lord Consume You

Be passionate for the Lord. Be zealous. In Romans 12:11, the Bible describes how we ought to be: "as to diligent zealousness, not slothful; in spirit fervent; serving the Lord" (DBT). Perhaps, as we are told in Revelation 2:5, you need to return to your first love for the Lord. Remember how fervent and zealous you were when you first knew the Lord? At the time, there was no sacrifice too great for you to make for the Lord, no price too high to pay, no valley too low to cross, no ocean too deep to traverse: You were completely and totally sold out for the Lord.

What has happened to your zeal, your passion, the fire that once burnt in your bones? God does not relish those who are lukewarm. From Revelation 3:15–16, it is clear that he prefers you either hot or cold. When you are hot, you are on fire for him, and that's his ultimate for you. If you are cold, he does not like it because you have no part in him, but at least he knows where you stand! Being *lukewarm*, on the other hand, is a complete no-no, especially when you are engaged in warfare with the enemy of your soul.

## FOOD FOR REFLECTION

- Have you believed that the devil is just a myth or fable?
- Why should Christians have no business playing around with ideas of the devil as a fun-loving, beer-swigging guy who just wants us to have a good time?
- What is the role of the Holy Spirit in ensuring that as a child of God you do not deliberately, knowingly, and habitually practice sin?
- In the "A–Z of Spiritual Warfare," what stands out the most for you, and why?
- How does one avoid the sin of prayerlessness?

## PRAYER FEATURES

- Lord, as I study the Scriptures, please give me a revelation of who the devil really is.
- Lord, help me to quit giving excuses so that I can go with you all the way.
- Lord, as you counseled the church in Ephesus in Revelation 2:1–7, help me to return to my first love for you.
- Lord, please help me to be totally committed to you.
- Lord, help me to demonstrate unconditional, sacrificial love—that is, *agape,* the God kind of love—in my dealings with others.
- Lord, please enable me to constantly examine myself.
- I prophesy and declare that I will stand before kings and not before ordinary men!

## ACTION POINTS

- Attempt to make up your own "A–Z of Spiritual Warfare" without replicating any of the points made in this chapter. Write it down in your journal. Then compare your list with the list in this chapter.
- Sing the hymns, "Take My Life and Let It Be" and "I Surrender All," which are included in this chapter under "C: Christ. Be Completely Christ-Controlled" and "Y: Yield. Give Yourself Fully to the Lord," during your personal devotions every day for the next week. Spend some time in quiet contemplation as you meditate on the words of these great hymns.
- Do you have a charity which you support financially on a regular basis? If you do, keep it up! If you don't, prayerfully select a well-established charity

which helps the poor and sign up for a program of regular giving to support their work. You do not need to be fabulously wealthy in order to give: your giving can be as little as US$5 or £4 a month. Such regular giving is one way of tapping into the blessing in Proverbs 28:27 that "whoever gives to the poor will have everything he needs" (NCV).

- In following the example of Jesus, who prayed all night before he chose his disciples, determine to have your own personal prayer vigil, say once a year. Set apart some time at night, perhaps between midnight and 6 a.m., when you sing praises to the Lord, pray, study the Scriptures, and just enjoy the Lord's presence in the comfort of your study, front room, bedroom, or basement. Start with a couple of hours and see how it develops.

Chapter Ten

# PUNISHING THE ENEMY'S PETULANCE

—⦿—

*Withstand him; be firm in faith [against his onset—rooted, established, strong, immovable, and determined], knowing that the same (identical) sufferings are appointed to your brotherhood (the whole body of Christians) throughout the world.*

1 PETER 5:9, AB

Rebellion comes naturally to the devil because he is a fallen angel. As Paul the apostle tells us in Ephesians 2:1–2, the devil—the commander of the powers in the unseen world—is the spirit at work in the hearts of those who refuse to obey God, or, as the New King James Version describes them, "the sons of disobedience." Satan revels in rebellion. The Bible says in 1 John 3:8, "He who sins is of the devil, for the devil has sinned from the beginning." He is the originator of sin, he is a sinner, and in fact, he is the chief of sinners. It should therefore not come as a surprise if the Evil One sometimes disobeys your lawful instructions as a child of God.

The second part of 1 John 3:8 tells us "for this purpose the Son of God was manifested, that He might destroy the works of the devil." The Amplified Bible says "The reason the Son of God was made manifest (visible) was to undo (destroy, loosen, and dissolve) the works the devil [has done]." By his death and resurrection, Jesus did not destroy the devil; he *destroyed all his work.* He undid what the devil has done. He stripped the devil of all his powers. In Colossians 2:15, we read, "In this way, he disarmed the spiritual rulers and authorities. He shamed them publicly by his victory over them on the cross" (NLT).

To help you understand what Jesus did to the devil, let us take a look at what happens when countries to go war. The Falklands War is a good example. It started on Friday, April 2, 1982, with the invasion and occupation of the Falkland Islands and South Georgia by Argentina. Great Britain then launched a naval task force to engage the Argentine forces and retake the Falklands. The war lasted just seventy-four days. It ended on June 14, 1982, when Mario Menéndez, the Argentine governor of the Falklands, surrendered to Major General Sir Jeremy Moore, the commander of the British forces. The two countries eventually signed a surrender document.

When Argentina surrendered to Britain, they gave up their arms and withdrew from the Falklands. However, the surrender did not make Argentina incapable of fighting. If the British had given back the ammunition to the Argentines, they could have continued the fight. Also, if the British were to decide to invite the Argentines back into the Falklands, they could stake their claim again. In the same way, although he has been disarmed, the devil can still operate in the lives of those Christians who *let* him. He still pretends to be a force to be reckoned with, even though Jesus stripped him of all his powers. That is one of the reasons why, as we saw in chapter 6, he goes about pretending to be a roaring lion, seeking whom to destroy (1 Peter 5:8).

Elsewhere in this book, we have made the point that if Satan disobeys your lawful instruction or opposes you as a Christian, you should be able to oppose him and avenge his disobedience or rebellion, and that God has made provision to enable you as a child of God to discipline Satan should such a situation arise. And rightly so, because the Bible tells us in 2 Corinthians 10:6 that we are to be "ready to punish all disobedience when your obedience is fulfilled."

As we saw in chapter 7, Satan disobeys the Christian if any of the following happens:

- If he ignores you
- If he resists or withstands you
- If he flouts your lawful instruction
- If he defies or refuses to obey you
- If he decides to go against you in any form
- If he refuses to comply with your command
- If he attacks you or rises up against you in any way
- If he decides to challenge or to contravene your prayers

## WHY DOES THE DEVIL DISOBEY?

Here are a few reasons why I think the Enemy withstands and opposes Christians. This list is by no means exhaustive. The important thing to point out here is that God has made sufficient provision for you to handle Satan's disobedience. For instance, the Bible says in Isaiah 54:17 that "'No weapon that is formed against you will prosper; and every tongue that accuses you in judgment you will condemn. This is the heritage of the servants of the LORD, and their vindication is from Me,' declares the LORD" (NASB).

Clearly, at the end of the day, it will be up to you to refute or condemn the devil's accusation and to punish his disobedience. But back to our topic: why does he disobey in the first place?

## IT IS IN HIS NATURE TO DISOBEY

It appears that disobedience is in the devil's genes. He can't help but resist you as a child of God. The Bible appears to accept the fact that he will resist you as given when it says in James 4:7, "So place yourselves under God's authority. *Resist the devil,* and he will run away from you" (GW, emphasis supplied). He wouldn't be the devil if he didn't oppose you as a child of God.

It is clear from the scriptural examples of Satan's insubordination which we saw in chapter 7 that there is no rhyme or reason to his disobedience. Sometimes he just disobeys. He is an opportunist; he will take advantage of any opportunity to oppose you. Don't be caught off guard by the devil. Take the view that he will oppose you, and be prepared to resist him!

## HE WANTS TO SEE IF YOU KNOW WHO YOU ARE

In chapter 2 we examined in detail the question of who we are in Christ Jesus. Do you know who you are? Unfortunately, a lot of Christians have no understanding whatsoever of who they are in the Lord. As we said in chapter 1, many Christians are spiritual millionaires in rags.

From time to time, it seems to me that the devil opposes Christians just to see how they will react. He probably thinks, "Let's see if I can get away with this." If you know who you are, I expect you to stand up to the devil, and he will run away from you! On the other hand, if you don't know who you are, instead of exercising authority when the Enemy confronts you, you start to tear your hair out, not knowing that the solution you seek is within your grasp.

## HE KNOWS HIS TIME IS SHORT

The devil knows that his time is very short, and he is furious. Because of that, he has declared an all-out war on the children of God! The Bible says in Revelation 12:12, "Be glad for this reason, heavens and those who live in them. How horrible it is for the earth and the sea because the Devil has come down to them with fierce anger, knowing that he has little time left" (GW). In the short time he has left, he wants to wreak as much havoc as possible. He is sending out false teachers and false prophets into the world. In Matthew 24:24, Jesus said that in the last days, "False Christs and false prophets will arise and will show great signs and wonders, so as to mislead, if possible, even the elect [those who know the Lord]" (NASB).

In his fury, the devil will overstep the mark and pretend that he doesn't know that he is a defeated foe. In trying to make up for lost time, he will push the boundaries and oppose you. It is up to you to remind him that Jesus disarmed him at Calvary.

## DEALING WITH SATAN'S REBELLION

So how do you chastise Satan for his defiance? What do you do in reaction to his petulance? How do you punish him when he is noncompliant?

### EXAMINE YOUR LIFE

> *Examine yourselves to see whether you are still in the Christian faith. Test yourselves! Don't you recognize that you are people in whom Jesus Christ lives? Could it be that you're failing the test?*
>
> 2 CORINTHIANS 13:5, GW

Self-examination is key. It was Socrates, the ancient Greek philosopher widely credited for laying the foundation for Western philosophy, who is quoted as saying that "The unexamined life is not worth living for a human being."[1]

If there is a show of disobedience by the Enemy to a child of God in any form, your first exercise should be one of self-examination. Search yourself, investigate your heart, examine your motives. Is there sin lurking, skulking, hanging about anywhere in your system, or are you in right standing and right living with God? It is important to eliminate yourself as the possible cause of the problem! If you are the source of the problem, then your obedience is not complete, and if your obedience isn't complete, you cannot punish the Enemy for his disobedience!

If you discover sin in your life, you need to deal with yourself immediately. If you need to repent, you must do so straightaway. If you need to forgive somebody, do it right away. Do whatever you need to do to get yourself back into fellowship and communion with God.

## SUBMIT YOURSELF TO GOD

*Submit yourselves therefore to God. Resist the devil, and he will flee from you.*

JAMES 4:7, KJV

For us to resist and stand against the Enemy, we first have to submit ourselves to God. This is a condition that we must first fulfill. What does submitting to God entail? One translation of the above verse says, "So place yourselves under God's authority. Resist the devil, and he will run away from you" (GW). In other words, to submit to God is to surrender and yield our hearts, our wills, and our lives to him. It is to:

- *Obey him.* To obey God is to do as God tells you. It is to comply with God's instructions to you as an individual. It is to act upon his Word, abide by his commandments, and conform to his will. Essentially, you are to just do what God wants you to do, how he wants it done, and when he wants it done. No more, no less!
- *Be faithful.* Faithfulness requires total, full, and wholehearted devotion to God and his service. Be loyal to God. Be so dedicated to God that you are sold out to him. Be fully, completely, and totally committed to him. Be trustworthy in whatever he has committed into your hands, recognizing the fact that someday you will be required to render an account of your stewardship to him (1 Corinthians 4:2). Be reliable; be dependable.
- *Entrust yourself to him.* Rely on God. Trust him. This trust should come from the revelation that God is able to do whatever he has promised, and secondly that God is your source—not your job, not your business, not even the economy of your country. He has promised, and he will never fail. He is dependable. So hang on him. Depend totally upon him.
- *Yield yourself to him.* God desires to have precedence in all things. You must seek him first. Surrender completely, totally, and absolutely to God. He wants to be your Savior and your Lord, not just your Savior. Be in

total submission to his will in all things. Yearn for him in the same way that the deer pants and longs for the water brooks (Psalm 42:1).

To submit to God is to trust and obey. Put differently, to yield to God is to *walk* the *talk*. Without total surrender and complete submission to God, we cannot firmly resist and stand firm against the Enemy.

## RESIST THE DEVIL

Resisting the Enemy means standing firm against him in prayer and opposing him with the Word of God. For this to happen, you must pray with the help of the Holy Spirit. Pray all manner of prayer. Speak the Word of God into the situation you are faced with. Address the Enemy and command him to back off in the name of Jesus. Tell him, "I resist you in the name of Jesus, and I command you to take your filthy hands off my family…my wife…my husband…my children…my ministry…my parents…my finances…my health…my career…my business…my investments…in the name of the Lord Jesus Christ."

## BIND HIM IN THE NAME OF JESUS

*Therefore, God elevated him to the place of highest honor and gave him the name above all other names, that at the name of Jesus every knee should bow, in heaven and on earth and under the earth, and every tongue confess that Jesus Christ is Lord, to the glory of God the father.*

PHILIPPIANS 2:9–11, NLT

In Matthew 12:29 Jesus asked, "For who is powerful enough to enter the house of a strong man like Satan and plunder his goods? Only someone even stronger— someone who could tie him up and then plunder his house" (NLT). Essentially, when the devil resists you, you must first lock him up and put him out of the way. That way, you can operate without any opposition or hostility. In the same vein, if in the course of a particular spiritual exercise the Enemy is fighting back, then perhaps you need to bind him before continuing.

On account of Jesus's death and resurrection, the apostle Paul tells us in Philippians 2:9–11 that God has elevated him to the place of highest honor and given him the name above all other names. Jesus acknowledged this when he declared in Matthew 28:18 that "All authority has been given to me in heaven and on earth."

Having been given all authority in heaven and earth, Jesus then decided to delegate his authority to you and me. In John 14:12, Jesus said, "I can guarantee this truth: those who believe in me will do the things that I am doing. They will do even greater things because I am going to the Father" (GW). The Amplified Bible puts it this way: "I assure you, most solemnly I tell you, if anyone steadfastly believes in Me, he will himself be able to do the things that I do; and he will do even greater things than these, because I go to the Father."

Basically, what you have as a child of God is delegated authority from Jesus over all the power of the Enemy, including the authority to bind the devil in Jesus's name (Mark 16:17, Luke 10:19). And because the name of Jesus is a name that is exalted above every other name, when we bind the devil, he cannot fight back, and so we have free access to plunder his possessions.

## Rebuke Him in the Name of Jesus

*And the Lord said to Satan, "The Lord rebuke you, Satan! The Lord who has chosen Jerusalem rebuke you! Is this not a brand plucked from the fire?"*

ZECHARIAH 3:2

To rebuke somebody is to reprimand them or scold them severely. Professional organizations reprimand their members for professional misconduct. Parents chastise their children if they are unruly or naughty. In the same way, you can rebuke the devil in the name of the Lord if the devil is wayward or mischievous.

Moses stands out as one of the greatest servants of God who ever lived in this world. The Bible tells us in Exodus 33:11 that the Lord would speak to Moses face-to-face, as one speaks to a friend. We don't know a lot about the circumstances surrounding Moses's death except what we are told in Deuteronomy 34:5–6. *The Message* tells us "Moses died there in the land of Moab, Moses the servant of GOD, just as GOD said. God buried him in the valley in the land of Moab opposite Beth Peor. No one knows his burial site to this very day."

Can you therefore imagine the devil attempting to lay his filthy, grubby hands on the body of Moses after Moses's death? "Incredible," you might say. Well, the devil did. He showed no reverence or respect whatsoever for the body of this mighty servant of God. In fact, he actually disputed the body with the archangel Michael. This was the height of insubordination and waywardness. Jude 1:9 tells us that the archangel had no choice but to tell him, "The Lord rebuke you!"

## PRAY IN THE HOLY SPIRIT

*But you, beloved, building yourselves up on your most holy faith, praying in the Holy Spirit…*

JUDE 1:20

One way of attacking the Enemy in spiritual warfare is to pray in the Holy Spirit. Paul also admonishes us to always pray in the Spirit. In Ephesians 6:18, he tells us to "pray in the Spirit at all times and on every occasion. Stay alert and be persistent in your prayers for all believers everywhere" (NLT). So how does one pray in the Spirit?

Some people equate praying in the Holy Spirit with praying in tongues. However, they are not one and the same. To pray in the Spirit is to pray *with the help, aid, and assistance of the Holy Spirit.* The God's Word Translation tells us in Jude 1:20, "Dear friends, use your most holy faith to grow. Pray with the Holy Spirit's help." You can therefore pray in the Spirit without praying in tongues (however, you cannot pray in tongues without praying in the Spirit).

Romans 8:26 tells us, "In the same way, the Spirit also helps us in our weakness, since we do not know how to pray as we should. But the Spirit himself intercedes for us with groans too deep for words" (ISV). Having said that praying in tongues is not *necessary* to pray in the Spirit, to my mind, the *easiest* way to pray in the Spirit is by praying in tongues. In 1 Corinthians 14:2 and 4, the Bible tells us that a person who speaks in tongues does not speak to men but to God, for no one understands him; however, in the spirit he speaks mysteries, and he edifies and builds himself. Furthermore, when you pray in tongues, you are entirely reliant upon the Holy Spirit. According to *The New York Times:*

Researchers at the University of Pennsylvania took brain images of five women while they spoke in tongues and found that their frontal lobes—the thinking, willful part of the brain through which people control what they do—were relatively quiet, as were the language centers. The regions involved in maintaining self-consciousness were active. The women were not in blind trances, and it was unclear which region was driving the behavior.

The images, appearing in the current issue of the journal *Psychiatry Research: Neuroimaging,* pinpoint the most active areas of the brain…In the study, the researchers used imaging techniques to track changes in blood flow in each woman's brain in two conditions, once as she sang a gospel song and again while speaking in tongues. By comparing the patterns created by these two emotional, devotional activities, the researchers could pinpoint blood-flow peaks and valleys unique to speaking in tongues.

Ms. Morgan, a co-author of the study, was also a research subject. She is a born-again Christian who says she considers the ability to speak in tongues a gift. "You're aware of your surroundings," she said. "You're not really out of control. But you have no control over what's happening. You're just flowing. You're in a realm of peace and comfort, and it's a fantastic feeling"…Contrary to what may be a common perception, studies suggest that people who speak in tongues rarely suffer from mental problems. A recent study of nearly 1,000 evangelical Christians in England found that those who engaged in the practice were more emotionally stable than those who did not. Researchers have identified at least two forms of the practice, one ecstatic and frenzied, the other subdued and nearly silent.

The new findings contrasted sharply with images taken of other spiritually inspired mental states like meditation, which is often a highly focused mental exercise, activating the frontal lobes.[2]

Pray in the Spirit at all times. If you can, also pray in tongues. The blessings are plentiful.

## SET HIS WORKS ALIGHT WITH GOD'S CONSUMING FIRE

*Fire goes before him and consumes his foes on every side.*

PSALM 97:3, NIV

Although in this warfare you cannot destroy the devil himself, you can completely extinguish and annihilate his works with God's fire.

I have been to prayer meetings where I have heard people tell the devil, "I burn you up in Jesus's name"; well, that won't happen because there is simply no provision for that in Scripture! However, Hebrews 12:29 tells us that our God is a consuming fire. This shows God as the Lord of heaven's armies, the Lord of Hosts. The imagery is of an intense and raging supernatural fire which cannot be put out by any Fire

Department. As a child of God, you can set the Enemy's works ablaze and totally incinerate them. You can destroy and totally wipe out his weapons, his plans, and whatever he has already set in motion in your life. Just like the Lord did to the house of Esau in Obadiah 1:18, you can command the specific work of the devil which you want to destroy to become "stubble" and to be destroyed by fire.

Listen to King David's testimony in Psalm 18:3–16:

*The Lord should be praised. I called on him, and I was saved from my enemies. The ropes of death had become tangled around me. The torrents of destruction had overwhelmed me. The ropes of the grave had surrounded me. The clutches of death had confronted me. I called on the Lord in my distress. I cried to my God for help. He heard my voice from his temple, and my cry for help reached his ears. Then the earth shook and quaked. Even the foundations of the mountains trembled. They shook violently because he was angry.*

*Smoke went up from his nostrils, and a raging fire came out of his mouth. Glowing coals flared up from it. He spread apart the heavens and came down with a dark cloud under his feet. He rode on one of the angels as he flew, and he soared on the wings of the wind…The foundations of the earth were laid bare at your stern warning, O Lord, at the blast of the breath from your nostrils. He reached down from high above and took hold of me. He pulled me out of the raging water.*

GW

### *Release Peals of Thunder and Hailstorms Upon the Enemy*

*Then God's temple in heaven was opened, and within his temple was seen the ark of his covenant. And there came flashes of lightning, rumblings, peals of thunder, an earthquake and a severe hailstorm.*

REVELATION 11:19, NIV

Peals of thunder and hailstorms here are symbolic of God's anger and fury. In spiritual warfare, I believe that you can disrupt, interrupt, and unsettle any assembly and gathering of the devil and his allies by raining upon them flashes of lightning, rumblings, peals of thunder, and a severe hailstorm from God's temple, because such a gathering is an unlawful assemblage. In Isaiah 54:15, the Bible says that

"Indeed they shall surely assemble, but not because of [the Lord]. Whoever assembles against you shall fall for your sake."

My belief is borne out by the fact that in Ezekiel 13:13, God releases his fury on the false prophets who mislead his people. The passage says, "Therefore this is what the sovereign Lord says: 'In my wrath I will unleash a violent wind, and in my anger hailstones and torrents of rain will fall with destructive fury'" (NIV). So you *can* stop that coven from meeting in your neighborhood! A note of caution however: don't use this against human beings, because, as we have seen elsewhere in this book, in this warfare, we do not fight against flesh and blood!

## PLUNDER HIS KINGDOM, SET SOULS FREE

*You know that God anointed Jesus from Nazareth with the Holy Spirit and with power. Jesus went everywhere and did good things, such as healing everyone who was under the devil's power. Jesus did these things because God was with him.*

ACTS 10: 38, GW

Whenever the Enemy got nasty during Jesus's earthly ministry, Jesus went out to plunder the Enemy's kingdom. For instance, in Matthew 14:1–28, when Jesus heard that John the Baptist had been beheaded by King Herod, he withdrew to be alone. He then healed the sick, fed five thousand men, walked on water, and healed more people!

In like manner, in Acts 5:40–42, the early apostles were flogged on the orders of the Jewish Council for preaching the gospel, after which they were told never again to speak in the name of Jesus. However, the apostles left the council meeting rejoicing that God had counted them worthy to suffer disgrace for the name of Jesus. Afterwards, they continued to teach and preach this message, "Jesus is the Messiah," every day in the temple and from house to house.

In the course of working with my editor on the manuscript for this book, I had a nasty attack from the devil. In reality, I had already sensed that the Enemy might want to attack since I am essentially unmasking him and his devices! Because of this, I was in the habit of backing up my work from my memory stick to the hard drive of my laptop computer.

You can therefore imagine my indignation on the morning of Sunday, August 14, 2011, when I lost my sermon for the church service as well as everything else on my memory stick, including about eight hours' work on my manuscript which I had not backed up. The last time I had backed up the manuscript was on Wednesday, August 10!

As a way of dealing with this attack of the Enemy, I decided to preach without my notes. Not only that, I made an altar call at the end of the message. The feedback I received afterwards was that it was a very powerful sermon. In addition, during the service and afterwards, I launched wave after wave of attack, in the place of prayer, against the devil and his evil schemes. I also started working on the manuscript immediately after I got back from the church service.

In the same way, whenever the devil shows any sign of disobedience to you, go and preach the gospel, lead people to Christ, heal the sick, feed the hungry, pray all night. Do the work of the ministry.

### SEND HIM TO THE WATERLESS PLACES IN THE NAME OF JESUS

*When an unclean spirit goes out of a man, he goes through dry places, seeking rest, and finds none.*

MATTHEW 12:43

To send the devil or any of his foul spirits to the "waterless places" is to drive them from their hideouts and make them homeless. The imagery is brilliantly depicted by *The Message* in Psalm 18:45, where we are told, "The foreign devils gave up; they came on their bellies, crawling from their hideouts." In the name of the Lord Jesus Christ, you can forcefully evict demonic spirits from anywhere which they consider to be their place of abode or domicile.

The demonic "apartment" may be a human being: Luke 11:24 tells us that "when an unclean spirit goes *out of a man,* he goes through dry places, seeking rest; and finding none, he says, "I will return unto *my house* from which I came." The home may be an animal: in Mark 5:12, we see demons begging the Lord to "send us to the pigs so we can live in them" (MSG). The house may even be a city, country, or region: in Revelation 18:2, we hear a loud voice, saying, "Babylon the great is fallen, is fallen, and has become a dwelling place of demons, a prison for every foul spirit, and a cage for every unclean and hated bird."

Demonic spirits detest the dry or waterless places. They would do anything to avoid going there, because they cannot find rest there. Where a demon spirit has been disobedient, one punishment that will really hurt it is to banish it to the waterless places by making it perpetually homeless. Albert Barnes explains:

> He walketh through dry places—That is, through deserts—regions of country unwatered, sandy, barren, desolate. That our Savior here speaks according to the ancient belief of the Jews that evil spirits had their abodes in those desolate, uninhabited regions, there can be no doubt; nor can there be any doubt that the Bible gives countenance to the opinion. Thus Revelation 18:2; "Babylon—is become the habitation of "devils" and the hold of "every foul spirit"; that is, has become "desolate"—a place where evil spirits appropriately dwell.[3]

## PERSIST IN PRAYER

> *Jesus told them a story showing that it was necessary for them to pray consistently and never quit.*

LUKE 18:1, MSG

Perseverance in prayer is a virtue which every child of God needs while on this side of eternity. In this ferocious warfare against the devil, you cannot afford not to carry through whatever you start. Nor can you think of looking back. You have to continue. You have to keep on keeping on! Nowhere is this more important than in the place of prayer. God expects you to persist.

To underscore this important spiritual principle, Jesus told his disciples a parable:

> *He said, "There was once a judge in some city who never gave God a thought and cared nothing for people. A widow in that city kept after him: 'My rights are being violated. Protect me!'*
>
> *"He never gave her the time of day. But after this went on and on he said to himself, 'I care nothing what God thinks, even less what people think. But because this widow won't quit badgering me, I'd better do something and see that she gets justice—otherwise I'm going to end up beaten black-and-blue by her pounding.'"*
>
> *Then the Master said, "Do you hear what that judge, corrupt as he is, is saying? So what makes you think God won't step in and work justice for his*

*chosen people, who continue to cry out for help? Won't he stick up for them? I*
*assure you, he will. He will not drag his feet."*

LUKE 18:2–8, MSG

It is also sometimes the case that, like he did to Daniel, the Enemy attempts
to withstand the answers to your prayers. If you feel that the Enemy is delaying
the answer to your prayer, just keep on praying. Don't give up! Delay is not
denial. The darkest hour of the night is just one hour before dawn. So hang in
there. Pray all manner of prayers. Pray in the Spirit. You must keep on praying
and praising until you see the physical manifestation of the answer to your
prayers.

## CALL HIS BLUFF: SHOW HIM THAT YOU ARE PREPARED TO DIE FOR WHAT YOU BELIEVE

*Shadrach, Meshach, and Abednego replied, "O Nebuchadnezzar, we do not*
*need to defend ourselves before you. If we are thrown into the blazing furnace,*
*the God whom we serve is able to save us. He will rescue us from your power,*
*Your Majesty.* But even if he doesn't, *we want to make it clear to you, Your*
Majesty, that we will never serve your gods or worship the gold statute
you have set up."

DANIEL 3:16–18, NLT, EMPHASIS SUPPLIED

The Enemy sometimes thinks that people are scared of death and that they
would rather deny God than die. Death is, of course, quite scary! *Everybody*
*Wants to Go to Heaven, but Nobody Wants to Die* is the title of a popular book.[4]
However, Jesus conquered death on the cross of Calvary, and as a result, death
has lost its sting. For the child of God, physical death is now but a passage
through which we go to eternal glory.

*And they have defeated him by the blood of the Lamb and by their testimony.*
*And they did not love their lives so much that they were afraid to die.*

REVELATION 12:11, NLT

When the Enemy pushes you into a tight spot, you need to call his bluff.
Let him hear your testimony. Tell him how God delivered you in the past, and

proclaim that he will deliver you again and again and again. Tell him that even if God does *not* deliver you, you still will not give in to him. Let him know in no unmistakable terms that you are prepared to die for your cause. Daniel was thrown into the lion's den; he survived. Joseph was thrown into prison; he came out victorious. Paul was stoned, beaten, and maligned; he emerged one of the strongest and most effective Christian witnesses this world has ever seen. Jesus was killed—and he rose from the dead on the third day.

## SPREAD YOUR SEED UPON THE WATERS

*Send out your bread upon the waters, for after* many days *you will get it back*

ECCLESIASTES 11:1, NRSV, EMPHASIS SUPPLIED

James 1:17 tells us that God is the source of every good and perfect gift. Everything you are, everything you have, and everything you own comes from God. And everything God gives you comes with a spiritual principle attached: each time you receive anything from God, you take delivery of both *seed* and *bread.* You eat your bread and sow your seed. Without sowing, you cannot reap a harvest. If you eat your seed and plant your bread, you will not receive, because bread does not germinate. Only seed does. It is your responsibility to determine what *seed* is and to differentiate it from bread. As a good rule of thumb, about ten percent of your income constitutes *seed.* This is over and above the tithe.

You sow your seed by giving to God's work, giving to charitable causes, giving to the poor and needy, saving, and investing. When you sow your seed, you "cast your bread upon the waters," and after many days, it will come back to you in multiples (Ecclesiastes 11:1). This is a spiritual principle.

The phrase "many days" as used by Solomon may mean different things to different people. In Genesis 26:1–12, Isaac sowed in a foreign land at a time when there was famine, and he reaped a hundredfold in the same year. On the other hand, Joseph put aside food for seven years before he saw it save lives in the eighth (Genesis 41:53–57). For some people the reaping may be in a day or a week. For others, it may be several days or many weeks. For another group of people, "many days" could be a month, a number of months, a year, a few years, or even more! Each individual case is different. However, you can be sure that no matter how long it may seem to take, in due season you *shall* reap, because the Bible says in Genesis 8:22 that as long as the earth remains, seedtime and harvest will not cease.

## FOOD FOR REFLECTION

- Who is in control of your life: you or Jesus?
- What is obedience?
- What have you found to be the most effective remedy for dealing with Satan's disobedience?
- What is the most effective way of carrying out self-examination?
- What is the longest period you have spent in persistent prayer?
- Do you consider yourself to be somebody who can rightly handle the Word of truth?
- How do you see death?
- What is the difference between bread and seed?
- How and where should we sow our seed?

## PRAYER FEATURES

- Teach me, Lord, to regularly examine myself to see if I still am in the faith.
- Lord, teach me to submit myself to you in all things.
- Lord, give me the grace to withstand and oppose the Enemy.
- Lord, give me a fresh desire for the Word of God.
- As I study your Word, reveal yourself to me. Speak to me through the pages of your Word.
- Help me to be skillful in handling the Word of truth.
- Lord, help me never to lose sight of the fact that without you, I am nothing.
- Lord, help me to depend on you in all things.
- Lord, please help me to distinguish between my seed and my bread.
- Lord, I turn over the reins of my heart to you. Be my Lord indeed.

## ACTION POINTS

- Take a moment to reflect on your life. Are you standing firm in the faith? If Jesus were to come through the clouds this minute, what would he say to you? Will it be "Well done, you good and faithful steward," or will it be "I do not know you, go away from me, you who do evil things" (Matthew 25:23)?
- If you don't already have one, set out a Bible study plan that will ensure that you regularly study and meditate upon God's Word.

- Take a moment to consider your regular income, whether it is by way of a salary, partnership drawings, dividends, fees, or interest on investments. Now, work out what is seed and what is bread. Determine where and how to sow your seed.

- In addition to the three reasons given in this chapter, try to come up with additional reasons why you think the Enemy withstands and opposes Christians. Make a note of them in your journal.

Chapter Eleven

# WALK THE TALK

—⟨∾∾⟩—

*The former treatise have I made, O Theophilus, of all that Jesus began*
*both to do and teach.*

THE ACTS OF THE APOSTLES 1:1, KJV

I have found that one of the most taxing things in life is for my life to be a mirror
image of my messages. To do what you expect of others is a real test of character!
When you don't practice what you preach, you are merely preaching at others.
The real challenge is making your lifestyle an epistle, an open letter of your opinions
and convictions. This is particularly germane in spiritual warfare.

The truth of the matter is that *talking* the talk is easy. You just talk! To
talk the talk is to express your personal opinion; you talk about the things you
have learned. You simply speak about what you believe, and that's it. As far as
you are concerned, your personal life is not relevant to your message. Your
lifestyle does not mirror your message. You adopt the philosophy of modern-
day politicians in the Western world who now think that they can separate
their private lives from their public lives. Your slogan becomes, "Do as I say
and not as I do."

But what about *walking* the talk? What does this mean? In the context of this
discourse, the *talk* signifies the Christian message. This is the good news of the
atonement, salvation, deliverance, and redemption. Salvation involves redemption
from sin as well as emancipation from the *Adamic curse.* It entails accepting the
death and resurrection of Jesus Christ and having a personal relationship with God.
It means becoming a new creation in Jesus Christ and, as a consequence of the
atonement, being able to enjoy life in all its fullness to overflowing. This is life in
abundance, which only comes through faith in Jesus. The *walk* connotes living
your life to please Jesus—not only being in right standing with God in a theological

sense, but also being in right living with him. To *walk* the *talk* is to walk worthy of your calling.

Jesus lived out every one of his teachings. He did everything he taught. His life was a reflection of his message. In other words, Jesus *walked* the *talk*. And so when Satan, the god of this world, came to Jesus, Satan could not find anything of his in him.

To be an effective warrior in spiritual warfare, you *must* walk the talk. What you do in your private moments is as important as what you do in public. Your lifestyle is critical. Your character is crucial. Character is what you get up to in private. It is what you do when the door is shut and the drapes are drawn. It is what you put into practice when you are not in church. Character is what you do when you are alone by yourself and there is nobody watching.

The apostle Paul put it succinctly and eloquently when he told the Corinthians, "Imitate me, just as I also imitate Christ" (1 Corinthians 11:1). How many people can make the same statement today? Can you ask your children to emulate you as you try to be like the Lord? What a challenge!

How do we walk the talk?

## PRACTICE WHAT YOU PREACH

Be an example. Be a *doer* of the word you speak, preach, and teach. Let your life be a reflection and a mirror image *not only* of your sermons, your public views, and your stated opinions, but also of what you expect of others. It is very easy to preach at others. It is more difficult to put those things into practice yourself. Remember that when you point a finger at somebody else, the remaining four fingers actually point back at you!

## LIVE THE WORD

As a Christian, your life should be an epistle (2 Corinthians 3:2–3). You are a letter to the world, penned by God and read by men. There are people who do not go to church, but who know how Christians should live, how they ought to behave, and how they are to comport themselves. They read your life with much more than a passing interest.

What message does your lifestyle communicate about Jesus to such people? Are they so impressed that they want to become like you and know your Jesus, or does your lifestyle put them off God?

## ARISE AND SHINE

You ought to let your light shine. In fact, in Isaiah 60:1, we are *commanded* to "Arise, shine" because our light has come. You have some part to play, because the word *arise* is a verb, an action word, and it means to get up, to come up, to stand up, and to rise. The time has come for people to see the greatness of God that lies hidden on the inside of you! You should let them see all the good stuff that is bottled up within you. The world should be a better place because of each one of us. Enough of hiding your light under a bushel! The whole of creation has been waiting for this time. This is your moment. You were created for this hour. Let that light shine forth, and let God receive all the glory!

## LISTEN FOR GOD

Faith comes by hearing the Word of God (Romans 10:17). It does not come by just *reading* the Word. As you study the Scriptures, God will speak to you. As we said in chapter 3 when looking at the sword of the Spirit, in your time of study, you might find a passage leaping at you or burning within your spirit. When that happens, that is a direct word from God for you.

Make no mistake about it: it is what you receive from God that builds your faith, *not just what you read.* Remember that in Matthew 4:4, Jesus said that man does not live by bread alone, but by every word that proceeds from the mouth of the Lord. It is the revelation *on* the written Word, that is, a specific *rhema,* that brings salvation, deliverance, breakthrough, healing, abundance, and transformation. It is this revelation that brings life.

Like CNN, BBC News 24, and any other twenty-four-hour television or radio station, God is sending out messages all the time. He is always speaking to his children. Unfortunately, many people do not hear God because they are too busy or so engrossed with their daily pursuits that they are unable to be quiet and still in the presence of God. As a born-again child of God, you are expected to listen. God expects you to hear him, to recognize his voice, and to do his bidding.

*After he has brought out all his sheep, he walks ahead of them. The sheep follow him because they recognize his voice. They won't follow a stranger. Instead, they will run away from a stranger because they don't recognize his voice.*

JOHN 10:4–5, GW

How does God speak? God speaks in various ways to us today: by means of the still small voice, through the Scriptures, by way of the inward witness of the Holy Spirit, by means of an impression on your spirit man, through the outworking of circumstances, or even through dreams, visions, and trances. However, whichever way God speaks to you, what he says cannot be in conflict with the Bible. God's written Word is the supreme and ultimate judge (Psalm 119:89). This is why it is necessary for you to know the Word and discern the spirits.

As a child of God, you can develop your ability to hear God. This happens as you seek his guidance, make an effort to listen for his voice, and obey him. Let me ask you, when was the last time you heard God? The tragedy of life is that many Christians do not hear God, and instead they hear the devil.

## BE THE BEST YOU CAN BE

Each one of us is unique: matchless, distinctive, special, and out of the ordinary. This is true notwithstanding what we may have been told about the circumstances of our conception and birth. Whether you believe it or not, *you as a person* are a stunning and spectacular success of creation, a magnificent work of art. God created you with the intention that the world should be better off because of you. And as a child of God, everything you need to fulfill your purpose was given to you at salvation.

To be effective in spiritual warfare and in the Christian life, you first need to discover who you are: you need to *uncover* the real you. Thereafter, you must work hard to attain, fulfill, realize, and release your full potential. You need to go all-out to do away with any and every form of mediocrity and set out to be excellent in all things. Break free from every satanic constraint, restraint, constriction, restriction, and limitation over your life. In Isaiah 10:27, the Bible says that "It shall come to pass in that day, [that] his burden shall be taken away from off thy shoulder, and his yoke from off thy neck; and the yoke shall be destroyed because of the anointing" (DBT). Today is that day! Break loose in the name of Jesus!

## HOPE: HOLD ON, PRAY EXPECTANTLY

In dealing with God, learn to be expectant. Expect the miraculous on a daily basis. When you pray, let your heart yearn for God with desire, expectation, and hope. Never quit or surrender, even if there appears to be a delay. Your vision is too precious to give up on! To surrender is to crucify Jesus afresh and humiliate him (Hebrews 6:6). You must hold on to God's Word and not give in. Never capitulate. To throw in the towel is to give the Enemy an advantage. You must persevere until you see the result. Your breakthrough is around the corner. Let Jesus be your example. He did not give up. He saw through the pain and the agony and the problems and the difficulties and the challenges on the road to Calvary. He is our example. He held on. So should you!

## WALK IN THE SPIRIT

In our life experiences, the Holy Spirit should normally guide the Christian. As a matter of fact, it is those who are led by the Spirit of God who are in reality the children of God (Romans 8:14). To be led by the Spirit is to walk in the Spirit. To walk in the Spirit is to be open to the guidance, direction, and supervision of the Holy Ghost in everything, on a daily basis, and to follow that direction when it comes. There is always the temptation to call upon on your experience or expertise; however, when you walk in the Spirit, you cannot depend on self; you must rely entirely and absolutely and wholly and unreservedly and wholeheartedly and unconditionally upon the Holy Spirit. When you walk in the Spirit, your spirit is in tune with the Holy Spirit, and it therefore becomes impossible for you to yield to the fleshly desires of your physical body (Galatians 5:16).

## ADD VALUE

As a child of God you can add value and worth to almost anything. To add value in the context of spiritual warfare is to bring your lifestyle of righteousness to bear on your surroundings, and in particular on:

- Your church
- Your home
- Your relationships
- Your business
- Your neighborhood

Your basic faith is the fundamental foundation of your spiritual life, which God has laid and upon which you need to build. Whatever you build on this foundation will be tested by fire when you stand before God in judgment, so you must be careful what materials you use to put up your structures upon it (1 Corinthians 3:10–15).

In 2 Peter 1:5–11, the Scriptures call on you to add to your basic faith good character, and to your good character you will most certainly need to append spiritual understanding. To spiritual understanding you will need to add alert discipline; to alert discipline, you will need to add a bit of passionate patience; to your passionate patience, some reverent wonder would be a welcome addition. God expects you to spice up your reverent wonder with a lot of warm friendliness; and to warm friendliness please add a sprinkling of generous love. (I'm indebted to Eugene Peterson's *The Message* for the memorable wording here!) This goes beyond your own character to the world around you. You can add value to your local church and make it more radiant, more relevant to the community, and more effective in its ministry. You can add worth to your home and make it a sanctuary, a safe haven, and a heaven on earth. You can enrich, enhance, and spice up a relationship you are in—perhaps by being less critical of the other person and displaying the God kind of love that is unselfish and unconditional. In the same way, you can also add value to a business and make the business more cost-effective and profitable. As a member of God's kingdom, you have the capacity and capability to add value and worth to the neighborhood where you live, no matter how notorious it may be, and to transform that neighborhood into a safer and better place to live.

To add value is to let the life of God blossom through you. As a child of God, you should bloom wherever you are planted. You do this as you let your light shine wherever you are located (Matthew 5:16). As your light shines, darkness is expelled, because the Bible says in John 1:5 that "The light shines in the dark, and the dark has never extinguished it" (GW). Letting Christ live through you, wherever you are, is the ultimate victory over the Evil One in this battle, because, as the Bible tells us in Proverbs 14:34, "Righteousness exalts a nation, but sin is a reproach to any people."

## FOOD FOR REFLECTION

- How do you walk the talk?
- Can you ask people to imitate you even as you imitate Christ?
- What is the difference between *walking* the talk and *talking* the walk?
- How do you avoid mediocrity?

- How would you define hope?
- How can you add value to your local church and make it more relevant to the local community?

## PRAYER FEATURES

- Lord, I receive the grace to be a doer of your Word and not just a hearer who is only deceiving myself.
- Lord, help me to talk the walk and to walk the talk.
- Lord, help me to be the best that I can possibly be.
- Lord, help me to add value and worth to my local church, my home, my relationships, and my neighborhood.
- Lord, help me to blossom where I am planted.
- Lord, I prophesy and proclaim that I am the head and not the tail (Deuteronomy 28:13)!
- Lord, I receive the grace not to give up and abort my vision.
- Lord, I reject the spirit of never completing.
- Lord, I receive staying power!

## ACTION POINTS

- Identify the areas of your life where you have been tempted to give up in the last six months. Make a list of them, and for each one, try to identify the reason(s) why you wanted to give in. Prophesy to yourself that you will not give up, and ask the Lord to give you staying power for each one.
- Determine to take an interest in the affairs of your neighborhood. Is there a group or committee which has oversight over the affairs of the area? If so, take an interest in the group or committee, and if possible, attend their meetings.
- If there is none, prayerfully consider setting one up. Ask God to open your eyes to see ways and means by which you can enrich the neighborhood and make it a better and safer place to live in.

Epilogue

# I HEAR THE SOUND OF ABUNDANCE

———⟿———

*Then Elijah said to Ahab, 'Go up, eat and drink; for*
*there is the sound of abundance of rain.'*

1 KINGS 18:41

As I conclude this book, a devastating downturn is being experienced in the economies of the world. The prophets of gloom and doom are having a field day. The news headlines are screaming "Recession," "Economic Crunch," "Economic Downturn," and "Housing Market Crash." Companies are laying off their employees in the thousands. The housing market is in turmoil. The cost of living is escalating. In many countries, mortgage lending is at its lowest in a decade. Around the world, property repossessions and foreclosures have reached record levels. Airlines are complaining of excessive fuel costs and threatening to pass all additional costs on to their passengers. Interest rates are at their lowest since records began.

The news is not good—and it's not limited to the United Kingdom. The economic crisis we're now seeing is a worldwide phenomenon. In point of fact, it started in the United States in 2006 with the subprime mortgage crisis. During 2007, nearly 1.3 million United States housing properties were subject to foreclosure activity, up 79 percent from 2006. This led to plunging property prices, a slowdown in the U.S. economy, and billions in losses by banks. In the wake of the crisis, the Wall Street bank Bear Stearns collapsed spectacularly when other banks lost confidence in the value of its investments in sub-prime mortgages. Bear Stearns, with fifteen thousand employees and assets of $385 billion in early 2007, was bought by J.P. Morgan Chase in March 2008 for a mere $240 million. How are the mighty fallen!

The credit crunch is destabilizing the world economy and has plunged many countries into recession. The Greek, Irish, Italian, and Spanish economies have recently been bailed out from the brink of collapse by other European countries. There have been riots in several countries, most notably Haiti, because of the hike in the price of basic foodstuff, and Greece, because of the austerity measures introduced by the government to stop the country from going bankrupt. In fact, the UN Food and Agriculture Organization (FAO) organized a World Food Summit in its headquarters in Rome in June 2008.

According to the FAO, this summit offered a unique opportunity for world leaders to adopt the policies, strategies, and programs that are required to overcome the new challenges to world food security. "We hope that world leaders coming to Rome will agree on the urgent measures that are required to boost agricultural production, especially in the most affected countries," FAO director-general Jacques Diouf said in a statement. He added, "At the same time [the measures should] protect the poor from being adversely affected by high food prices."[1]

In America, people are beginning to see previously unthinkable increases in the price of gasoline. It has been reported that with the price of gas approaching $4 a gallon, more commuters are abandoning their cars and taking the train or bus. Mass transit systems around the country are seeing standing-room-only crowds on bus lines where seats were once easy to come by. Parking lots at many bus and light rail stations are suddenly overflowing with automobiles.

According to the *Sunday Herald,*

> It is the new face of hunger. A perfect storm of food scarcity, global warming, rocketing oil prices and the world population explosion is plunging humanity into the biggest crisis of the 21st century by pushing up food prices and spreading hunger and poverty from rural areas into cities.
>
> Millions more of the world's most vulnerable people are facing starvation as food shortages loom and crop prices spiral ever upwards. And for the first time in history, say experts, the impact is spreading from the developing to the developed world…
>
> More than 73 million people in 78 countries that depend on food handouts from the United Nations World Food Program (WFP) are facing reduced rations this year. The increasing scarcity of food is the biggest crisis looming for the world, according to WFP officials. At the same time,

the UN Food and Agriculture Organization has warned that rising prices have triggered a food crisis in 36 countries, all of which will need extra help.[2]

What should the Christian response be to such widespread crisis? There is a sense in which I feel that history is beginning to repeat itself *again*. Life works in cycles. Like the Bible says in Ecclesiastes 1:9, there is nothing new under the sun. Whatever you are going through today as an individual has most certainly happened to somebody else in the past. And it will definitely happen to another person in the future. That is just the way life is. In addition, you need to be aware that you are merely *going through,* or *passing through,* these challenges and difficulties. If you persevere, if you do not give up or give in, you will eventually pass through and come out on the other side!

One of the greatest lessons of history is that history *keeps on* repeating itself. The tragedy of history and of life, however, is that nobody seems to learn anything from the lessons of history. Certainly not our political leaders! For instance, how many countries, companies, families, or even individuals were prepared for the current economic squeeze? It appears that we have all lived as though the good times would never end! Many of us have not even bothered to put a little away in savings for a rainy day.

Israel faced a similar situation in the time of Elijah, the Old Testament prophet, when Ahab was king and Jezebel his queen. It was a period of pessimism, hopelessness, economic depression, and national crisis. There was no rain or dew in the whole country for three and half years because Elijah had prayed that there should be no rain. For a country whose economic mainstay was agriculture, the effect can only be imagined. The farms did not yield anything. Livestock died in droves. People could barely feed themselves. Until Elijah prayed for the rain to begin again, the nation faced an acute shortage of essentials.

In the midst of the current economic catastrophe and financial upheaval, I hear in my spirit the sound of the abundance of rain. I see God providing for those of his children who will totally rely on him. I see him meeting their every need. I see him empowering those who seek first the kingdom of God and his righteousness with the ability to acquire wealth. God is the source and ultimate provider of every good and perfect gift (James 1:17). He owns the silver and the gold (Haggai 2:8). The cattle on a thousand hills are his also (Psalm 50:10). He is able to provide regardless of what the economic forecast says. He can supply all we need according to his riches in glory through Jesus Christ (Philippians 4:19). I ask you the same question that the Lord asked both Abraham and Jeremiah the prophet: "Is there anything too hard for the Lord to do?" (Genesis 18:14; Jeremiah 32:26–27).

The question is really a rhetorical one, because of a certainty, there is nothing too difficult for him to do. With God, nothing will be impossible (Luke 1:37).

## BUT WHY WOULD GOD PROVIDE FOR YOU?

Why would God provide for you? What makes you so special, so important, and so exceptional that God would make supernatural and miraculous provision for *you* in the current economic conditions? Indeed, why would God supply your needs in *any* economic climate?

I can think of at least nine different reasons, all based in Scripture, why God would *always* meet your *every* need:

### 1. YOU ARE A CHILD OF GOD

If you are born again, then you are God's child. You are born of God. The divine seed dwells within you. He has redeemed you, you are called by his name, and he takes delight in you.

> *Can a woman forget her nursing child,*
> *And not have compassion on the son of her womb?*
> *Surely they may forget,*
> *Yet I will not forget you.*
> *See, I have inscribed you on the palms of My hands;*
> *Your walls are continually before Me.*
>
> ISAIAH 49:15–16

In much the same way that earthly parents look after their children and provide for them, God looks out for you and will provide for you. Hebrews 4:15 tells us that in Jesus "we do not have a high priest who is unable to empathize with our weaknesses, but we have one who has been tempted in every way, just as we are—yet he did not sin" (NIV). And so he understands what we are going through. He understands when we are hungry, when we cry, when we are in need.

## 2. HE HAS PROMISED, AND HE WILL NEVER FAIL

God is dependable, reliable and trustworthy. You can rely on him. Numbers 23:19 tells us that God is not a man that he should tell lies. If he has promised, he will do it.

*The Lord is my shepherd. I am never in need.*

PSALM 23:1, GW

From time to time, we may need to remind God of his promises—not because he forgets, but because that is just the way it is sometimes. Remind him of his promises. He watches over his words to ensure that they come to pass. So hold on to his Word and the promises he has made to you.

## 3. HE HAS DONE IT IN THE PAST

Our God is the great provider. Jesus Christ is the same through all eternity (Hebrews 13:8). He is unchanging. Whatever he has done in the past, he can do for you. With him there is no favoritism, there is no preferential treatment, there is no partiality, there is no nepotism, and there is no discrimination what-soever (Acts 10:34–35). In Christ, we all start on an equal footing. He reaches out to those who make contact with him.

*I have been young, and now am old;*
*Yet I have not seen the righteous forsaken,*
*Nor his descendants begging bread.*

PSALM 37:25

David's testimony is that throughout his life, he has never seen a righteous person forsaken by God, nor their children begging for food. That is why God is called Jehovah *Jireh,* "God my provider." This powerful testimony of divine provision can be a reality in your life if you are a born-again child of God. God is able to meet not only your needs, but also those of your offspring after you. He did it in the time of King David, and he can do it again.

## 4. You Are a Joint Heir of the Grace of Salvation with Jesus Christ

In Christ Jesus, as a born-again child of God you become God's heir, a joint heir with Jesus (Romans 8:17). God will not withhold any good thing from you, seeing that you are a co-heir of the blessings of the Lord.

> *What then shall we say to these things? If God is for us, who can be against us? He who did not spare His own Son, but delivered Him up for us all, how shall He not with Him also freely give us all things?*
>
> ROMANS 8:31–32

Think about it: having given Jesus for you, why would God withhold any good thing from you? All the resources and storehouses of heaven are within your grasp and are at your disposal. All you need do is appropriate and receive them to yourself.

## 5. You Are the Apple of His Eye

You are the apple of God's eye. But what does it mean to be the apple of somebody's eye? In its literal meaning, the "apple of the eye" is the middle aperture of the eye. Figuratively, the apple of one's eye is usually someone whom we value, cherish, esteem, take pleasure in, and treasure more than anybody else. God loves you, and he treasures, esteems, and values you above everything else that he created. Because of that, he will provide for you and meet your needs.

> *For thus saith the Lord of hosts; After the glory hath he sent me unto the nations which spoiled you: for he that toucheth you toucheth the apple of his eye.*
>
> ZECHARIAH 2:8, KJV

## 6. His Thoughts Toward You Are of Good, Not of Evil

God actually thinks about you! Can you imagine that? He is not too busy to be concerned about you. You occupy his thoughts. To put this in focus, let us see what God told the prophet Jeremiah about you and me through the eyes of four very different translations of the Bible:

> *For I know the thoughts that I think toward you, saith the Lord, thoughts of peace, and not of evil, to give you an expected end.*
>
> JEREMIAH 29:11, KJV

> *I know what I'm doing. I have it all planned out—plans to take care of you, not abandon you, plans to give you the future you hope for.*
>
> JEREMIAH 29:11, MSG

> *"For I know the plans I have for you," says the Lord. "They are plans for good and not for disaster, to give you a future and a hope."*
>
> JEREMIAH 29:11, NLT

> *I know the plans that I have for you, declares the Lord. They are plans for peace and not disaster, plans to give you a future filled with hope.*
>
> JEREMIAH 29:11, GW

Not only does God think about you, he actually has good, excellent, and delightful plans concerning you! His thoughts and desire concerning you are for a future filled with his peace, his provision, and his hope. If he thinks about you, then there is no reason why he will not provide for you!

## 7. HE CARES ABOUT YOU

Not only does God cherish and treasure you above all else, he actually cares for you. He is interested in your welfare. He looks out for you. When you go through trials and tribulations, he understands and empathizes with you.

> *Casting all your anxiety upon Him, because He cares for you.*
>
> 1 PETER 5:7, NASB

*I look up to the mountains; does my strength come from mountains? No, my strength comes from God, who made heaven, and earth, and mountains.*

PSALM 121:1–2, MSG

The Bible tells us in Romans 8:34 that Jesus Christ is at God the Father's right hand, interceding and praying for you. And because he cares for you, he is willing and able to provide for you and meet all your needs, no matter the state of the economy in the country where you live. Although you look up to the mountains, in reality your help, your sustenance, your protection, and your provision come *not* from the mountain, not from your job, not from your business, not from your savings, not from your investments, not from man, not from the economy, but from the Most High God.

## 8. HE LOOKS AFTER THE FLOWERS AND THE BIRDS

Let us take a moment to consider the flowers of the field as Jesus urged us to do in Matthew 6:28–30. God takes care of them and clothes them in beautiful colors. They don't spin thread to make clothing, yet as Jesus said, not even King Solomon in all his glory was ever dressed like one of them. They appear today, but the day after, they are either scorched by the sun or picked by man and eventually thrown away. What of the birds of the air? They neither plant nor do they reap; they are always fed and taken care of by God—and this is notwithstanding the fact that most of them have little or no value in man's eyes. If God cares for the flowers of the field which appear today and are shortly destroyed, as well as for the birds of the air which are worth little or nothing, why will he not care for you, who are made in his image and have been redeemed by him? He will do much more for you!

## 9. HE DELIGHTS IN YOUR PROSPERITY

The road to Calvary was arduous. Our Lord Jesus Christ didn't have to die. However, Jesus shed his precious blood to pay the ransom for your soul and my soul and to win our true prosperity in all things.

*Beloved, I pray that you may prosper in all things and be in health, just as your soul prospers.*

3 JOHN 1:2

Jesus went through all that pain, torture, anguish, and agony so he could redeem you back to God. For that reason, *you* are the fruit of his death and resurrection. Therefore, he wants you to prosper, to flourish, to thrive, to do well, and to get on in all things—to be in good health even as your soul prospers. The Bible tells us in Isaiah 53:11 that "He shall see of [the fruit of] the travail of his soul, [and] shall be satisfied: by his knowledge shall my righteous servant instruct many in righteousness; and he shall bear their iniquities" (DBT). Without a shadow of doubt, he will provide for you.

Why would God care so much about the fruit of his work? Because scarcity and want signify the following:

- *Unfruitfulness.* Mediocrity in any area of one's life is symptomatic of barrenness. It may be in your spiritual life, where God has called you to bear two types of fruit—the fruit of the Spirit in terms of displaying Christian character and in being more and more Christlike, and the fruit of your witness in leading people to Christ. These new believers become your spiritual sons and daughters and therefore your fruit. It may be in your finances: as we have seen, poverty and lack are a manifestation of the *Adamic curse.* Barrenness in the area of the fruit of the womb is not necessarily God's will for you, because he has mandated you to be fruitful and to multiply. In your career, he expects you to arise, shine, and be the very best that you can be.

- *Going round in circles.* There are people who appear to all intents and purposes to be doing well, but in reality they are just going round and round in circles. This happens when there is no iota of progress or growth or development or advancement or positive change in their lives. They have movement, but they do not make any progress. The children of Israel are a classic example. They spent forty years going through the wilderness on a journey that should have taken forty days! That equates to thirty-nine years and three-hundred-and-twenty-five days just going through the motions. This is indicative of dryness, drought, and a lack of fire. God expects you to make progress in every facet of your life, even if you are only taking little steps at a time.

- *Toil.* Toil is real hardship. This came as a result of the fall, when Adam and Eve committed treachery. It is prolonged labor; working long and hard to earn a living. It is real drudgery where you have to sweat to eke out a living. Remember that man had to till the garden of Eden and look after it even before the fall, so *God created work as a good thing.* However, *toil* is not of God. There is a very thin line between hard work created by God and toil which came as a result of man's fall. Toil is suggestive of barrenness, unfruitfulness, infertility, adversity, poverty, and hardship. God requires you to be diligent, conscientious, scrupulous, meticulous, and hardworking, but he does not expect you to toil. Jesus has redeemed you from the *Adamic curse.*

- *Every possible kind of difficulty.* Whereas some people have the Midas touch and whatever they touch turns to gold, some have the accursed touch. Anything they handle simply disintegrates! Whatever they lay their hands upon falls apart. Any path they choose invariably ends up being problematic and difficult. Doors are constantly shut against them. When this happens consistently, it is indicative of somebody who is probably operating either under a curse or under a closed heaven—or even both. If you find that the heavens appear closed to you, then you need deliverance. However, it must be pointed out that if rightly handled, *normal* problems can become raw materials for future development and growth.

## ROOTS OF LACK

How do people get into situations like the above? What leads to a lack of prosperity in the Christian life? There are several possible culprits.

### Curses

A curse is a solemn utterance intended to invoke a supernatural power to inflict harm or punishment on someone or something.[3] It is a negative word spoken by a person in a position of authority, like a parent over the life of his or her child. Curses are real. They exist and affect real people. Some people suffer hardship because of curses. When Adam and Eve sinned, they fell under the *Adamic curse.*

There are two main types of curses:

- *Generational or ancestral curses.* These are curses which run through families principally because of something an ancestor did in ages past.

There are some families where nobody lives beyond a certain age. They all die just before they reach the age of forty, or forty-five, or fifty. There are also families where every marriage falls into crisis, and they all end up in divorce. If you suspect a generational curse in your life, ask the Lord to set you free. You can base your prayer on Colossians 2:14.

- *Curses brought on oneself.* This would normally happen as a result of one's own actions. Sin and disobedience to God lead to curses. Sin creates a gulf between God and man and leads to the heavens being shut against us. The Scriptures tell us in Isaiah 59:1–2 that God's hands are not too short that he cannot save, nor are his ears too dull that he cannot hear, but our sins have made a separation between us and him. If you fall into this category, you need to repent and ask the Lord for mercy.

Generally, for a curse to perch and have effect, there must be a basis for it. This is because it is a spiritual principle that a causeless curse does not alight or take effect, no matter how potent or powerful the curse itself may be (Proverbs 26:2). Furthermore, it is difficult to place a curse upon a born-again child of God who is in right standing and right living with God. (The same cannot be said of a child of God who is living in sin, as such Christians have broken the hedge of protection over their lives.)

In Jesus, we are redeemed from the *Adamic curse*, and so curses can be broken, no matter how deeply rooted or potent. In Christ Jesus, you can be set free from the effect of any curses that may have been pronounced on you.

## DECISIONS

We are all products of decisions. Your choices dictate your present circumstances. Your circumstances determine your chances in life. To put it differently, you are where you are today because of decisions made for you by your parents or guardians when you were younger, as well as the choices you have made for yourself since becoming an adult. Your choice of schools, your choice of a career, your choice of a spouse, your decision whether or not to have children, and your choice of domicile have all contributed to a large extent into making you the person you are—they have led you to where you are at today. And where you are today dictates your prospects for the future. You are the sum of all your experiences.

You are reading this book because you decided to. Every time a decision is to be made, you are at a crossroads. You have at least two options. When you make a decision, you effectively choose one door, and the other door is automatically shut against you. You are in debt because you chose to borrow. People in the Western world are generally in financial difficulty, not necessarily because they do not earn well enough, but because of their lifestyle. Your lifestyle is a choice. You can decide to keep up with the Joneses and try to acquire the latest cars, the hottest jewelry, the most up-to-date electronic gadgets, and the clothes in fashion even if you have to borrow to buy them. If that's your decision, you will probably spend money you don't have on things you don't necessarily need to impress people you don't really like. On the other hand, you can decide to live within your means. You need to remind yourself, as Paul tells us in 1 Timothy 6:6, that godliness with contentment is great gain!

## LACK OF FORESIGHT

In Pharaoh's dream of Genesis 41, the seven years of famine and drought came *after* the seven years of abundance and prosperity. Joseph had the God-given wisdom and foresight to put away one fifth of all the crops produced in Egypt during the years of abundance and opulence. He had the foresight not to squander resources during the good years, but to save and put them aside for the rainy day (or the dry day, in this case!). He piled up huge amounts of grain in warehouses throughout the whole of Egypt. When the years of scarcity and shortage began, there was so much food in Egypt that people traveled from the neighboring countries to Egypt to buy food.

Anybody who fails to put a little aside during the good times will inevitably suffer in the days of adversity. This is just lack of foresight. We have much to learn from the ant, as Solomon advised. Tiny as it is, it puts away a bit more during the summer months and so has enough to live on during the cold months of winter.

Did you know that half the population of the United Kingdom would survive for just seventeen days if they suffered an unexpected loss of income?[4] This is because half the population have less than two months' salary tucked away in savings, and 27 percent of the population have no savings at all! Even more alarming is the fact that nearly one in three adults in the United Kingdom failed to save a penny from January to December 2006, while a further fifth said they had not saved as much as they had planned.[5]

There is also a culture of waste in the Western world that must be tackled. People waste food. People waste power. People waste fuel. People waste water. As a typical example, at a time when millions of children die of hunger and starvation, one third of all the groceries bought in the United Kingdom end up in the bin.[6] What a waste!

## SIN

As we have seen, sin is disobedience to God. Whereas righteousness exalts a nation, sin is a reproach to any group of people (Proverbs 14:34). Sin creates a barrier, obstruction, or barricade between God and human beings (Isaiah 59:1–2). Sin can also result in lack and scarcity as well as drought. This is simply because God, who cannot behold sin, will not always continue to protect you and provide for your needs when you disobey him and sin against him. A case in point is the Old Testament nation of Israel. Every time they sinned against God, God eventually stopped protecting them, and their enemies overpowered them.

## IT MAY BE PART OF YOUR DESTINY

It is not always the case that barrenness is caused by sin. For instance, we do not know a lot about Zechariah and his wife Elizabeth apart from the fact that they were the parents of John the Baptist, the precursor of Jesus. Zechariah was, of course, from the lineage of Judah, and Elizabeth was a cousin of Mary, the mother of Jesus. However, one thing we do know for sure is that they were righteous in God's eyes, careful to obey all his commandments. Notwithstanding the fact that they were holy, godly, and in right standing with God, they were barren and infertile. Their story can be found in Luke 1:5–7. In effect, you *can* be barren but blameless.

It may be the case that what you are going through is part of your cross. Passing through the fire, difficult as it may seem, may be part of God's refining strategy to burn out and destroy the dross in your life and bring out the gold in you. If your challenges are part of your cross, then you will have to bear them with quiet dignity. No amount of fasting and prayer will remove your cross from you. Crosses are to be borne. One thing you can be sure of is that God would not let you pass through the fire except he knows that it will work out for your good in the end. He told the nation of Israel that he made them go through the wilderness for forty years, he humbled them, he made them hunger, and he fed them with manna, all in order to do them good in the end (see Deuteronomy 8). So you can have confidence in his competence and compassion!

## LESSONS FROM THE OLD TESTAMENT NATION OF ISRAEL

It may surprise you, but there is a lot for us to learn from the ancient nation of Israel in this day and age. In these difficult times, when even the top-notch AAA credit rating of the United States, the most powerful nation on earth, has recently been downgraded by Standard & Poor's (one of the world's leading credit rating agencies), we can draw some parallels from the Israelites of old as recorded in the Bible. Instead of losing heart and succumbing to despair, I intend to bring out, in this section, five principles from the lives of the Israelis of old which can help you survive these challenging times.

### 1. EVEN WHEN THERE IS A PROMISE FROM GOD, WE STILL NEED TO PRAY IT INTO EXISTENCE

After three years of drought, famine, and one of the worst economic recessions in Israel, God told the prophet Elijah in 1 Kings 18:1–2 to announce to King Ahab that there would soon be rain. This was a clear message from God to Elijah. Notwithstanding the fact that Elijah heard God clearly, we are told in 1 Kings 18:41–46 that he climbed to the top of Mount Carmel, and there he bowed himself and prayed for rain with his face between his knees. He continued in prayer until his servant saw a tiny dark cloud in the sky. Even though Elijah had God's word, he had to *bring forth* the promise in the place of prayer.

God told Abraham that his offspring would go into slavery in a foreign land, and that after four hundred years he would liberate them and take them to the Promised Land, a land flowing with milk and honey. However, the Old Testament nation of Israel was in Egypt for four hundred thirty years. Why did they spend an extra thirty years in captivity and bondage? They remained in slavery until they began to pray. We are told in Exodus 2:23–24 that when the burden of slavery became too great for the Israelites, they groaned and cried out to God for help. Their cry rose up to God, who remembered his covenant with Abraham, Isaac, and Jacob and decided to send a deliverer in the person of Moses to redeem them. Although they had a promise, they had to pray it into existence; they had to *birth* the promise in the place of prayer.

In Daniel 9, we are told that Daniel understood from reading the prophesy of Jeremiah that the Israelites were to be in exile for seventy years. At this time, they had been in captivity in Babylon for seventy years. He then took it upon himself to fast, pray, and seek God. He asked God to remember his word and to carry it out. Although Daniel and the people had God's promise, they had to *make it happen* in the place of prayer.

Has God given you a word or spoken into your life? Between every promise of God and the actual performance, there ought to be prayer. If you have a promise from God that is yet to come to pass, introduce the missing link, which is prayer. Your prayer closet is the delivery suite in the hospital maternity unit where you *give birth to* and *bring forth* the promises of God.

## 2. LIKE ELIJAH, YOU MUST PERSIST IN PRAYER

Elijah persisted in prayer. In 1 Kings 18:42–44, we are told that Elijah prayed seven times. He continued in prayer until he received an answer. Seven is the number of perfection. It is God's number. In effect, Elijah prayed the mind of God; he prayed the will of God; he prayed until he received his breakthrough; he prayed in the Spirit. He prayed that there should be rain, and after three and a half years of no rain, there was rain. Earlier, he had prayed that there wouldn't be rain, and for three and half years there was no rain (1 Kings 17:1; James 5:17–18).

The interesting thing is that Elijah was a human being like you and me (James 5:17). Although a great and mighty man of God—in fact, he was one of the greatest prophets that ever lived—he was subject to the same temptations you and I are. He had the same kind of needs, desires, wishes, and interests. Let us take a look at some of his human limitations and inadequacies:

- Elijah sometimes got it wrong! Would you believe that such a mighty and great prophet would get things wrong? But he did! For instance, there was a time when he thought he was the only righteous person alive in Israel. And God had to remind him that he had reserved unto himself seven thousand people who were righteous, holy, and separated to him, and who had not bowed to the god Baal (1 Kings 19:13–18).
- Immediately after the miracle of Mount Carmel, when God showed up and the fire of the Lord fell from heaven upon Elijah's sacrifice, Eli-

jah was so scared that (wait for it) Jezebel, a woman, would kill him that he ran for his life. A man who had called down fire from heaven only a few days earlier was so scared that Jezebel would kill him that he took to his heels and ran for dear life (1 Kings 19:1–4).

So if Elijah, frail and human as he was, could prevail in prayer, so can you, because God is no respecter of persons. Acts 10:34 tells us that there is no favoritism with him. In 2 Chronicles 16:9, the Bible says that God's eyes are constantly looking throughout the entire world to find those whose hearts are right for his purpose so that he may reveal himself to them and show himself strong and powerful on their behalf.

## 3. WE NEED TO TRAVAIL TO PREVAIL

The Bible says in James 5:16 that the effectual, fervent, passionate, earnest prayer of a righteous person avails much; such a prayer has much effect. Note that there are two conditions which must first be fulfilled: fervency and righteousness. In other words, the passionate prayer of a person who is in right standing with God and in right living has much effect.

However, for your prayers to avail, you need to learn to travail in the place of prayer.

> *Who hath heard such a thing? who hath seen such things? Shall the earth be made to bring forth in one day? or shall a nation be born at once? for as soon as Zion travailed, she brought forth her children.*
>
> ISAIAH 66:8, KJV

How do we travail in prayer? It is by praying with passion, fervor, desire, expectation, and "groanings" that are too difficult to be uttered in human words. It is our birth pangs, wordless sighs, and aching groans in the place of prayer as we seek to bring forth into physical manifestation those things which God allows our spiritual eyes to see.

> *Meanwhile, the moment we get tired in the waiting, God's Spirit is right alongside helping us along. If we don't know how or what to pray, it doesn't*

*matter. He does our praying in and for us, making prayer out of our wordless sighs, our aching groans.*

ROMANS 8:26, MSG

In the garden of Gethsemane just before his betrayal and arrest, we see our Lord Jesus travailing in prayer. He was in such anguish, pain, and distress that his sweat was like blood (Luke 22:44). He travailed and prevailed. Travailing *in* prayer helps you to prevail and triumph over the Enemy.

## 4. WE MUST ASK IN FAITH

Prayer must be in faith. The Bible tells us in James 1:6–7, "But let him ask in faith, with no doubting, for he who doubts is like a wave of the sea driven and tossed by the wind. For let not that man suppose that he will receive anything from the Lord." But what is faith? Faith is the fuel that powers the engine that carries your breakthrough. Faith enables you to anticipate the result; it makes it possible for you to see the answer to your prayer even before its physical manifestation. Hebrews 11:1 tells us that faith is the evidence of things not seen.

When you pray, you must expect an answer. There must be an expectation in your heart that God will do what you have asked of him. To do otherwise is to either doubt God or be double-minded. Doubt does to faith what cancer does to the human body: it destroys and annihilates it. And double-minded people do not receive from God, because such people are unstable in all their ways (James 1:7–8).

## 5. IF YOU FIND YOURSELF IN A HOLE, STOP DIGGING

Let me give you good, honest advice: if you find yourself in a hole, please stop digging. This may sound straightforward enough; however, when in a hole, the reality is that your natural tendency will usually be to dig further. However, if you don't stop digging, you will only make your situation worse. As an example, if you are in debt, the tendency may be for you to borrow more money to pay off some debtors and consolidate some of your debts. However, this solution only takes you further into debt. You need to stop digging: do not take any additional or further borrowing, no matter how tempting it may be!

## HOPE FOR THE FUTURE

I hear the sound of abundance. With the eyes of my spirit, I see God's abundant provision for his children. God is making a demarcation and separation between his people and everybody else, much like he did in Egypt just before the Passover (Exodus 8:22–24). God is willing and able to provide for his own. What sound do you hear? What do you see? Open your heart to receive from the Most High God. Accept his divine provision today. All he asks of you is that you should be willing and obedient.

# A POEM-LORD I NEED YOU, I REALLY DO

Sweet Jesus, oh how I love your name
You are today and forever the same
I am yours, O Lord Jesus, so marvelous
My Redeemer, my Savior, you are glorious
Lord, help me in your Word to always tabernacle
Help me your Word to accord highest pinnacle
I know whatever is mine is thine
Help me know whatever is thine is mine
Your throne of grace, I approach to embrace
As I run with patience and face this race
Let your light shine right through my night
For in your sight my darkness takes flight

*Lord, I need you*
*You can see I really do*
*You are more precious than silver and gold*
*You are more valuable to me than riches untold*
*As I confront my worries and what I most fear*
*Lord, help me know you are forever here, always near!*

My King, I cannot but sing and tell the story
Of the splendor of your grandeur and glory
My Prince of Peace, your praises I cannot but raise in a chord
Adoration, exaltation, and veneration to you I accord
For you are my Savior, Redeemer, and Lord
Though you are God's eternal Word
I need you, yes Lord, I need you every hour
Manifest yourself in your magnificent power
Like a balmy, blooming, blossoming fragrant flower

*Lord, I need you*
*You can see I really do*
*You are more precious than silver and gold*

# CRUSHING THE DEVIL

*You are more valuable to me than riches untold*
*As I confront my worries and what I most fear*
*Lord, help me know you are forever here, always near!*

You make me stay in the way
In the right path away from wrath and decay
You make me talk the talk not just talk the walk
You make me walk the walk and walk the talk
Your blood like a flood, priceless, treasured, precious
So pure, such a cure makes me virtuous, righteous
Your peace never ceasing like a fountain
Flowing down from your holy mountain
At the sight of your light so bright, not by might
All my personal pride perishes in blistering blight

*Lord, I need you*
*You can see I really do*
*You are more precious than silver and gold*
*You are more valuable to me than riches untold*
*As I confront my worries and what I most fear*
*Lord, help me know you are forever here, always near!*

Lord, I proclaim and name your name
Glad you don't play the blame game
Lord, such fire in me you inspire
Such passion, such desire
Oh what fervor, such fire
Such craving about you to enquire
Such awesome power
Every hour
I sing my psalms to thee
Unto thee shall my desires be
Lord, you are to me very dear
Help me know you are near

# POEM

*Lord, I need you*
*You can see I really do*
*You are more precious than silver and gold*
*You are more valuable to me than riches untold*
*As I confront my worries and what I most fear*
*Lord, help me know you are forever here, always near!*

A bright sight, your light, neither tight nor slight
Ever so vivid, so brilliant, so bright
Dazzling, ascending, never ever ending
Such splendor springing forth and stringing
Descending upon my head you bring
Into my life healing upon your wing
My faith flaunt I, yet yield I and wield I as a shield
Against the fiery darts of the devil in the battlefield
Now shall I arise in the power of your might
And be wise and walk by the Spirit, not by sight
I will to your holy hill flow
In desire, hunger, and thirst more of you to know
Now no more unbelief
Thank God, what a relief

*Lord, I need you*
*You can see I really do*
*You are more precious than silver and gold*
*You are more valuable to me than riches untold*
*As I confront my worries and what I most fear*
*Lord, help me know you are forever here, always near!*

Jesus proclaimed and ordained by God
Appointed and anointed by God to trod
Upon Satan, the adversary, our foe
And in one go all his affliction and woe
Lord, when I gawp and gawk into your face
I see why John couldn't undo your shoelace

Because of your unmerited favor I cannot fail
You have blessed me so much I must prevail
On the throne of grace
Your grace becomes my ace
Victorious you were through the cross
The devil through the cross suffered loss
Hurray! No more satanic oppression or repression
And now an end to all human indiscretion and transgression

*Lord, I need you*
*You can see I really do*
*You are more precious than silver and gold*
*You are more valuable to me than riches untold*
*As I confront my worries and what I most fear*
*Lord, help me know you are forever here, always near!*

Jesus, you once were dead
Your blood at Calvary shed
You rose triumphant from the grave
Gave yourself voluntarily and willingly to save
All mankind who like sheep have gone astray
From you, the truth, the life, and the way
All who from grace have fallen down
Losing their authority and their crown
You stopped their agony and their anguish
Now there is no more need for man to languish
You said "It is finished," then you ascended beyond the cloud
Unto the right side of the Father in glory with a shout so loud

*Lord, I need you*
*You can see I really do*
*You are more precious than silver and gold*
*You are more valuable to me than riches untold*
*As I confront my worries and what I most fear*
*Lord, help me know you are forever here, always near!*

## POEM

Jesus, name above every name
All creation your glory proclaims
Jesus, once slain, now you reign
I need you again and again and again
Without the coat of your righteousness
I am poor, filthy, useless, and helpless
Sweet Jesus, please meet me today I pray
As I travail to prevail and avail in the way
Help me, Lord, in your awesome presence
Forever to make my residence and existence

*Lord, I need you*
*You can see I really do*
*You are more precious than silver and gold*
*You are more valuable to me than riches untold*
*As I confront my worries and what I most fear*
*Lord, help me know you are forever here, always near!*

# END NOTES

CHAPTER 1: RIGHT, CAPACITY, ABILITY

1. "Teacher leaves million dollar legacy." News report by the Alberta Teachers'
   Association which appears at:
   http://www.teachers.ab.ca/Publications/ATA%20News/Volume%2041/Num-
   ber%204/Fact%20or%20Fiction/Pages/Teacher%20leaves%20million%20do
   llar%20legacy.aspx (Accessed July 31, 2011)
2. "Meet the surprisingly rich. Does your eccentric old aunt secretly have millions?
   Stranger things have happened." Article by Les Christie, which appears at
   http://money.cnn.com/2003/07/31/pf/millionaire/surprisinglyrich/ (Accessed
   January 10, 2009)
3. "Recluse leaves £6 million to hospice." News report in *The Telegraph* which
   appears at http://www.telegraph.co.uk/news/uknews/1564361/Recluse-leaves-
   6-million-to-hospice.html (Accessed January 10, 2009)
4. "Millionaire priest dies in squalor, relatives to inherit $." News report by Tom
   Gallagher in *The National Catholic Reporter* which appears at
   http://ncronline.org/blogs/ncr-today/millionaire-priest-dies-squalor-relatives-
   inherit-0 (Accessed July 31, 2011)
5. "World's top maths genius jobless and living with mother." News report in
   *The Sunday Telegraph* (London), Sunday, August 20, 2006.
6. Strong's number 1849. *New Strong's Concise Dictionary of the Words in the Greek
   Testament.* Nashville, TN: Thomas Nelson, 1995.
7. "Lost altar masterpieces found in spare bedroom fetch £1.7m." News report
   in *The Guardian* (London), Friday, April 20, 2007. "£1.7m for £200 paintings." *Metro,* April 20, 2007.
8. "Chinese vase found in Pinner home fetches record-breaking £43 million at
   auction." News report in *The Harrow Times* which appears at http://www.har-
   rowtimes.co.uk/news/8633388.Chinese_vase_fetches_record_breaking___43
   _million_at_auction/ (Accessed December 24, 2010)
9. If you would like to invite Jesus into your heart to become your Lord and
   Savior, you will need to pray the sinner's prayer. Please say it out loud:

"Lord Jesus, I acknowledge that I am a sinner. I believe with my heart that you died for my sin and that you were raised from the dead for my justification. Your Word says in Romans 10:9 that "if you confess with your mouth the Lord Jesus and believe in your heart that God has raised Him from the dead, you will be saved." I confess with my mouth that you are my Savior and my Lord. I invite you to come into my heart and make me a new creation. Thank you, Lord Jesus, for saving me. Please write my name in your Book of Life. In Jesus's name I pray. Amen."

If you have just prayed that prayer sincerely, with all your heart, then you have now become a child of God. Congratulations! Please arrange to obtain a Bible if you don't already have one. You can start reading from John 1. In addition, kindly join the membership of a local, Bible-believing church, where your new faith can be nurtured.

CHAPTER 2: WHO ARE YOU?

1. H. Enoch. *Evolution or Creation*. London: Evangelical Press, 1976. 144.
2. Letter by Dr. Wernher von Braun. Originally published in Edward F. Blick, *Special Creation vs. Evolution*. Oklahoma City: Southwest Radio Church, 1988. 29–31.
3. "Blood Vessels. Tubular Circulation": The Franklin Institute. http://www.fi.edu/learn/heart/vessels/vessels.html (Accessed August 1, 2011)
4. "The Human Brain": The Franklin Institute. http://www.fi.edu/learn/brain/ (Accessed January 10, 2009)
5. Michael J. Behe. *Darwin's Black Box: The Biochemical Challenge to Evolution*. New York: The Free Press, 1996. 193.
6. Michael Denton. *Evolution: A Theory in Crisis*. Bethesda, MD: Adler and Adler, 1986. 69.
7. "All About Fingerprints." Article by Maria Timmins which appears at http://www.norfolk.police.uk/article.cfm?catID=671&artID=7765&bctrail=0 (Accessed January 10, 2009)
8. Excerpted from Hamlet's speech in Act II, Scene 2 of *Hamlet* by William Shakespeare. *Heinemann Advanced Shakespeare: Hamlet*. Harlow, UK: Pearson Education Limited, 1996. 97.

## END NOTES

CHAPTER 3: SPIRITUAL WARFARE

1. Strong's number 4182. *New Strong's Concise Dictionary of the Words in the Greek Testament.* Nashville, TN: Thomas Nelson, 1995.

2. Marilyn Hickey. *The Power of Prayer and Fasting: 21 Days that Can Change Your Life.* Nashville, TN: FaithWords, 2006. 4–5.


CHAPTER 4: STRATEGY IN SPIRITUAL WARFARE

1. "It All Began with a Man: A Biography of Walt Disney," article which appears at http://d23.disney.go.com/archives/it-all-began-with-a-mana-biography-of-walt-disney/ (Accessed September 6, 2011)

2. "Susan Boyle, Top Seller, Shakes Up CD Trends," article by Ben Sisario, *The New York Times,* December 2, 2009, which appears at: http://www.nytimes.com/2009/12/03/arts/music/03sales.html?scp=2&sq=susan%20boyle&st=cse(Accessed August 15, 2011)

3. "Susan Boyle celebrates after getting THREE Guinness World Records," article in *The Daily Mail* (London), September 19, 2010, which appears at http://www.dailymail.co.uk/tvshowbiz/article-1313401/Susan-Boyle-celebrates-getting-THREE-Guinness-World-Records.html (Accessed August 15, 2011)


CHAPTER 5: YOUR AUTHORITY OVER THE ENEMY

1. Strong's number 1228. *New Strong's Concise Dictionary of the Words in the Greek Testament.* Nashville, TN: Thomas Nelson, 1995.

2. Strong's number 2190. *New Strong's Concise Dictionary of the Words in the Greek Testament.* Nashville, TN: Thomas Nelson, 1995.

3. Strong's number 4190. *New Strong's Concise Dictionary of the Words in the Greek Testament.* Nashville, TN: Thomas Nelson, 1995.

4. Strong's number 894. *New Strong's Concise Dictionary of the Words in the Hebrew Bible.* Nashville, TN: Thomas Nelson, 1995.

5. Strong's number 6865. *New Strong's Concise Dictionary of the Words in the Hebrew Bible.* Nashville, TN: Thomas Nelson, 1995.

6. Strong's number 1849. *New Strong's Concise Dictionary of the Words in the Greek Testament.* Nashville, TN: Thomas Nelson, 1995.

7. *Oxford Dictionary of English.* Electronic version. Second edition. Oxford University Press, 2010

CHAPTER 6: DEMONIC SCHEMES AND METHODS

1. "The Lion's Roar: More Than Just Hot Air," an article by Jon Grinnell in *Zoogoer*, May/June 1997, which can be accessed at http://nationalzoo.si.edu/Publications/ZooGoer/1997/3/lionsroar.cfm

2. Try personalizing Psalm 91 this way:

   "I dwell in the shelter of the Most High and rest in the shadow of the Almighty. I will say of the LORD: He is my refuge and my fortress, my God, in whom I trust. Surely he will save me from the fowler's snare and from the deadly pestilence. He will cover me with his feathers, and under his wings I will find refuge; his faithfulness will be my shield and rampart. I will not fear the terror of night, nor the arrow that flies by day, nor the pestilence that stalks in the darkness, nor the plague that destroys at midday. A thousand may fall at my side, ten thousand at my right hand, but it will not come near me. I will only observe with my eyes and see the punishment of the wicked. Because I say, 'The LORD is my refuge,' and I make the Most High my dwelling, no harm will overtake me, no disaster will come near my home. For he will command his angels concerning me to guard me in all my ways; they will lift me up in their hands, so that I will not strike my foot against a stone. I will tread on the lion and the cobra; I will trample the great lion and the serpent. Because I love the LORD, he will rescue me. He will protect me, for I acknowledge his name. I will call on him, and he will answer me. He will be with me in trouble; he will deliver me and honor me. With long life he will satisfy me and show me his salvation."

3. American Psychiatric Association. *Diagnostic and Statistical Manual of Mental Disorders*, 4th ed. Washington, DC: American Psychiatric Association. 2000. 631.

4. "What are panic attacks?" Article published at www.mind.org. http://www.mind.org.uk/help/diagnoses_and_conditions/panic_attacks#What_are_panic_attacks_ (Accessed January 10, 2011)

5. Blurb at: http://www.myspace.com/leonardcohenspace (Accessed June 6, 2009)

6. Yoga is a Hindu practice. Hindu disciples will meditate on a word, phrase, or picture for hours, days, months, or even years, attempting to achieve a state of

transcendence or an internal harmony with the universe. Yoga is a tool espoused by Hindus to help with meditation: it involves meditation, chanting, postures, and breathing exercises. Hinduism is one of the key foundations of the New Age and Transcendental Meditation. Hindus believe in many gods, but Brahma is the chief god, the omnipresent one who is father of the Brahman Trinity. He has four heads, three of which can be seen from any point of view. In Hinduism, Jesus Christ is seen as a teacher, a guru, or an avatar (an incarnation of Vishnu). He is a son of God as are others. His death does nothing toward atonement for sins, and he did not rise from the dead. Salvation is the release from the cycles of reincarnation by achieving a state of transcendence or an internal harmony with the universe. This can take many lifetimes. Salvation is achieved through yoga and meditation. Repeated reincarnations may be required as a person gradually moves to higher and higher levels till he leaves the cycle. He must bring this about by his own effort. The gods may help, but there is no concept of a Supreme Being who pays the penalty of sin on behalf of the sinner. Final salvation is ultimately absorption or union with Brahman. Clearly, by partaking in yoga, you are agreeing with the notion of salvation by Hinduism and accepting their teaching that Jesus did not rise from the dead and that his death does not atone for sin!

7. *Chambers 21st Century Dictionary.* Edinburgh, UK: Larousse, 1996.
8. Richard David Thompson. *Almost Midnight.* Chichester, UK: New Wine Press, 2008. 215–216.

CHAPTER 7: HOW DOES THE ENEMY DISOBEY?

1. Winston Churchill, in a speech to Harrow School entitled "Never Give In." The Churchill Centre: http://www.winstonchurchill.org/learn/speeches/speeches-of-winston-churchill/103-never-give-in (Accessed August 7, 2011)
2. John Gill. *An Exposition of the New Testament.* Published electronically by www.sacred-texts.com. Quote taken from "Acts 3:6": http://www.sacred-texts.com/bib/cmt/gill/act003.htm (Accessed August 6, 2011)

CHAPTER 8: FULFILLING YOUR OBEDIENCE

1. Albert Barnes. *Notes on the Bible.* Published electronically by www.sacred-texts.com. Quote taken from "Daniel 11:28":

http://www.sacred-texts.com/bib/cmt/barnes/dan011.htm (Accessed August 19, 2011)

2. William Carey (1761–1834), in a sermon to the Association of Baptist Pastors in Nottingham on Wednesday, May 31, 1792. Quote found in "William Carey," http://www.gfamissions.org/missionary-biographies/carey-william-1761-1834.html (Accessed August 19, 2011)

3. Adam Clarke. *Commentary on the Bible*. Published electronically by www.sacred-texts.com. Quote taken from "1 Peter 3:6": http://www.sacred-texts.com/bib/cmt/clarke/pe1003.htm (Accessed on 6 August 2011)

CHAPTER 9: PREPARATION FOR BATTLE: THE A–Z OF SPIRITUAL WARFARE

1. Frances Ridley Havergal. "Take My Life and Let It Be." Written 1874. Words and music are found at http://nethymnal.org/htm/t/m/tmlalib.htm

2. Excerpted from Portia's speech in Act IV, Scene 1, of *The Merchant of Venice* by William Shakespeare. *Oxford School Shakespeare: The Merchant of Venice*, edited by Roma Gill. Oxford, UK: Oxford University Press, 1979. 73.

3. Judson W. Van DeVenter. "I Surrender All." Written 1896. Words and music are found at http://nethymnal.org/htm/i/s/isurrend.htm

CHAPTER 10: DEALING WITH THE ENEMY'S PETULANCE

1. Socrates. Quote found in Debra Nails, "Socrates," in *The Stanford Encyclopedia of Philosophy*. http://plato.stanford.edu/archives/spr2010/entries/socrates/. (Accessed August 10, 2011)

2. "A Neuroscientific Look at Speaking in Tongues." Article by Benedict Carey in *The New York Times*, November 7, 2006: http://www.nytimes.com/2006/11/07/health/07brain.html (Accessed August 15, 2011)

3. Albert Barnes. *Notes on the Bible*. Published electronically by www.sacred-texts.com. Quote taken from "Matthew 12:43": http://www.sacred-texts.com/bib/cmt/barnes/mat012.htm (Accessed August 12, 2011).

4. David Crowder and Mike Hogan. *Everybody Wants to Go to Heaven, but Nobody Wants to Die*. Grand Rapids, MI: Zondervan, 2009.

# END NOTES

Epilogue: I Hear the Sound of Abundance

1. http://www.fao.org/foodclimate/conference/doclist/en/?no_cache=1 (Accessed on May 10, 2010)

2. "2008: The year of global food crisis." Special report by Kate Smith and Rob Edwards, *The Sunday Herald* (Scotland), March 8, 2008. Article is found at http://www.sundayherald.com/news/heraldnews/display.var.2104849.0.2008_the_year_of_global_food_crisis.php (Accessed May 10, 2010)

3. *Oxford Dictionary of English.* Electronic version. Second edition. Oxford University Press, 2010

[4.] 4. Research by Combined Insurance reported in page 5 of "Debt Facts and Figures - Compiled 1st November 2006" by Credit Action. http://www.creditaction.org.uk/assets/PDF/statistics/2006/november-2006.pdf

5. "Up to 12 Million Brits Failed to save a Penny in 2006." Results of a survey by Alliance and Leicester, published December 23, 2006. http://www.alliance-leicester-group.co.uk/upload/pdf/PR1812064.pdf (Accessed May 10, 2010)

6. "Buy one, bin one free: How cynical supermarket offers make us throw away food by the ton," *Daily Mail*, August 14, 2009:
http://www.dailymail.co.uk/debate/article-1205911/Buy-bin-free-How-cynical-supermarket-offers-make-throw-away-food-ton.html